Eva-Sabine Zehelein, Andrea Carosso, Aida Rosen[...]
Family in Crisis?

For our families

Eva-Sabine Zehelein is an adjunct professor of American studies at Goethe-Universität Frankfurt and fellow at the Brandeis Women's Studies Research Center. She specializes in 20th and 21st century North American literatures and (popular) cultures and leads the international and interdisciplinary research group "Family Matters".

Andrea Carosso is a professor of American literature and culture at the Department of International Languages and Literatures at Università di Torino, where he coordinates the post-graduate program in English and American Studies. His books include *Cold War Narratives. American Culture in the 1950s* (2012), *Urban Cultures in the United States* (2010), and *Invito alla lettura di Vladimir Nabokov* (1999).

Aida Rosende-Pérez is an assistant professor at the University of the Balearic Islands, where she teaches in the fields of American literature and culture, as well as gender studies. Her research has focused primarily on the politics and poetics of transnational feminism, with emphasis on the narratives and (audio)visual productions of contemporary Irish women writers and artists.

Eva-Sabine Zehelein, Andrea Carosso, Aida Rosende-Pérez (eds.)

Family in Crisis?

Crossing Borders, Crossing Narratives

[transcript]

Bibliographic information published by the Deutsche Nationalbibliothek
The Deutsche Nationalbibliothek lists this publication in the Deutsche National-
bibliografie; detailed bibliographic data are available in the Internet at http://
dnb.d-nb.de

Cover layout: Maria Arndt, Bielefeld
Cover illustration: Santhosh Kumar
Printed by Majuskel Medienproduktion GmbH, Wetzlar
Print-ISBN 978-3-8376-5061-7
PDF-ISBN 978-3-8394-5061-1
https://doi.org/10.14361/9783839450611

Printed on permanent acid-free text paper.

Contents

III.
FAMILY – SOCIETY – TOGETHERNESS:
Centrifugal and Centripetal Forces

Introduction: Family in Crisis?
What Crossing Borders and Crossing Narratives Tell Us About the State of the Family (Today)

Eva-Sabine Zehelein, Goethe Universität Frankfurt / Brandeis University WSRC

Families are in all their rainbow-colored appearances and life forms – mono- or pluripaternal, with, e.g., hetero-, homosexual, or transgender adults/parents – fundamental and reliable core elements of social existence and action. Families are intimate networks which are constitutive of all social architectures, central actors in multiple (trans)national/global networks, and it is here where nearly all (inter)national political decisions, ethical, moral, and religious systems, and socio-cultural practices crystallize. Various centrifugal and centripetal forces work on, influence, and shape the families, demand that they cross national, cultural, moral, ethical, and legal borders, and thus trigger change within the families. Sometimes, families "fight back" and through their lived realities force laws to be (re)written, ask for attitudes and norms to change or adapt, question long held belief systems and tear down pillars of thought.

Thus, families are an ideal prism through which central contemporary national as well as transnational and international, yes, also global, phenomena, interconnections and crises can be highlighted and debated. We believe that to examine families requires interdisciplinary and intersectional perspectives. Such an endeavor may bear potential for controversy, yet it is of fundamental importance in order to shape the futures of our societies.

The following contributions by German, Italian, Spanish and American scholars with an exceptionally broad range of backgrounds – English and American Studies, sociology and anthropology, law, media and gender studies, as well as history – highlight through select examples how today's families cross borders, and how cultural texts (de)construct, take part in, and mirror family discourses around topics such as fatherhoods and motherhoods, reproductive decisions, adoption, marriage and divorce, poverty and welfare, and the rhetoric of the nuclear family.

As all articles make very clear, the nuclear family model defined as consisting of a person identifying as a man, a person identifying as a woman, ideally married, and living together with their mutual genetic children, underlies all discourses and debates and often also practices of "doing family" (Schneider 72). Astonishingly enough, this model describes a *Way We Never Were*, as social historian Stephanie Coontz has so aptly phrased it for the US American context. Although at best only with an ephemeral prime existence, say, from the late 1940s into the 1960s (cf. e.g. Brown 11, also Giddens 27, Coontz, *The Way We* 14, 28), it has written itself and been written into each and every family narrative, be that political, legal, social, or cultural. It underlies as a foil or silent goal all lived family practices, and seems to be and have been dangling like a 'master carrot' in front of too many donkeys' noses for way too long. In 2015, 46% of children in the US younger than 18 were living in a home with two heterosexual parents in their first marriage; in 1960, the number had been at 73% (Pew). In Germany, the number of families (very broadly defined![1]) was in 2018 at 68.3% (down from 79.1% in 1996); yet 35% of all children have unmarried parents, 20% of families are single parent families (www.deutschland.de). In Spain, the households consisting of a couple (either married or cohabiting) with children made up only 34.4% in 2017 (single person households were astonishingly high at 25.4%, and couple households without children were at 21.3%) (Instituto Nacional de Estadística). In Italy, data from 2019 indicate that out of a total of 16.1 million households (down from 16.5 million in 2015), families with children accounted for 31.6% of total families (down 2.3 % from 2015), whereas single parent households were 9.3% of the total (up 0.4% from 2015) (http://dati.istat.it).

All these statistics and the varieties of families or households they describe already illustrate how complex and differentiated families' lives are today. The stereotypical monolith from the 1950s – white and middle class – had cherishable moments, such as general prosperity and reassuring stability, yet also sparkled with a variety of rather negative facets, e.g. the 'separate spheres', the somewhat rigid role for men as bread-winner fathers, and the isolation of women as full-time mothers in the suburban 'bla', today revived in predominantly repressive concepts such as "new momism" (Douglas and Michaels).[2] Cultural texts have contributed decisively to the formation and cementation of the nuclear family narrative. Fleshed out versions of the ideal are constantly (re)inscribed and most often employed for tongue-in-cheek (re)presentation, persiflage, or outright critique of social mores. For the US American context, for example, we might think of a nearly endless line of TV-series from *Father Knows Best* (1954-60) and *Leave It to Beaver* (1957-63) to more contemporary shows such as e.g. *Weeds* (2005-12), which, even in its trailer features

---

1   The Statistisches Bundesamt defines family very broadly as all parent-child-communities, with two parents or one, with at least one child younger than 18 living in the same household. This also includes families with step children, foster care children, or adopted children (Statistisches Bundesamt 65).

2   "The new momism is a highly romanticized view of motherhood in which the standards for success are impossible to meet" since "a woman has to devote her entire physical, psychological, emotional, intellectual being, 24/7, to her children" (Douglas and Michaels 4).

the "Little Boxes, made of ticky-tacky, little boxes all the same" (a 1962 song originally by Malvina Reynolds), yet then focusses on how a family *sans* bread-winning
dad can earn a living, selling weed. Or the recent comedy-drama series *Transparent*
(2014-19) might come to mind, featuring a Jewish nuclear family in LA in which
the father comes out as transgender after his retirement, implodes the nucleus,
and upsets the notoriously fragile family tectonics even further. Or we could delve
deeply into a long tradition of literary texts from, say, Nathaniel Hawthorne's *The
Scarlet Letter* (1850) all the way to, say, Celeste Ng's *Little Fires Everywhere* (2017), or
the 'global phenomenon' of the Neapolitan Saga by the unidentified Italian writer
Elena Ferrante.

The abstract idea(l) that the man earns the living outside the home and the
woman stays at home and takes care of household and children is to this day dying a
long and thus terrible death in lived practice. Not the least due to financial reasons.
Single income families with more than one adult are today a minority and that not
only because many people want to be (fulltime) members of the global workforce,
but often first and foremost, because a single wage in a family with children is
simply not enough to stay financially afloat. Single parent families with children
have a specifically high risk of being or becoming and staying poor; often, they even
fall into deep poverty (Thévenon et al.). Family and economics, family and welfare,
and family and poverty are thus core themes of serious concern when we look at
families today, and thus the focus of the first part of this volume.

Chiara Saraceno provides a rare glimpse at what it means to be born and growing up poor in Italy with a specific focus on health and cognitive development. She
shows that social justice and equality are nearly unattainable for children born into
poverty, with significant – negative – impact on their development and later life as
adults. Poorer children, and especially in the South of Italy, have access to limited
educational resources which are, in addition, of lower overall quality, as compared
to children whose parent(s) have higher incomes and live in the North. Saraceno
thus calls for adequate economic and material resources for all children, but also
for parental employment at decent wages to combat a (transgenerational) family
crisis she conceptualizes as "educational poverty," which, although it has recently
become part of a governmental initiative, might, as she fears, remain "experimental, and therefore, in all probability, transitory" (p. 33).

A transatlantic look reveals somewhat similar findings, albeit via a different
route. **Maurizio Vaudagna** draws attention to the connection between the American welfare reforms and their impacts on families, but also to the (ideological)
conception of family which guides and has guided welfare reform measures. After
all, family politics are influenced by moral and ethical frameworks, as well as by
images of the 'ideal' family that deserves to be supported or fostered. Vaudagna
sketches the transition from the "Reagan Revolution" – aimed to strengthen the,
by then already declining, practice of the nuclear family and the concomitant con-

servative family values, and thus weakening the social safety net – via Clinton's "New Covenant" which constituted "the end of welfare as we know it" and completed the shift from a politics of entitlement to 'responsible' behavior along predefined, again traditional, normative values (Clinton). Under Clinton, AFDC (Aid to Families with Dependent Children) was replaced by TANF (Temporary Assistance for Needy Families). TANF defines welfare no longer as entitlements you can in theory receive for life, but as a temporary (maximum of 5 years in a lifetime!) monetary assistance based on the idea of 'welfare to work'. The results have been catastrophic – inequality and poverty have increased, and neither the Obama administrations, nor the Trump administration have so far initiated substantial modifications. Quite the contrary: under Trump and with the appointment of two anti-abortion justices to the Supreme Court, the federal government has continued a strongly conservative attitude, to the detriment of reproductive justice for many. Just like Saraceno, Vaudagna closes his historical overview and analysis on a pessimistic note; whereas in many European states, active measures are taken by federal governments to improve the work life and its family compatibility, such as paid (maternity) leave, paid sick days, and affordable childcare, "the nature of the 'healthy family' and the government's duty to support it, are in today's US an embattled terrain, open to multiple interpretations, values, and legislative programs, which are unlikely to soon come to rest" (p. 44).

When families break apart, they often require a court or judge to settle aspects of their crisis. **Antonio Legerén-Molina** highlights the three areas of antenuptial agreements in anticipation of rupture, alimony, and child support within Spanish family law. What his contribution makes very clear is that the law establishes "suitable tools to solve the problems that arise from the frequent family crises" (p. 55) brought about by the lived realities of today's families. Under Spanish law, he shows, the family has become a "configurable unit by the individuals or society at large" (p. 48) and is no longer a "natural reality" based on matrimony (p. 48). In Spain, just as in many other western countries, marriage is no longer the or a major factor for the building and maintenance of family ties. Marriage rates in general decline, people marry later in life,[3] yet marriage is still for many family forms a

---

3   The crude marriage rate (marriages per 1.000 persons) in Germany, Italy, Spain, and the US dropped significantly between 1970 and 2017 (Germany: from 7.4 to 4.9; Italy: from 7.3 to 3.2; Spain: from 7.3 to 3.7; US: from 10.6 to 6.9 (OECD 2017). The mean age of marriage for first-time marriages rises in many European countries and the US. In Germany, the mean age was 28.2 in 1990 for men and 25.5 for women; in 2017 34.0 for men, and 31.2 for women (OECD 2017). In Italy in 2017, first-time grooms were 35 years old, first-time brides 32.3 – an increase of some seven years since 1990 (28.9 / 25.9) (ISTAT; OECD 2017); in Spain, the numbers are comparable: in 2017, men were 35.4 and women 33.2 when they married for the first time – an increase of roughly eight years since 1990 (27.8 / 25.6; OECD 2017). In the US, the mean

ticket towards more safety, stability, and equality. For instance, as Laura Briggs argues in *How All Politics Became Reproductive Politics*, the fight for same-sex marriage[4] was and is for many couples not motivated primarily by a desire to marry and thus buy into or emulate specific normativities of an institution generally considered sexist, but rather, marriage was and still is in many countries, also in Europe, the only way to try and end a second-class status and receive legal protections, primarily and crucially against "losing children in custody cases, guardianship of partners with severe disabilities, and the inability to protect the right to care for partners or hold on to common property" (Briggs 168).

"Making Parents" and being parents are, indeed, processes and practices with their very own "ontological choreography" (Thompson). New family constellations and the challenges they pose for the law are discussed in the first contributions of the second part of this volume. Families can be conceptualized as groups which are very often formed on the basis of the human longing to belong. And belonging is characterized not only by genetic descent, but also by social forms of togetherness based on consent, and can thus, e.g., cause family situations of multiparentality. This is why the second part of this volume is titled "Family – (Multi)parentality – Belonging: "It Takes a Village." **Josep Ferrer-Riba** employs the conceptual distinction suggested by Andrew Bainham between parentage (biological or genetic progenitor), parenthood (father or mother in the legal sense) and parenting (individuals exercising parental responsibilities) (p. 62) to flesh out the varieties of multiparentality from a legal perspective. He then focusses on parenthood – by natural reproduction, by adoption, and by ARTs – to illustrate how the (Spanish) law can and should respond to modern reproductive choices and families of choice in order to respect individual identities, autonomy, and preferences, as well as the children's best interests. Ultimately, says Ferrer-Riba, family law needs to be(come) "more flexible, diversified and adjusted to each case" (p. 75), in acceptance and (legal) understanding of families as unions based on contracts and consent.

Although "families we choose" (Weston) and families flourishing through ART should have legal protection and be equal before the law, the field research carried out by anthropologist **Gloria Álvarez Bernardo** shows how so not this is the case in Spain at the current moment. Despite the promise of Spanish law that all women, "independent of their sexual orientation and/or civil status, can have access to assisted reproductive treatments" (p. 80), a specific order establishes that

---

age increased from 26.1 for men and 23.9 for women in 1990 to 29.5 and 27.4 in 2017 (OECD 2917). See also Coontz, *Marriage...*

4   In Spain, same-sex marriage has been legal since 2005, in the US it was finally legalized with the Supreme Court decision in the case *Obergefell v Hodges* in 2015, in Italy it is still only rudimentarily legal through a civil unions law (May 2016) – access to ART as well as step-child adoption or joint adoption are still exempted; in Germany same-sex marriage was fully realized as "Ehe für alle" in October 2017.

the crucial access requirement to ARTs is a woman's infertility, thus excluding most single women and lesbians from treatment and also from motherhood and family creation. Álvarez Bernardo demonstrates how deeply ingrained notions of the nuclear family still are, and how strong the belief that a child needs a father (figure). In her ethnographic field work with 11 lesbian couples she could show that most couples had to revert to treatments in private clinics due to the discriminatory regulations, but that they consider their motherhood as "whole and complete," and that a father figure is neither missing nor desired (p. 84). Interestingly enough, sperm donation in Spain is only legal as anonymous donation. Thus, neither the parents, nor the child can ever know the donor's identity. Such a regulation has its very own (archaic, regressive) logic – if ARTs are only 'okay' and thus legally accessible for infertile women in heterosexual relationships, then donor anonymity keeps the thin veneer of an ideal 'nuclear family' intact. Donor anonymity and even fertility doctors' advice to patients not to tell the children they were donor-conceived was practiced in Germany, too, with the saddening result that thousands are now unable to ever find their genetic fathers. The legal situation changed only in Juli 2017, with the *Gesetz zur Regelung des Rechts auf Kenntnis der Abstammung bei heterologer Verwendung von Samen*. Donor conceived adults now have the legal right to know who their donor is/was, however, many clinics did not even archive their donor profiles and the patients' records, so that much information is forever lost (www.spenderkinder.de).[5]

The same-sex parents in Álvarez Bernardo's study emphasized the importance of informing the child from an early age about its origins and family situation. Potential scruples that a child might demand to know its genetic heritage and origin were countered by arguments that love and affection are central for the upbringing of a child, and not the presence of a specific gender relation, and that families need not follow the patriarchal heteronormative model. We know from extensive longitudinal kinship research that children with same-sex parents do not fare worse in their development than children from traditional families, quite the contrary; we also know, though, that donor conceived children have generally a high interest in knowing who their genetic parent(s) is/are (Golombok; Scheib et al.). Many researchers in sociology, anthropology and psychology, as well as many legal scholars today argue with growing consensus that donor conceived children have the right to know their genetic heritage, since it is part of their identity to know about their ancestry and their medical background, and significant to finding a place in

---

5   In Italy, sperm and egg donation became – sort of – legal in 2014, when a total ban from 2004, turning Italy into one of the most conservative nations in Europe, was finally lifted after a decade of fierce and bitter contention. However, many groups – single women, same-sex couples – are still barred from access to ARTs (Riezzo et al.). In the US, sperm donation is regulated on the state level.

the world (Harper et al.). Although many family forms de-emphasize genetic essentialism, there remains an ineradicable perception of the significance of genetic inheritance, not just for medical reasons (e.g. inheritable diseases), but also for who we are, where we belong, and where we come from (Zehelein, "Family Trees...;" Nordqvist and Smart).

Eva-Sabine Zehelein's analysis of the reality docu-diary *Generation Cryo* (2013) takes a look at the inside dynamics of ARTs families, in this case, of sperm donor families in the US. The show presents in an entertainment format what the long-term and in-depth sociological field work of Hertz and Nelson, published as *Random Families*, has empirically illustrated – sperm donation can create large networks of families all connected to each other through the donor's genetic material, and all members have to (re)write their roles and identities and negotiate practices of belonging. Bree, who has two mums, sets out to meet as many of her donor siblings as possible and ultimately to track down the anonymous donor. She meets single mum families, but also 'nuclear families' in which the father's infertility necessitated the use of donor sperm. One focus of the show is to highlight how all the parents construct their identities as husbands and wives, as mothers and fathers, as co-parents and single parents by choice, and how deeply troubling the potential appearance of the donor is for all family constellations, and also for the children. Fundamentally, *Generation Cryo* is, argues Zehelein, an (auto)biographical project of a donor conceived child and its donor siblings to piece together their identities and autobiographical narratives by learning more about the man who "did his thing in the cup." But all involved have to determine: can/will he be family?

Virginia Pignagnoli and **Margarita Navarro Pérez** also zoom in on gender relations in cultural texts, namely in the American HBO series *Big Little Lies*, and in the short story "Erewhon" by the British writer Helen Simpson. **Pignagnoli**, and to a degree also Pérez, draw attention to a further, important aspect tearing at many family fabrics, namely abusive relationships and intimate partner violence, in combination with a discussion of the social construction of mothers, motherhood, and mothering. *Big Little Lies*, Pignagnoli argues, employing James Phelan's concept of "narrative ethics" (p. 102), "conveys an ethics of motherhood as collective agent of change" (p. 101) by highlighting in two plot strands – narrating stories of domestic violence and rape – how mothers, through collective action (spoiler alert: by more or less accidentally killing the perpetrator) assert their agency in the face of massive failure by American institutions to protect them from violence and abuse committed by men. Deeply ingrained notions of "intensive mothering" (a term introduced by Hays in 1996) and "new momism" (cf. Douglas and Michaels) strangled the women into subservient and disenfranchised positions of constant guilt and reduced self-worth, and made them cover up domestic abuse and intimate partner violence for far too long. The promise of empowerment inherent in mothering, namely what O'Reilly has labelled "feminist mothering," a negation of patriarchal motherhood, can here only be fulfilled through a (collective) act of retributive violence.

In Helen Simpson's short story "Erewhon," published in the 2015 collection *Cockfoster*, the obvious allusion to Samuel Butler's 1872 novel of the same title serves, argues **Pérez**, to present contemporary readers with an equally dystopian scenario. Via the literary technique of estrangement, going back to Russian formalists such as Victor Shklovsky, but also to Brechtian political theater, the social constructedness of gender and thus power relations is highlighted which discriminates against and suppresses specific groups. In Simpson's short story, the prevalent gender constructions and performativities, privileging men over women, are reversed. Women are in power and at work, men are disenfranchised, often victims of domestic violence, and caught in socio-political inferiority and powerlessness (p. 119). This form of matriarchy, the "natural order" (p. 120), is, however, understood by Pérez as "a dooming construction of femininity" (p. 120), as not intended as a projected hailed future victory of women over men, but rather as a 'what if' scenario that ultimately aims for gender equality.

Sonia Di Loreto takes a look back into American (literary) history and at the story of adoptions during the late 19th century within the frames of property and inheritance, as well as race and class. Di Loreto shows that on the basis of biblical justification patterns as well as (first) legal regulations (*Massachusetts Adoption of Children Act* (1851), sentimental America hid under a thin veneer of charity (performed by the adopter) and deep gratitude (demanded from and performed by the adoptee), that adoption – just as slave labor or indenture – was essentially all about "transferring and accumulating property, but while in the case of adoption property remains within the family, ensuring in fact, a clear hereditary line of succession, bound labor is connected to the accumulation of property for the employers and the public (state), but certainly never for the child, whose welfare is distributed among a number of different agencies (asylum for the orphans or other benevolent institutions, employer, the public), thus diffusing all social responsibility while avoiding direct accountability" (p. 126). Harriet Wilson's autobiographical novel *Our Nig* (1859) illustrates, argues Di Loreto, that despite the sentimental promise of salvation through virtue for adopted children, this did not hold true for non-white children who remained property and were deprived of the possibility to become propertied. "It seems that every time the sentimental tide rises, it crashes against economic and capitalist issues, without being able to produce a valid material alternative" (p. 128). Narratives about white adopted children, however, such as "The Adopted Daughter" (*Youth's Companion* 1845) or "The Orphan" (*Olive Branch* 1844), illustrate the sentimental notion of redemption and "heavenly ascent" for the blessed children rescued by benevolent adults and initiated into their families.

The third part of our collection is devoted to "Family – Society – Togetherness: centrifugal and centripetal forces." It focusses on a variety of cultural texts which all showcase how external factors impact families and how the families constitute and reassert their unity in the face of centrifugal forces. In Philip Roth's 2005 novel *The Plot Against America*, it is the dystopian setting of a 1940s America governed by the fascist and anti-Semitic President Charles Lindbergh that serves as background for the illustration of how a Jewish family adapts to socio-cultural as well as political and ideological pressures. **Alice Balestrino** understands Roth's novel as one out of many of his autofictional texts in which "the simplicity yet exceptionality of the family as a paramount interest" is asserted. For Roth, says Balestrino, the family is "the earliest and most essential instance of society; the milieu where one's mindset and value system become radical (in the sense of constitutional and powerful) and germinate in broader contexts (Newark, the Jewish American experience)" (p. 136). By imagining an America and an autobiographically infused Roth family under Lindbergh, Roth "approximates the Holocaust in a narrative that aims to be faithful to reality (the autobiographical details) yet detached from it (the counterfactual apparatus)" (p. 136), and which zooms in on (personal) family dynamics as (political) national dynamics (p. 138). The fictional(ized) Roth family under pressure of anti-Semitism "proves to be an elastic structure" (p. 139), one of unity based on the centripetal force of the father's patriarchal Jewish ethics and value system, with shifting members "at their kitchen table in times of high vulnerability for their community" (p. 139).

Two more versions of 'circling the wagons' to protect families against centrifugal forces are highlighted in **Brigitte Georgi-Findlay's** and **Lee Herrmann**'s contributions on US television Westerns and the horror film *The Hills Have Eyes*. **Georgi-Findlay** reminds us that the Western genre as "American founding narrative" (p. 146) and the West/the frontier as the place/space where the 'national character' is formed provide an ideal prism through which to look at family discourses over the decades (1960s to 1980s). Georgi-Findlay analyzes three iconic TV series: *Bonanza*, *The Big Valley* and *Little House on the Prairie*. In all three, she argues, "family provides the context for enacting learning processes tied to the paradoxes of the American historical experience" (p. 151). And all three series present their viewers with atypical, that is non-nuclear, family constellations which, in the context of the frontier settings, understood as sites of crisis, both affirm gender roles and dare to transgress them – *Bonanza* with the patchwork family of a father *cum* three-time widower and his sons; *The Big Valley*, featuring the widowed matriarch with four own children and a son fathered by her late husband with another woman; and *Little House on the Prairie* centered around a rather traditional nuclear family model in challenging frontier settings. Before the backdrop of centrifugal forces such as the Cold War, Vietnam, and 1960s counterculture, "[a]ll of the series stress the importance of home and belonging beyond the 'natural' birth family" (p. 153); family is "not about heredity, but about the freedom of choice" (p. 149), and it is "a bulwark of emotional and economic stability against a hostile, dangerous environment (p. 150).

A "modern Western" reverberating classics such as *The Searchers*, is, argues **Herrmann**, the horror movie *The Hills Have Eyes* (1977), commenting critically on America's recent past and contemporary situation, e.g. on the war in Vietnam and 1960s hippie counterculture – here presented as the evil Other, with obvious references to the Manson Family. The nice American Carter family – moral, civilized, and above all white Americans – are "pushed to savage violence against a monstrous Other in the name of vengeance and survival" (p. 159). Drawing on Richard Slotkin's classic *Regeneration Through Violence*, Lee argues that the film "is a conservative narrative writ over-large, of cannibal mutant hippies-gone-Red-Indian destroying religious, patriarchal, and parental authority, undermining the family, defiling one's daughters, and eating one's babies" (p. 161).

Another attempt at forging alternative modes of kinship, togetherness and solidarity, this time during the 1980s and 1990s, is portrayed by **Stefano Morello**. What he calls "punk kinship" (p. 167) should be understood as a form of resistance or "iterative symbolic performance of negation, a kind of undoing – acts of communal conscious disruption, both on and off the stage" (p. 171) *vis à vis* an America under Reagan that fostered feelings of alienation and discontent, e.g. through a nostalgic celebration of 1950s white middle-class nuclear family ideals, accompanied by reduced governmental social spending, stagnating real wages, and thus a widening gap between rich and poor. Punks, shows Morello, disillusioned with the American Dream rhetoric, "turned to themselves, then to each other, and collectively crafted alternative worlds, modes of sociality, and forms of desire" (p. 173). Punk houses such as the Maxi-Pad in North Oakland created the conditions for punk life. And, as Morello illustrates, punk was more than just music or a youth subculture; it was also "a meeting ground for those rejected by society and those who reject it *as is*. As a mode of belonging in unbelonging, punk seeks alternative modes of lived care and relationality free from the self-perpetuating motives of capital and the nation" (p. 177; italics in original).

The third part of the book closes with two contributions that highlight family planning, from an American studies/media studies perspective (Andrea Carosso) and through the lens of a historian (Claudia Roesch). Both employ cultural texts – a 1960s American Disney propaganda film and 1980s German family planning brochures – in order to illustrate once more how ideologically charged, how political private matters, and how private political matters, such as family building, can be(come).

Andrea Carosso takes a close look at Disney's 1967 propaganda animation film *Family Planning*. He understands it as a cultural crystallization point of ideas and ideologies circulated at the time by women's rights advocates, neo-Malthusian activists, and proponents of eugenics to control population growth and to foster a specific – nuclear – family model. Carosso shows that Paul Ehrlich's *The Population Bomb* (1968) was just the photogenic and media-suitable tip of a broad international movement that had been advocating population control for decades. In clear reference to the looming danger of the atom bomb, population growth was considered a massive threat, especially from "Third World" and communist countries and for the West. Planned Parenthood and the Population Council brought together international experts and policy makers to make suggestions for family planning (a.k.a. fertility control) at home, as part of Johnson's War on Poverty, but first and foremost abroad in nations such as Japan or India, as well as in Latin America. Ten minutes long and available in 25 languages, *Family Planning* argued, in a nutshell, that only small families are healthy and prosperous families – contrasting the American ideal nuclear model with the allegedly super-fertile (and poor and destitute and futureless) families in the target countries. The character of Donald Duck served the colonialist program to hammer home the message that the golden key for each family is family planning, the power provided by contraceptives to build a better life, and become, as Carosso argues, good consumers, too.

Claudia Roesch zooms in on the activities of the German family planning agency Pro Familia which, during the 1980s, motivated by Western feminist thought, attempted to promote birth control and other forms of female empowerment through brochures and community outreach measures. Supported by the analysis of at the time widespread cultural texts, such as brochures as well as the *Pro Familia Magazin* "Of Turkish Women and Other Foreigners" (1982), Roesch criticizes the Pro Familia activities as insensitive measures to assimilate Turkish women into German mainstream culture and as ignorant of who these women and their actual problems were – e.g. "women faced more severe health and housing problems, [...] connected to bad working conditions and insecure immigration statuses" (p. 202). Roesch states that the Pro Familia activists also learned that "most women wanted two children and actively requested the pill or abortions," and interprets this as an indicator that they thus "proved their own agency and subscribed to the Western concept of the nuclear family" and employed personal networks as well as sympathetic counsellors to make their own reproductive decisions (p. 202).

All the stories about families we tell in these pages remind us of how central to our societies families as fundamental social structures are. And no matter what we define as family and no matter how we live family, it is always the expression of a universal longing to belong, a strong desire and human right to find shelter and comfort, protection against and retreat from outside forces and pressures. Over the centuries and across the globe, families have constantly shifted and adapted, in form and in size, as well as in their rhetoric. As many of our articles vividly illustrate, notions of the so-called 'nuclear family' have served a plethora of social, but also political, moral, ethical and legal agendas, first and foremost about the 'right' norms and values, and too often with repressive and restrictive intent.

In her monograph *Modern Families* (2015), Susan Golombok has asked a very important question: what about children in today's families? How do – if at all – family constellations impact the well-being of children? And on the basis of longitudinal, in depth, and multifaceted research by her own research center, the Centre for Family Research at the University of Cambridge, but also by new kinship researchers around the world, she argues that "family processes are better predictors of children's psychological adjustment than family structure" (204).[6] She thus closes *Modern Families* with this summary:

> Families come in all shapes and sizes. Whether children have one parent or two, whether their parents are male or female, whether their parents are of the same sex or the opposite sex, whether they have a genetic or gestational link to their parents, and whether they have been conceived naturally or through assisted reproduction, seem to matter less for children than does the quality of family relationships, the support of their community and attitudes of the society in which they live. (127)

In a world characterized by plurality and demands for and practices of individual choices, frequently in the teeth of stigmatization, discrimination, and outright disenfranchisement, a 'nuclear' formula is nothing more, but also nothing less than one out of many lived realities of family life. More than 20 years ago, Judith Stacey in her by now canonical work *In the Name of the Family* called for more "individual resilience, flexibility, courage, and tolerance while we work collectively to provide the best forms of social and cultural supports we can devise" (12). Today, major reforms and legal changes have finally given more (reproductive) rights to more people and families – same-sex marriage or step-child adoption being just two – and these need defending and supporting in countries where they already exist and are sometimes under siege (let's just mention abortion rights in the US), as well as in those countries where the path to more equality and social justice is still longer than in others. What an advertisement for the American reproductive justice organization Sister Reach declared in the context of Black women and their reproductive rights certainly holds true for all families everywhere: "Our family's success requires: lots of love, a living wage, affordable housing, a safe environment, healthcare, reliable transportation, safe and robust schools, a chance" (quoted in Ross and Solinger 165).

In times of severe conservative backlash in parts of the US as well as in many EU states, cutting back on state support and reproductive rights, and endangering not only reproductive freedoms, but also causing internal rifts tearing at the social

---

6   See also Lynda Ross (139) for the same argument.

fabric, cultural texts help us comprehend and talk about the crises many of today's families face. Cultural texts invite us to enter important and rich discourses, and to lobby for policies fostering equality and justice, and to support all practices of (European) family life that seek unity in diversity.

We encourage readers to delve into this interdisciplinary, multiperspectival, European-American transatlantic comparative project, to (re)think and (re)consider, and to raise their voices, and to take a stand.

We thank the DAAD (German Academic Exchange Service) and the German Auswärtiges Amt (Federal Foreign Office) for their generous (financial) support in the context of the "Hochschuldialog mit Südeuropa."

Bibliography

Briggs, Laura. *How All Politics Became Reproductive Politics. From Welfare Reform to Foreclosure to Trump.* U of California P, 2017.

Brown, Susan L. *Families in America.* U of California P, 2017.

Clinton, Bill. "Transcript of Speech by Clinton Accepting Democratic Nomination." *The New York Times*, 17 July 1992, section A, p.14.

Coontz, Stephanie. *The Way We Never Were: American Families and the Nostalgia Trap.* Basic Books, 1992.

—. *Marriage, a History: How Love Conquered Marriage.* Viking, 2005.

Deutschland.de, https://www.deutschland.de/de/topic/leben/wie-familien-in-deutschland-leben. Accessed 20 March 2020.

Douglas, Susan J., and Meredith W. Michaels. *The Mommy Myth: The Idealization of Motherhood and How It Has Undermined All Women.* Free P, 2004.

Eurostat. *Statistics Explained.* June 2019, https://ec.europa.eu/eurostat/statistics-explained/index.php/Marriage_and_divorce_statistics. Accessed 20 March 2020.

Eurostat/Instituto Nacional de Estadística. *Marriages and Births in Spain.* June 2015, https://ec.europa.eu/eurostat/statistics-explained/index.php?title=Archive:Marriages_and_births_in_Spain&oldid=258019. Accessed 20 March 2020.

Giddens, Anthony. "The Global Revolution in Family and Personal Life." *Family in Transition. 15th edition*, edited by Arlene S. Skolnick and Jerome H. Skolnick, Pearson Education, 2010, pp. 25-31.

Golombok, Susan. *Modern Families. Parents and Children in New Family Forms.* Cambridge UP, 2015.

Harper, Joyce C., et al. "The End of Donor Anonymity: How Genetic Testing Is Likely To Drive Anonymous Gamete Donation out of Business." *Human Reproduction*, vol. 31, no. 6, 2016, pp. 1135-40.

Hays, Sharon. *The Cultural Contradictions of Motherhood*. Yale UP, 1996.

Hertz, Rosanna, and Margaret K. Nelson. *Random Families. Genetic Strangers, Sperm Donor Siblings, and the Creation of New Kin*. Oxford UP, 2019.

INE-Instituto Nacional de Estadística. *Continuous Household Survey 2017. Released April 2018*, https://www.ine.es/en/prensa/ech_2017_en.pdf. Accessed 20 March 2020.

ISTAT–Istituto Nazionale di Statistica. "Press Release: Marriages, Separations and Divorces," https://www.istat.it/en/archivio/192521. Accessed 20 March 2020.

Nordqvist, Petra, and Carol Smart. *Relative Strangers: Family Life, Genes and Donor Conception*. Palgrave Macmillan, 2014.

OECD. *Family Database*, www.oecd/els/family/database.htm. Accessed 20 March 2020.

O'Reilly, Andrea, editor. *Feminist Mothering*. SUNY P, 2008.

Pew Research Center. "Parenting in America: Outlook, Worries, Aspirations Are Strongly Linked to Financial Situation." 17 December 2015, https://www.pewresearch.org/wp-content/uploads/sites/3/2015/12/2015-12-17_parenting-in-america_FINAL.pdf. Accessed 15 March 2020.

Riezzo, Margherita, et al. "Italian law on medically assisted reproduction: do women's autonomy and health matter?" *BMC Women's Health*, vol. 16, no. 1, 23 July 2016, pp. 1-9.

Ross, Loretta J., and Rickie Solinger. *Reproductive Justice. An Introduction*. U of California P, 2017.

Ross, Lynda R. *Interrogating Motherhood*. AU P, 2016.

Scheib, Joanna E., et al. "Who Requests Their Sperm Donor's Identity? The First Ten Years of Information Releases to Adults with Open-Identity Donors." *Fertility & Sterility*, vol. 107, no. 2, 2017, pp. 483-93.

Schneider, David M. *A Critique of the Study of Kinship*. U of Michigan P, 1984.

Spenderkinder. https://www.spenderkinder.de. Accessed 20 March 2020.

Stacey, Judith. *In the Name of the Family. Rethinking Family Values in the Postmodern Age*. Beacon P, 1996.

Statistisches Bundesamt. *Statistisches Jahrbuch 2019*, https://www.destatis.de. Accessed 20 March 2020.

Thévenon, Olivier, et al. "Child Poverty in the OECD: Trends, Determinants and Policies to Tackle It." *Employment and Migration Working Papers*, OECD Publishing.

Thompson, Charis. *Making Parents: The Ontological Choreography of Reproductive Technologies*. MIT P, 2005.

Weston, Kath. *Families We Choose. Lesbians, Gays, Kinship. Revised Edition with a new Preface*. Columbia UP, 1997.

Williams, Joan C., and Heather Boushey. "The Three Faces of Work-Family Conflict: The Poor, the Professionals, and the Missing Middle." *Center for Ameri-*

can Progress 25 Jan. 2010, https://www.americanprogress.org/issues/economy/reports/2010/01/25/7194/the-three-faces-of-work-family-conflict/. Accessed 20 March 2020.

Zehelein, Eva-Sabine."Mothers, ART and Narratives of Belonging." *CoSMo*, vol. 12, summer 2018, pp. 77-94.

—. "Family Trees: Mnemonics, Identity and Cultural Memory." *Trees in Literatures and the Arts: Humanarboreal Perspectives in the Anthropocene*, edited by Daniela Fargione and Carmen Concilio, Lexington Books, 2020, pp. tba.

I.
FAMILY – STATE – ECONOMY: Poverty, Welfare, Benefits

The Long-Term Impact of Growing Up Poor – the Italian Case

Chiara Saraceno, Collegio Carlo Alberto Torino

Introduction

Family origin is still to a large degree a destiny, even in democratic societies. Not only does it determine to a large degree the life chances, the constraints, and opportunities one encounters while growing up and becoming an adult – via social and cultural capital, as well as family income. It also shapes from the start, in some cases even already in the fetal phase, a child's chances to develop his or her own capabilities as well as his/her health throughout the life course.

Inequalities among children tend therefore to become inequalities among adults. Although one cannot totally rule out the role of genetic differences/inequalities and of their intergenerational transmission as an explanation of social inequality among adults (see e.g. Herrnstein and Murray; Jensen), there is a substantial body of research that points to social, not genetic, factors which impact both on child development and on children's life chances. This impact is particularly negative at the bottom end of the social stratification model, in so far as it affects all the dimensions of an individual's life chances. This impact is multifold. It concerns e.g. survival at birth, infant mortality, health throughout the life course, cognitive development, as well as social opportunities and outcomes.

Inequalities among children, therefore, particularly those affecting those who happen to enter the world at the bottom of the social scale and in very disadvantaged situations, pose issues of social justice and equality in a more radical way than those experienced by adults. As Ermisch, Jäntti and Smeeding state in their introduction to an edited volume that explores the weight of the parental transmission of life chances:

> parental SES [socio-economic status] may be associated with any stage or outcome of the development process, and any outcome at an earlier life stage may be related to later outcomes all the way up to adulthood. For example, parental education or income may be related to birth weights in the birth year, or to test scores and socioemotional behavior in early childhood, which, in turn, may be as-

sociated with various outcomes at any of the subsequent developmental stages up to adulthood. (10)

In this paper, I will focus on the impact of being born unequal, and particularly at the bottom of social stratification, in the fields of health and cognitive development, in Italy.

Literature Overview

As synthetized in an OECD (2018) report on (failed) social mobility in developed countries, health and epidemiological research indicate that parents influence the health of their children already before the children are born through their own health endowment, health behavior, and socio-economic status. The coefficient for the impact of early childhood conditions is highest in some Southern countries (Spain and Greece).

Economic difficulties can contribute to the impaired physical and mental health of children also post-birth and then while they are growing up. Because of lower housing costs, poorer families, in fact, might live near to sources of pollution. Exposure to harmful environmental factors such as pollution, violence, and stress have been linked to poorer infant health. A recent study also found that children coming from lower income households had differences in brain surface area in comparison with children from higher income families (Noble et al.). At the same time, children with poor neo-natal health born to more educated families are more likely to overcome their initial health shortcomings than those from less educated families. Studies examining especially the association between mothers' socio-economic status and their children's health have confirmed the importance of maternal education (Currie and Moretti; Cutler and Lleras-Muney).

The link between childhood social disadvantage and lower levels of cognitive development and educational attainment has been a matter of substantial theoretical debate in the educational, sociological, and health literature (for critical overviews see e.g. Shavit and Blossfeld; Duncan and Brooks-Gunn 2000; Burkam and Lee; Machin). Although explanations may differ concerning the emphasis they put on which is the specific mechanism that activates this link (for an overview see Fergusson et al.) – constraints deriving from material circumstances, parental, and particularly mothers' caring and interaction styles (e.g. Bradley), genetics, inefficacy of the school system – they all start from the evidence that family income is a strong and consistent predictor of multiple indices of achievement, including standardized test scores, grades in school, and educational attainment (e.g. Duncan and Brooks-Gun 1997; Mayer; Duncan et al.; Duncan and Brooks-Gun 2000, Bradley and Corwyn). The income-achievement gap is already present by kindergarten and accelerates over time (e.g. Heckman; Evans and Schamberg; Bradbury et al.) in all the countries studied, although there are cross country differences. Investigations of what the mechanisms are, in addition to health conditions and possibly genetics, that link income to cognitive development, have found that both home environment and quality of out of the home child care are important. Linver et al. (1999, 2002) for instance, found that a variety of family factors, including maternal distress, authoritarian parenting, and low levels of cognitively stimulating activities, mediated the link between low income and poorer educational outcomes. Studying the performance in international test scores of children belonging to different socio-economic backgrounds, researchers have found confirmation of these socially structured inequalities in cognitive development. Perrons and Plomien, studying the PISA results, found that on average children belonging to households in the lowest income quartile exhibit an 83 points difference in math competences compared to those who belong to the highest quartile. Jerrim and Micklewright identified a striking similarity in the relationship between test scores and a measure of a family's cultural and socio-economic background – the number of books in the home – at both ages, and in all countries.

The good news is that the severity of this problem differs across developed countries and that much might be done to mitigate it, not only addressing inequalities among parents, but with specific measures addressed to children which might prevent, or mitigate, some of the worst consequences of being born and growing up in disadvantaged circumstances (e.g. Smeeding et al., eds.; Ermisch et al., eds.). For instance, early maternal investment has a positive and persistent impact on the child's cognitive development (Del Bono et al.). And good quality early child care, good after school programs that incentivize the learning skills and cognitive development of children, have a positive impact particularly on the educational outcomes of children coming from low income households (e.g. Dumas and Lefranc; Bingley and Westergård-Nielsen; Del Boca et al.). Perrons and Plomien found important cross-country differences in the degree and persistence of socially structured cognitive gaps. The lowest differences were found not only in countries such as the Northern European ones – Finland, Sweden, Denmark, the Netherlands – which have comparatively low levels both of poverty and of income inequality, but also in some Eastern European countries, such as the Czech Republic, Slovakia, Slovenia, and Croatia, which have higher levels of poverty, but a comparatively low level of intergenerational persistence of low education. This last aspect, as suggested by a study based on EU-Silc data (Grundiza and Lopez-Vilaplana), is an important driver of the intergenerational transmission of poverty. Italy, instead, is among the countries with a high intergenerational transmission of education levels (OECD 2018).

Overall, as Fergusson et al. state on the basis of their findings of a longitudinal study on a cohort of children from birth until age 25, there are "pervasive relationships between socioeconomic status at birth and childhood material, cognitive, family and school factors. These correlations clearly suggest the presence of large variations in the mix of individual, family, economic and school conditions experienced by children from different social strata" (288).

Growing Up Poor in Italy

Italy is one of the developed countries where, since the mid-1990s, children's poverty has started to increase and the incidence of poverty is greater among children than among the adults (and the elderly) (European Commission 2009; Saraceno 2014).

The causes of this phenomenon are multiple: high unemployment or sub-employment rates among men and in-work poverty, particularly in the South, where poverty is concentrated, comparatively low rates of women's employment and activity, particularly in the South and among women/mothers with low levels of education, as well as a fragmentary and little generous family policy (Saraceno 2014). The result is not only a high concentration of poverty in the South, but also among large households with (three or more) dependent children and, more recently, among foreign households. Things have worsened with the 2008 financial crisis (Natali and Saraceno), also because Italy has been among the countries more severely hit, the low-income groups suffered more, recovery started later and is slower (Ólafsson and Stefánsson). Children's anchored poverty worsened considerably after 2010, peaking to 32.6% in 2013, up from an already high 24.7% in 2008. Data are even worse, and still increasing, with regard to absolute poverty, which reached 9% in 2013, up from 4.9% in 2008. It increased constantly also in the subsequent years, involving 12.6% of all underage children in 2018, compared to the already high 8.4% of the entire population. The percentage is much higher for children with a migrant background.

The reasons for this high percentage of children's poverty are manifold. Among them, the following should be mentioned: large territorial differences, with the South having a persistently higher incidence both of unemployment and of poverty; a comparatively low women's labor force participation, with large regional differences and differences in the level of education; consequently, a high incidence of single earner households, particularly when children are present, when the mother has limited education, in the South, and among foreign households; and finally, a fragmentation and redistributive inefficiency of child-linked income transfers.

Research on the impact of being born and growing up poor in Italy is very recent and relatively scarce. The most systematic studies are those promoted, on the one hand, by the Istituto Superiore della Sanità among primary school children, and on the other hand by Save the Children, with the support of a scientific committee. They are in line with what is known from the international research results.

With regard to the impact of poverty on chances at birth, the evidence is indirect, but worrisome. The geographical gradient in infant mortality, in fact, overlaps with that of poverty, with a 2.9% infant mortality in the Northern regions, and a 3.8% infant mortality rate in the Southern regions. The study by the Istituto Superiore della Sanità (2016) monitoring the health of children attending primary school, finds that inequalities in parental income and labor position, combined with region of residence, affect inequalities in exposure to children's illnesses and health risks. The case of child obesity is particularly dramatic, with the poorer Southern regions exhibiting much higher rates than the richer Center and Northern regions. The same occurs in the case of children with parents with limited education compared to those with parents who have attained higher levels of education.

Based on survey data on children's parents, the Istituto Superiore di Sanità (2016) found that children of poor parents (particularly mothers) with limited education eat less fruit and vegetables and do not eat breakfast regularly. They are also less physically active and practice sports less often than their better off contemporaries, particularly if they live in the South. There are also gender differences, with girls being less active and practicing sports less frequently than boys. From this perspective, girls living in poor households suffer from a double deprivation. The survey, however, did not find differences between native and foreign children in these behaviors, once controlling for income and education.

Own elaboration of data of the ISTAT 2013 survey on health shows that children living in poor households are highly likely not to be followed regularly by a doctor, even if in Italy the National Health Service is universal and the general practitioner (a pediatrician in the case of children under 12) is free. This risk is much higher if, in addition to being poor, children live in the South. About 32% of 0-3-year old children living in poor households have not been seen by a doctor in the previous 12 months at the national level, ranging from 29% in the North East to 34% in the South and Isles. Their health is not monitored properly and there is no possibility of prevention, or early intervention. The percentage of children living in poor households who never see a doctor during a year increases with age, involving 45% of the 4-6-year old children at the national level, 50% in the South, 55% in the Isles.

Scores on the international cognitive test PISA document the impact of household income inequalities. 36% of 15-year-old children whose household is in the first income quintile do not achieve the minimum competencies in math and reading, compared to respectively 10% and 7% of their contemporaries in the fifth quintile (Save the Children 2015, fig. 8). Also, in this case, there is a regional gradient overlapping the poverty gradient. Foreign children are the worse off, with 42% of children of first-generation parents not reaching the minimum competencies both in math and in reading compared to respectively 19% and 15% of Italian born children. Low socio-economic status combines with lack of local cultural capital. A 2019 cross-national test performed by the Ministry of Education (Invalsi) arrived at similar findings.

Attendance of early child care seems to have a positive effect on low income children's cognitive development throughout adolescence, at least as measured by performance in math tests at age 15 (Save the Children 2015). But the likelihood that children from low income households attend such a service from a very early age is very reduced, for various, interacting, reasons: cultural models concerning the proper care of very young children, lower labor market participation among low income mothers with limited education, as well as lower availability of these services in the very regions where there is a higher concentration of children's poverty. Kindergarten attendance, in fact, is almost universal in Italy for children aged 3 to 5. Kindergartens, defined as *scuole dell'infanzia* (infant schools), are part of the universal school system, although quality is uneven across the country and in the Southern regions kindergartens often operate on a half-day basis only. Both coverage and attendance of nursery schools for children under the age of 3, on the contrary, is limited, involving 24.2% of 0-2-year-old children at the national level in 2016, thus 9 points below the 33% coverage set as a goal for all EU countries (Dipartimento politiche per la famiglia et al. 2018). Coverage is also very uneven across regions. Center-Northern regions, although not always reaching the 33% coverage, are much closer to it than the Southern ones, some of which do not even reach 10%.

Coverage – taking together public and private nurseries – in fact, is to a large degree linked to women's labor force participation rates. Thus, regions with a high incidence of child poverty are those where the offer of early child care and education is lower. For this reason, Pavolini and van Lancker have pointed to the risk of a Matthew effect in the uses of early child care and education services. The risk of a Matthew effect in childcare attendance (Pavolini and van Lanker), in so far as it is skewed towards the children of better off and more educated mothers, is particularly high in Italy, where education is a selective determinant for women's, and particularly mothers', labor force participation, with better educated women being much more likely than less educated ones to enter the labor market and remain within it also when they become mothers. Highly educated mothers, furthermore, are also more inclined to choose an institutional, professional service over other forms of informal or family (grandparental) care for their very young children.

Although nursery schools, analogously to what had happened before to kindergartens, have recently been formally integrated in the overall system of basic schooling, their scarcity, which in turn imposes the definition of priority criteria for access, and the presence of fees (although on a sliding scale), while excluding the majority of children, supports the persistence of an image of these services as a surrogate for a working mother's care or as a social assistance service for particularly problematic families. This image, in turn, helps to legitimize the low coverage offered by available services and discourages from putting pressure on policy makers for their development.

Also the quality of schools for older children is uneven across regions as well as within the same municipality, with the regions and neighborhoods which see a concentration of poverty and other disadvantages often having also a lower quality of school buildings and infrastructures, as well as fewer resources for extracurricular activities (Save the Children 2015; Save the Children 2019), which research has found of crucial importance for the development of children's capabilities. Poorer children, therefore, are generally offered by the public system fewer educational resources that are, in addition, of lower quality, which, therefore, strengthens, rather than compensates for, the developmental disadvantages of growing up poor.

Conclusion

Granting children adequate economic and material resources, supporting their parents' employment at decent wage levels is, of course, of utmost importance to prevent children's poverty. 34% of children living in a jobless household, but also 16.2% of those living in a single earner household were in absolute poverty in 2018. The figure dropped by 3.9% if they lived in a two-parent dual earner household, indicating the crucial importance of supporting mothers' employment. Other needs of poor children, however, must be addressed as well, in order to grant them equal opportunities in developing their capabilities, both supporting parental skills and enlarging access to non-family-linked developmental resources. Italy is lacking on both counts, given the high incidence of children's poverty and the scarcity of good quality developmental resources available in particular to children living in the poorer areas. There are exceptions, of course. But only very recently has "educational poverty" entered the political agenda, with a special fund allocated to initiatives in the field. They remain, however, experimental, and therefore, in all probability, transitory.

Bibliography

Bingley Paul, and Niels Westergård-Nielsen. "Intergenerational Transmission and Day Care." *From Parents to Children. The Intergenerational Transmission of Advantage*, edited by John Ermisch et al., Russel Sage Foundation, 2012, pp. 190-204.

Bradbury, Bruce, et al. "Inequality in Early Childhood Outcomes." *From Parents to Children. The Intergenerational Transmission of Advantage*, edited by John Ermisch et al., Russel Sage Foundation, 2012, pp. 87-119.

Bradley, Robert H. "Environment and Parenting." *Handbook of Parenting. Vol. 2: Biology and Ecology of Parenting. 3rd edition*, edited by Marc H. Bornstein, Erlbaum, 2002, pp. 281-314.

Bradley, Robert H., and Robert Corwyn. "Socioeconomic Status and Child Development." *Annual Review of Psychology*, vol. 53, no. 1, 2002, pp. 371-99.

Brooks-Gunn, Jeanne, and Greg J. Duncan. "The Effects of Poverty on Children." *The Future of Children*, vol. 7, no. 2, 1997, pp. 55-71.

Burkam, David T., and Valerie E. Lee. *Inequality at the starting gate: Social background differences in achievement as children begin school*. Economic Policy Institute, 2002.

Currie, Janet, and Enrico Moretti. "Mother's Education and the Intergenerational Transmission of Human Capital: Evidence from College Openings." *The Quarterly Journal of Economics*, vol. 118, no. 4, 2003, pp. 1495-1532.

Cutler, David, and Adriana LLeras-Muney. "Understanding Differences in Health Behaviors by Education." *Journal of Health Economics*, vol. 29, no. 1, 2010, pp. 1-28.

Del Boca, Daniela, et al. "Investments in Early Education and Child Outcomes: The Short and the Long Run." *ifo DICE Report*, vol. 15, no. 1, 2017, pp. 43-48.

Del Bono, Emilia, et al. "Early Maternal Investment and Early Child Outcomes." *The Economic Journal*, vol. 126, no. 596, 2016, pp. 96-135.

Dipartimento politiche della famiglia/Centro Nazionale di documentazione e analisi sull'infanzia e l'adolescenza. *Monitoraggio del Piano di Sviluppo dei Servizi Socio-Educativi per la Prima Infanzia*. Istituto degli Innocenti (Firenze), 2018.

Dumas, Christelle, and Arnaud Lefranc. "Early Schooling and Later Outcomes." *From Parents to Children. The Intergenerational Transmission of Advantage*, edited by John Ermisch et al., Russel Sage Foundation, 2012, pp. 164-89.

Duncan, Greg J., and Jeanne Brooks-Gunn. "Family poverty, welfare reform and child development." *Child Development*, vol. 71, no. 1, 2000, pp. 188-96.

Duncan, Greg J., and Jeanne Brooks-Gunn, editors. *Consequences of Growing Up Poor*. Russell Sage Foundation, 1997.

Duncan, Greg J., Jeanne Brooks-Gunn, and Pamela K. Klebanov. "Economic Deprivation and Early-Childhood Development." *Child Development*, vol. 65, no. 2, 1994, pp. 296-318.

Duncan, Greg J., et al. "How Much Does Childhood Poverty Affect the Life Chances of Children?" *American Sociological Review*, vol. 63, 1998, pp. 406-23.

Ermisch, John, et al. "Advantage in comparative perspective." *From Parents to Children. The Intergenerational Transmission of Advantage*, edited by John Ermisch et al., Russel Sage Foundation, 2012, pp. 3-31.

Ermisch, John, et al., editors. *From Parents to Children. The Intergenerational Transmission of Advantage*. Russel Sage Foundation, 2012.

European Commission. *Joint Report on Social Protection and Social Inclusion 2009.* European Commission, 2009, www.srseuropa.eu/publications5/2009_EU%JR. pdf. Accessed 20 Feb. 2020.

Evans, Gary W., and Michelle A. Schamberg. "Childhood poverty, chronic stress, and adult working memory." Proceedings of the National Academy of Science USA, vol. 106, no. 16, 2009, 6545-9.

Fergusson, David M., et al. "The transmission of social inequality: Examination of the linkages between family socio-economic status in childhood and educational achievement in young adulthood." *Research in Social Stratification and Mobility*, vol. 26, no. 3, 2008, pp. 277-95.

Grundiza, Sigita, and Cristina Lopez-Vilaplana. *Is the likelihood of poverty inherited?* Eurostat, 2013.

Heckman, James J. "Skill Formation and the Economics of Investing in Disadvantaged Children." *Science*, vol. 312, no. 5782, 2006, pp. 1900-2.

Herrnstein, Richard J., and Charles Murray. *The Bell Curve: Intelligence and Class Structure in American Life.* Free P Paperbacks, 1994.

INVALSI. Il *Rapporto INVALSI 2019*, https://www.invalsiopen.it/risultati/rapporto-prove-nazionali-invalsi-2019/. Accessed 23 Feb. 2020.

Istituto superiore della Sanità. *Okkio alla Salute.* ISS, 2016.

Jensen, Arthur R. "The g factor." *Nature*, vol. 381, no. 729, 1996, p. 729.

Jerrim, John, and John Micklewright. "Children's Cognitive Ability and Changes over Age in the Socioeconomic Gradient." *From Parents to Children. The Intergenerational Transmission of Advantage*, edited by John Ermisch et al., Russel Sage Foundation, 2012, pp. 262-84.

Linver, Miriam R., et al. "Parenting behavior and emotional health as mediators of family poverty effects upon young low-birthweight children's cognitive ability." *Annals of the New York Academy of Sciences*, vol. 896, 1999, pp. 376-78.

Linver, Miriam R., et al. "Family processes as pathways from income to young children's development." *Developmental Psychology*, vol. 38, no. 5, 2002, pp. 719-34.

Machin, Stephen. "Social Disadvantage and Education Experiences." *OECD Social, Employment and Migration Working Papers*, no. 32, 2006.

Marmot, Michael. The Health Gap: The Challenge of an Unequal World. Bloomsbury Publishing, 2015.

Mayer, Susan. *What Money Can't Buy: Family Income and Children's Life Chances.* Harvard UP, 1997.

Natali, Luisa, and Chiara Saraceno. "The Impact of the Great Recession on Child Poverty: The Case of Italy." *Children of Austerity*, edited by Bea Cantillon et al., Unicef/Oxford UP, 2017, pp. 170-90.

Noble, Kimberly G., et al. "Family Income, Parental Education and Brain Structure in Children and Adolescents." *Nature Neuroscience*, vol. 18, no. 5, 2015, pp. 773-78.

OECD. *A Broken social elevator? How to Promote Social Mobility.* OECD, 2018.

Ólafsson, Stefán, and Kolbeinn H. Stefánsson. "Welfare Consequences of the Crisis in Europe." *Welfare and the Great Recession. A Comparative Study,* edited by Stefán Ólafsson, et al., Oxford UP, 2019, pp. 15-42.

Pavolini, Emmanuele, and Wim van Lancker. "The Matthew effect in childcare use: a matter of policies or preferences?" *Journal of European Public Policy,* vol. 25, no. 6, 2018, pp. 878-93.

Perrons, Diane, and Ania Plomien. *Why socio-economic inequalities increase? Facts and Policy responses in Europe.* Publication Office of the European Union, 2010.

Saraceno, Chiara. *Il lavoro non basta. La povertà in Europa negli anni della crisi.* Feltrinelli, 2014.

Save the Children. *Illuminiamo il futuro 2030.* Save the Children, 2015.

Save the Children. *Il miglior inizio. Disuguaglianze e opportunità nei primi anni di vita.* Save the Children, 2019.

Shavit, Yossi, and Hans-Peter Blossfeld, editors. *Persistent Inequality: Changing Educational Attainment in Thirteen Countries.* Westview P, 1993.

Smeeding Timothy, et al., editors. *Persistence, Privilege and Parenting: The Comparative Study of Intergenerational Mobility.* Russel Sage Foundation, 2011.

World Health Organization (WHO). *Nurturing care for early child development.* WHO, 2018, https://www.who.int/maternal_child_adolescent/documents/nurturing-care-early-childhood-development/en/. Accessed 28 Dec. 2019.

Family Change and Welfare Reform in the United States Since the 1970s

Maurizio Vaudagna, Università del Piemonte Orientale

Since its origins in the second half of the 19th century, the history of American welfare has interacted with that of the family. Chiara Saraceno has stressed that "[a] significant relationship exists between social policy and civil law definitions of who or what constitutes family" (229).

Poverty and need were particularly frequent in domestic environments, and the family characterized the origins of the social provision in many ways: as an inspiration, as women social reformers saw public protection as a development of the womanly care work for children and the elderly; as a source of values for the whole national community; as a safety net in case of unemployment and low pay; and as a welfare recipient. At the same time, social family policies were to encourage preferred family values and structures.

This essay aims to develop the family-welfare link along two interacting guidelines, and focus them from the 1970s through the present: on the one hand, it will highlight which family values prevailed at any moment in time, were projected unto society as a whole, and were extolled as moral and fair in the public conversation. On the other hand, I aim to show, how social family policies tried to embody such value preferences and encouraged family arrangements to stick to them.

Since the 1960s, the core American discussion on the family-welfare relationship has dealt with whether the social provision was to either re-establish the supposedly morally superior and socially more stable "breadwinner family," or to adapt to the new plurality of family setups. Since then, historian Robert O. Self has argued that the "breadwinner model," characterized by the husband/father as the sole earner of the family's monetary income upon which children and wife "depended," while the latter cared for domesticity and child rearing, was largely obsolete (273-76). In the 1960s and 1970s, increasing family diversity, single parenthood and changing gender expectations, shaped by the sexual revolution, the rise of divorce, and the women's movement, weakened the traditional family ideal, and inaugurated the era of the 'pluralist family' characterized by a variety of setups and lifestyles.[1] The consequence was the relative decline of the middle-class family model that had ideally prevailed in the earlier century and a half.

Moreover, the family revolution meant that even the sense of what constituted a family was under discussion. The family declined as the foundation of legal prerogatives *vis à vis* the individual. The simultaneous revolution in family law recognized individual rights as superior to public needs or family membership. In the noted 1965 case *Griswold v Connecticut*, the Supreme Court ruled that matrimony was a fundamental *private* right of American citizenship.[2] Historian Nancy Cott emphasized that these legal trends contributed to putting an end to "matrimony's preeminent position as a 'pillar of the state'" (198). What emerged were "children's rights," "privacy rights," "gender-equality rights," and "reproductive rights," and courts ruled that the government could not define the family in restrictive terms. Rights emphasized individual personality *vis à vis* family membership to such a point as to limit parental authority over minor offspring.

Since the 1970s, however, innovations have been so drastic as to prevent a general consensus on what a family, and, even less, on what the 'right' family is, which became an uninterrupted battlefield of American public life. While the pluralist family has maintained its social predominance ever since, the 1980s inaugurated a change of direction in the perceptions of the 'healthy family' throughout American public life. Against the individualistic spirit of the late 1960s and 1970s that had debunked the concept of 'family values', the trend in the family-welfare policies of the last 40 years has been significantly modified in both, values and goals, by the "Reagan Revolution" of the 1980s[3] and Clinton's "Third Way" of the following decade. The neoconservative surge of the 1980s revived the ideal catchword of 'family values' to contrast the pluralist family and re-establish its nuclear precedent which had supposedly peaked in the 1950s. Against the legacy of the radical decades, the family was redefined as the fundamental source of social and national values, the patriotic cornerstone of what it meant to be American. In terms of actual familial welfare measures, the Republicans' dislike of government social protection had made their interpretation of the "social safety net" very restrictive. They believed that public support engendered passivity and a dangerous sense of entitlement within and outside the family. The new market fundamentalists feared dependence and illegitimacy as the pernicious effects of assistance to the poor, who were 'worthy' of protection only if they conformed to the traditional nuclear family model. Republicans were weary of the government as social security distributor, and preferred

---

1   Compare Andrea Carosso's contribution on Disney's 1967 propaganda animation film *Family Planning*.

2   See the contributions by Antonio Legerén-Molina and Josep Ferrer-Riba for elaborations on this concept within (Spanish) family law.

3   See also Stefano Morello's article on punk kinship of the 1980s as alternative family forms.

services to be provided by private actors and be bought on the market, possibly helping purchasers with tax deductions. Republicans shared with many Democrats the notion of the somewhat shameful status of being on welfare. Critics of Johnson's Great Society prevailed by the mid/late 1970s and transformed the former commitment to the War on Poverty into its opposite, the War on Welfare (Lo and Schwartz 267-301). The Democrats' appreciation of family life was also changing: the so called "New Democrats," the new party leadership that emerged in the 1990s as a response to the neoconservative success in the former decade, distanced itself from the New Deal legacy in favor of a "new centrism," and borrowed from conservatives a strong suspicion of welfare, which sounded increasingly as a bad word, as getting something for nothing.

At the beginning of the 1990s, the "New Democrat" Bill Clinton publicized his preference of "family values," even if colored by a progressive tone (Clinton). Away from the radical 1970s and the neoconservative 1980s, especially in the presidential campaign of 1992, Clinton's "New Democrats" tried to steal away from Republicans their cherished theme of "family values," to become the cornerstone of a "New Covenant" of progressive politics that would put an end to the long Republican hold of power. Clinton's new stance was the result of a long-term liberal change of mind regarding the link between welfare and family prosperity. Under the shock of the family revolution, and the pressure of conservative ideas on 'welfare as a way of life', labor unions, antipoverty activists, and liberal groups, that is the "antipoverty coalition" of the 1960s, condemned the culture of entitlements and federal programs like AFDC (Aid to Families with Dependent Children, in support of poor mothers with infant children) for creating family "dysfunction," discouraging marriage, and forcing couples to split so that women could qualify for welfare benefits.

The Clintonian shift away from assistance and poverty relief consisted in pairing opportunity and responsibility. Republicans objected, Democrats were loudly proclaiming "family values," but were doing basically nothing, except issuing moral tirades, to actually help "healthy families." Compared to Republicans, said Clinton, we "will demand more from families, but [...] will offer more, too" (as quoted in McClain 1627). Nobody had a right to public protection, said Clinton. The government was no more to dispense welfare, but to create opportunities, especially work opportunities, that people in need had to responsibly take advantage of via activation programs, new training, moving from welfare to work, and following responsible family and parental behaviors. "The new legislation," said sociologist Sharon Hays, "was to train poor families in 'mainstream' American values" (4). As "New Democrats" identified the 'disease' of American life in the "crisis of the middle class," then it was middle class values that had to be restored. No more "politics of entitlement," therefore, as in President Johnson's Great Society: liberals fought instead to extend the fading promise of the breadwinner's family wage to poor white and black families through massive federal investment in full employment and income support (Rose 153-86). Citizens had to work hard, play by the rules, and give back to society something in exchange for the opportunities it had made available to them. Jobs and responsible family ways would liberate the poor from the shame of dependence. Local welfare offices started being decorated with "inspirational phrases like 'perseverance', 'seizing opportunities', 'determination', 'success'" (Hays 3).

Whether understood in a liberal or conservative vein, "family values" had plenty in common: both interpretations stressed the social engineering task of government legislation and family social policy: benefits and opportunities were to be framed in such a way as to encourage family arrangements that were deemed more moral and socially beneficial. Scared by out-of-wedlock births, teenage pregnancy, the rise of divorces, and family desertion, both parties emphasized that legislation was to foster the 'right' family life. What it actually meant, however, differed: in its own version of family responsibility, Clintonism redefined the concept of a "healthy family," and did not select the legal, nuclear family as the only admissible model: cohabiting, remarried, or single parents could very well fall within the boundaries of the healthy family. The accent fell on "responsible fatherhood" to continue supporting his children's emotional, educational, and economic lives, and keeping constructive contacts with their children's mother.

In terms of family legislation, Clintonism moved in different, contradictory directions. For example, on the topic of gay marriage. In 2013, the Supreme Court repealed DOMA (Defense of Marriage Act), approved in 1996 under Clinton. The law was deeply in contrast with Clintonian principles, the president signed it at night with no fanfare due to political expediency, and has recently repudiated it. It barred the federal government from recognizing same-sex marriages legalized by individual states, and prevented same-sex couples from receiving benefits provided to other married couples under federal law. In the opposite direction, the Medical and Family Leave Act of 1993 has made available 12 weeks of unpaid family leave to mothers of newborns, and is the source of the present debate on paid leave.

But the peak family legislation in the Clintonian opportunity and responsibility vein was the "welfare reform" of 1996 that cancelled AFDC, thus overturning 60 years of federal responsibility for poor children and their caregivers. The program was important not only as the leading measure of federal support for poor families, but also because since the 1930s, in contrast with the predominant middle-class nuclear model, it had built a system of money transfers in favor of nontraditional families headed by unmarried, poor women with children. By the 1990s, welfare had few supporters, and it is ironic that it was up to a Democratic president to put an end to it. It is a symptom of its unpopularity that, in spite of the debatable results of its repeal, a similar welfare measure has never again come up for discussion.

AFDC was substituted by the TANF (Temporary Assistance for Needy Families) program, much shorter in time limits, less generous in monetary subsidies, and conditioned by compulsory retraining and searching for a job (the so-called welfare-to-work, or activation precondition). AFDC's successor devolved responsibility for poor families to states and counties. As a step in the war against the notion of "social rights," under TANF no individual or family is "entitled" to welfare, and members are limited to a total of five-year assistance in a lifetime. In an effort to "moralize" the American poor family, TANF also promotes marriage, discourages teenage pregnancy, and tries to limit the number of their children: minor parents cannot receive TANF benefits unless they are living at home with their parents or in another adult-supervised setting. Another issue is that TANF subsidies can be managed and distributed by private nonprofit or for-profit agencies, which may result in reducing service access to highly needy, and therefore 'costly' clients. Moreover, its so called "charitable choice" encouraged states to expand the role of religious organizations as qualified service providers, as was the case with George W. Bush's controversial "faith-based initiative," where religious groups provided social-service programs without breaching the separation of church and state.

According to its framers, the elimination of AFDC and the arrival of TANF was a "success," as it saw welfare rolls plummet at the cost, however, of increasing inequality and poverty. Blessed by the prosperity of the 1990s, welfare rolls "registered a dramatic decline – from 12.2 million recipients in 1996, to 5.3 million in 2001. Although nearly 2/3 of former welfare clients had found some kind of work, half of those were not making wages sufficient to raise them out of poverty" (Hays 8).

Different from Clintonism legitimizing diverse family setups, it was for Republicans to proclaim that the only way to family responsibility was marriage. In George W. Bush's welfare plan *Working Toward Independence*, it was openly stated that child well-being and responsible fatherhood were achieved via work and legal marriage. In 2002, during the Bush administration, the Department of Health and Human Services launched a "healthy marriage" initiative, based on "demonstration projects" performed by public or private actors involved in family support. In the Republican understanding of the link of healthy families and family welfare, only the 1950s-style nuclear model was the 'right' one (McClain 1650-51).

Obama's social family policy mainly followed Clintonian guidelines, that is, pairing responsibility and opportunity, work and family, in a cooperative spirit of community, while distancing himself from welfare as assistance and entitlement. The Obama administration introduced, however, some new perspectives. As legal scholar Linda C. McClain has emphasized,

> one striking feature is the way in which he [Obama] and First Lady Michelle Obama have made the personal political in relating the stories of their upbringing, marriage, and experience as parents to concrete policies such as workplace flexibility, promoting responsible fatherhood and healthy marriage [...moreover,] the Obama administration's distinct focus on women and girls [has insisted] that

many economic and social issues are not just 'women's,' but affect families, men, the economy, and the nation. (McClain 1716)

According to the Pew Research Center, the presidential couple's focus on gender issues has convinced many American women to favor bigger government and its social services. Women's support stands at 58% against 36% opposed, while earlier it was evenly divided (in mirror-like contrast, 59% of men are opposed to bigger government against 37% in favor) (Hartig).

The present president, a "plutocratic populist" in the definition of distinguished public commentator Fareed Zakaria, comes from neither of these welfare traditions. Trump has not placed "family values" at the center of his message. The focus on healthy domestic units is usually aimed to encourage national cohesion, because of the universality of the family condition. Trump's populist message is divisive, stressing "us" versus "them," and "family values" is not fitting with his narration (Zakaria). Trump is perceived to have widened the gender gap more than his presidential predecessors. This has deepened the gap between men's and women's evaluation of his presidential performance. While in the late spring of 2019, men's opinion was evenly divided, 63% of women were instead critical, while only 32% were supportive (Hartig). This is not surprising, as Trump's access to power has been interpreted as the backlash of whiteness and masculinity against the Democrats' "political correctness." Still, on individual family issues, the present president has erratically fluctuated, mostly responding to personal popularity goals and electoral expediency. Trump has supported abstinence campaigns against sexual education, as well as anti-contraceptive advertising, because condoms would incite "risky" sexual behavior. After many oscillations, the president has prohibited public funding to family planning agencies if abortion was mentioned in their pamphlets, has appointed new anti-abortion justices to the Supreme Court, but has avoided focusing on the repeal of *Roe v Wade*. He has stated that marriage is by nature heterosexual, but has equally held that the Supreme Court DOMA sentence that legalized same-sex marriage may be here to stay (McClain 1630).

The same volatility shows in Trump's vision of the work-family balance. In his words, pregnancy is an inconvenience for employers, equal pay requires women to prove they are as good as men on the job, work requirements should be extended to other welfare programs like food stamps, and childless families are free riders, because children will pay our entitlements in decades to come. But once again the president's stance has been more complicated, especially on matters of childcare. In the 2016 presidential campaign, Trump, recognizing the increasing women's participation in the labor market and under the influence of his daughter Ivanka, pledged to make childcare more affordable for working families via tax deductions. Little concrete measures have followed these promises.

While the Republican Senate opposes government "interference," public spending, and favors decentralizing welfare matters to states, still one important family measure has been at the center of much public and congressional debate: paid maternal or family leave, after the unpaid version that has been legislated in 1993. More than 80% of women and 3 out of 4 men are in favor.

Both leading Republican and Democratic senators have introduced bills on paid leave that show important differences regarding recipients, length and ways to fund it. Democratic senator Kirsten Gillibrand's bill provides for a 12-weeks family leave, available to both mothers and fathers, to be funded by a payroll tax paid by both employers and employees and supported by a government subsidy. Republican senator Marco Rubio's project envisages instead a six-weeks maternal leave totally funded by the recipient's Social Security pension, to be proportionately delayed in time or reduced in quantity when the parent will retire. Both projects incite controversy: Republicans want no new taxes, Democrats object that maternal leave reiterates the sexist notion that domesticity and child rearing are women's burdens, and that the individual discretion to advance Social Security money not only violates a fundamental social right, but condemns people in need to a retirement of scarcity (Vesoulis).

Since the 1980s, the "healthy family" has had a comeback as a signpost of the "American way" and Clinton's famous line of 1996 on the "end of welfare as we know it" is the exemplary slogan of the welfare-family history from then to the present. Different from northern and central Europe, where childcare public services are quite popular (Ferrera 9-10), in the United States the ambiguity of the family ideals has not been resolved. In spite of the vast female employment, the dream of the breadwinner model where the stay-at-home mother/wife requires less family services and allegedly creates the best environment for successful children, family stability, and national good health, is still very alive in conservative circles. Often the politicians who support cuts in family benefits and poor mothers' obligation to find a job, are the same who cherish "family values" based on stay-at-home moms, and denounce women's tiring second shift. Differently from Europe, which has generally adopted the model of the two-, or one-and-a-half family earners, in the US the notion that women's work-family balance requires quality services and caretakers to temporarily replace working mothers is still guilt ridden.[4]

Alone among the advanced capitalist countries, the US has never provided a universal family allowance program, and childcare services emphasize another typical feature of the American welfare provision: a strong public/private link where services are provided by private non-profit or for-profit actors. The government has introduced no national childcare legislation or universal childcare programs,

---

4   See also on this aspect the analysis of the Italian situation by Chiara Saraceno.

and often utilizes only tax credits and deductions to help families buy childcare on the market (Olsen).

In a nutshell, the nature of the "healthy family" and the government's duty to support it, are in today's US an embattled terrain, open to multiple interpretations, values, and legislative programs, which are unlikely to soon come to rest.

Bibliography

Clinton, Bill. "Address at Notre Dame University, South Bend, Indiana, September 11, 1992," http://www.nytimes.com/1992/09/12/us/the-1992-campaign-democrats-clinton-says-foes-sow-intolerance.html/. Accessed 12 Oct. 2019.

Cott, Nancy F. *Public Vows. A History of Marriage and the Nation.* Harvard UP, 2000.

Ferrera, Maurizio. *La società del Quinto Stato.* Laterza, 2019.

Hartig, Hanna. "Gender Gap Widens in Views of Government's Role – and of Trump." *Pew Research Center*, 11 April 2019, https://www.pewresearch.org/fact-tank/2019/04/11/gender-gap-widens-in-views-of-governments-role-and-of-trump/. Accessed 9 Oct. 2019.

Hays, Sharon. *Flat Broke with Children. Women in the Age of Welfare Reform.* Oxford UP, 2003.

Lo, Clarence Y.H., and M. Schwartz. *Social Policy and the Conservative Agenda.* Blackwell, 1998.

McClain, Linda C. "Federal Family Policy and Family Values from Clinton to Obama, 1992 to 2012 and Beyond." *Michigan State Law Review*, vol. 1621, 2013, pp. 1621-1718.

Olsen, Gregg M. "Toward Global Welfare Convergence? Family Policy and Health Care in Sweden, Canada, and the United States." *The Journal of Sociology and Social Welfare*, vol. 34, no. 2, 2007, pp. 148-51.

Rose, Elisabeth. "Head Start Growing Beyond the War on Poverty." *LBJ's Neglected Legacy*, edited by Robert W. Wilson et al., U of Texas P, 2015, pp. 153-86.

Saraceno, Chiara. "Family Matters: Social Policy, an Overlooked Constraint on the Development of European Citizenship." *Democracy and the Welfare State. The Two Wests in the Age of Austerity*, edited by Alice Kessler-Harris and Maurizio Vaudagna, Columbia UP, 2018, pp. 229-48.

Self, Robert O. "Breadwinner Liberalism and Its Discontents in the American Welfare State." *Democracy and the Welfare State. The Two Wests in the Age of Austerity*, edited by Alice Kessler-Harris and Maurizio Vaudagna, Columbia UP, 2018, pp. 273-76.

Vesoulis, Abby. "Paid Family Leave Has Stalled in Congress for Years. Here's Why That's Changing." *Time Magazine*, 4 May 2019, https://timedotcom.

files.wordpress.com/2019/04/paid-family-leave-gillibrand-trump-rubio.jpg. Accessed 12 Oct. 2019.

Zakaria, Fareed. "The Normalization of Trumpism and the End of Globalization." *Washington Post*, 23 Jan. 2020, https://fareedzakaria.com/columns/2020/1/23/the-normalization-of-trumpism-and-the-end-of-globalization. Accessed 14 Feb. 2020.

Patrimonial Benefits Arising from Family Crises[1]

Antonio Legerén-Molina, Universidade da Coruña

Introduction

If this book's goal is to ask from different international and disciplinary perspectives whether the family is in crisis, this chapter will only address the Spanish situation and from a legal viewpoint. In spite of such delimitation of the object of analysis, it is worth suggesting early on that it is impossible to conclude whether the family as a whole – at least in Spain – is or is not in crisis, primarily for three reasons.

The first: because Spanish legislation does not set forth any normative definition of what the family is; so, it is impossible to determine whether what is actually practiced in daily life coincides with any particular definition.[2] Second: because most of Spanish families live 'outside the law'. Or more accurately: they live 'outside the conflictive dimension of legal rules' – which are resolved by courts – and such families apply family law in a peaceful and nonjudicial way. Since the courts do not account for millions of people and legal operators who apply 'legal rules' on an informal and non-contentious basis – thus avoiding, to a certain extent, the situation typically resolved by judges – it is not easy to determine, on a larger scale,

---

1   I want to expressly thank Brian McCoy and Marc Doherty for their valuable suggestions to this paper.

2   The only existing references to the family at constitutional level are included in sections 32 and 39 of the current *Spanish Constitution* of 1978. The first provides that "1. Man and woman have the right to marry with full legal equality. 2. The law shall make provision for the forms of marriage, the age and capacity for concluding it, the rights and duties of the spouses, the grounds for separation and dissolution, and their effects." And the second section states that: "1. The public authorities ensure social, economic and legal protection of the family. 2. The public authorities likewise ensure full protection of children, who are equal before the law, regardless of their parentage, and of mothers, whatever their marital status. The law shall provide for the possibility of the investigation of paternity. 3. Parents must provide for their children, whether born within or outside wedlock, with assistance of every kind while they are still under age and in other circumstances in which the law so establishes" (*Spanish Constitution*).

the current legal reality of the family. And third: due to reasons of space it is impossible to examine here the plethora of current trends in Spanish family law from at least, say, a legal, jurisprudential and sociological perspective, in order to offer a more definitive answer regarding whether the alleged family crisis actually exists.

Among the abovementioned difficulties, the most relevant at this stage is the first. Indeed, in the last several decades, the family has experienced an intense evolution at the social and legal level. In this last area, it may be affirmed that while previous Spanish family law sought to emphasize equality between spouses and children, nowadays the regulations place greater emphasis on the freedom and diversity within family units (Espinosa de Soto 73).[3] As a result, the legal system does not refer to 'a family model', but accepts several realities which citizens can choose with the intention of fulfilling the function performed by a family, e.g. single parent families, nuclear or extended families, reconstituted or blended families, cooperative living arrangements, etc.[4] The family, therefore, has evolved from a 'natural reality', which in its nuclear form was given to human beings, into a configurable unit by the individuals or society at large (Martínez de Aguirre 29). In this context, a privatization trend has emerged and family law norms have been losing the imperative character which characterized them years ago, allowing for a greater latitude and autonomy to configure interests and relationships within the family context. That does not, however, eliminate the existence of imperative norms outside the freedom of agreement in order to protect the most vulnerable members of the community.[5]

Thus, given the absence of a legal definition of 'the' family model which encompasses the diverse family realities of today; in view of the fact that judicial dec-

---

3   Some of the most important laws enacted in Family Law in Spain in recent years are: Law 13/2005, 1 July, on same sex marriage; Law 15/2005, 8 July, on divorce; Law 14/2006, 26 May, on assisted reproduction; Law 54/2007, 28 November, on international adoption; Law 15/2015, 2 July, on voluntary jurisdiction; Law 8/2015, 22 July and Law 26/2015, 28 July, on the modification of the system for the protection of children and teenagers.

4   Together with typology mentioned in the main text, current families are also linked to international, intercultural or interreligious elements; aspects which, for instance, have revived, among others, the problem of marriages of convenience.

5   One of the corollaries of the indicated trends is the dejudicialization of family issues. In this regard, Law 15/2015 is very significant in Spain, because one of its main purposes was to subtract from judicial scope those functions not strictly jurisdictional, maintaining its intervention to defend fundamental rights or the aforementioned people. On the other hand, there is also an evolution from a collective vision of the family to a more individual one, where elements such as the free exercise of fundamental rights are stressed, while matters such as family responsibilities or concepts such as "interest of the family" lose their importance (cf. art. 67 of the *Spanish Civil Code*; hereinafter CC). Such evolution has also been accompanied by a more focused view, at a large scale, on adults' wishes than on the children's interests, creating, in the opinion of Glendon, "an adult-centered Family Law" (xiii).

larations address only a small portion of the family law situations; and inasmuch as it is impossible to carry out a thorough examination of every matter related to that area of the legal system, it seems impossible to conclude definitively whether the family is in fact in crisis. For this reason, instead of on the crisis of the family, the following pages will be focused on family crises, which, unfortunately, constitute a frequent phenomenon from particularly a sociological point of view.[6] More specifically, based on Spanish Supreme Court decisions, the main benefits of a patrimonial nature that arise from marital or partner separations and ruptures will be examined.[7] Focusing this chapter's goal on the analysis of the main patrimonial benefits derived from family crises – antenuptial agreements in anticipation of rupture, alimony and child support – it will be left to the reader to determine whether the present-day family is experiencing a crisis.[8]

Prenuptial Agreements in Anticipation of Rupture and Alimony

One of the consequences of the evolution mentioned in the previous section is the spouses' or partners' greater autonomy to configure the legal status of the family

---

6   According to the Spanish National Statistics Institute (www.ine.es), the average number of annulment, separation and divorce judgements between 2010 and 2017 is 108.382 annually, excluding those relating to *de facto* unions in which, as is well known, there is no formal procedure. The average of those couples with minor children is 52.8%. Likewise, and although marriage is still the majority type of union in Spain, there is an increasing number of *de facto* unions and a correspondent decrease of the nuptiality rate. Beside this, and as a result of the modification of divorce procedures introduced in 2005, 9 out of 10 ruptures are divorces, so that separation and nullity are playing just a residual role. The 97% of divorced couples with children have a high level of conflict, which explains the quantitative increase of resolutions on custody, use of family home and alimony (Asociación Española de Abogados de Familia 3). Finally, along with family crises, another typical core of problems of the current family sociological map is the care for dependent people. Figures such as powers of attorney, support or curatorship, among others, try to figure these questions out; their discussion exceeds the purpose of this contribution.

7   The interest of resting on jurisprudence resides, on the one hand, in the fact that they are *real* cases of *real* people, and, on the other, in the fact that sometimes innovations have been introduced through the judges updating or interpreting existing legal criteria; i.e. the recognition of the *de facto* filiation.

8   The first two measures analyzed in this paper are more focused on the couple itself, and the last one more on the children; those respond to the dispositive principle and parties must request it (arg. *ex* art. 97 CC) and the last can be established *ex officio* (arg. *ex* art. 93 CC). Along with these benefits, other consequences of family crises are, in the economic order, the use of family home and distribution of furniture, as well as the division of marital property; and with personal content, the exercise of parental rights, child custody, and, where appropriate, the regime of visits.

and some family relationships. That fact could be understood as an informal recognition of their best position to decide which is most appropriate for their diverse family situations. However, when a divorce or notarial separation takes place and there are children of legal age, they, too, must give their consent to the measures that affect them, which gives them some decision-making authority in configuring the ultimate result.

Regarding couples, it is commonly understood they can reach two types of prenuptial agreements: those through which they can alter their rights established by law, either by modifying or eliminating them – i.e. waiving alimony in married couples for example[9] – and those which attribute rights *ex novo*, not specifically contemplated by law.[10] Although such agreements do not have an explicit recognition in the Civil Code, there is a broad consensus regarding their admissibility. In particular, the Supreme Court has approved them on several occasions, using, as legal authority, articles 1.323 and 1.325 of the Spanish Civil Code, which are a specification of the autonomy of will regarding contracts contained in article 1.255 CC, but included in the primary matrimonial economic regime and premarital contracts sections (cf. Supreme Court judgements of 24 June 2015 [RJ 2015, 2657] and 31 March 2011 [RJ 2011, 3137], among many others).

Admitting such possibility, the aforementioned agreements are subject to a triple examination: an initial one at the time of its drafting in order to guarantee freedom of consent, a second one regarding the content itself, and a third one at the time of its execution.[11]

With regard to the first examination, it attempts to ensure that both parties enjoy a truly autonomous position, not only from a legal point of view, but also from an economic, social or cultural perspective, thus guaranteeing the independence of will necessary to form a contract (Scherpe 62-63). To achieve this goal, several legal regimes have introduced supplementary measures to ensure and strengthen such autonomy – i.e. providing relevant financial information to each other and/or receiving independent legal advice.

---

9   Other matters that can be the content of such agreements are financial compensation due to domestic work (cf. art. 1.438 CC), or the allocation of the use of family housing (cf. art. 96 CC). As an example, a waiver agreement for both alimony and the use of housing is contained in Supreme Court judgement [hereinafter SC]] of 30 May 2018 [R] 2018, 2358].

10   Some examples of agreements admitted by jurisprudence are the prenuptial in which a life annuity in favor of the wife is settled (cf. SC] of 31 March 2011 [R] 2011, 3137] and 24 June 2015 [R] 2015, 2657]), the agreement whereby the husband will pay a pension to his wife if she does not work in his business, the agreement by which one of the spouses agrees to pay the mortgage alone, or, finally, the one which settles a pension that will be paid to the other spouse even when s/he enters the labor market, provided s/he earns less than a specified amount. About different types of agreements see Quicios Molina 1007-8.

11   On this topic, see García Rubio 102.

Regarding the second form of examination, the central issue under discussion here are the limits of the aforementioned agreements. In this regard, it must be examined whether they respect the minors' interests and preserve the principle of equality; the latter not only meaning that neither party suffers any kind of subordination nor enjoys supremacy over the other, but also meaning the benefits are truly reciprocal, especially in the first type of prenuptial agreements – those through which they alter the rights established by law.[12] However, this does not prevent a party from freely accepting non-reciprocity or making an early waiver of benefits. Once autonomy is verified in the formation and issuance of consent and the knowledge of the consequences takes place, such clauses and waivers must be admitted.[13]

And with respect to the third form of scrutiny, in parallel with the *rebus sic stantibus* doctrine, it is appropriate to examine the agreement again at the time of its execution, in order to avoid that it makes an obligation for one of the parties particularly onerous or that the agreement becomes seriously detrimental due to a substantive alteration of the circumstances involved.[14]

More specifically, regarding the alimony that derives from article 97 CC, in view of the high number of cases that have reached the Supreme Court, it is difficult to establish definitive general guidelines about it. In any case, the possibility of waiving marital cohabitation as a termination cause – as is established by article 101 CC – has been approved by the Supreme Court (cf. SCJ of 11 December 2015 [RJ 2015, 5414]). Also, it has been declared several times that alimony does not pretend equity-matching between spouses' estates, but to repair a real imbalance when it exists (cf. SCJ of 23 January 2012 [RJ 2012, 1900]). That imbalance is an element that has to be proven with respect to the moment of the rupture only, inasmuch as it is impossible to take into account subsequent events (cf. SCJ of 27 November 2014 [RJ 2014, 6034]). Likewise, it is also part of the Supreme Court doctrine on alimony that such benefit does not eliminate the obligee's obligation to procure his or her own support, since alimony does not constitute a lifetime income or a life insurance. As

---

12   SCJ of 30 May 2018 [RJ 2018, 2358] refers to the two limits mentioned in the text, using the analogy with section 90.2 CC. Vid., over that judgment, Rodríguez Guitián 261-77. Vid. also SCJ 24 June 2015 [RJ 2015, 2657].

13   What is mentioned in the text must be considered just as a general principle: in that context many other elements that can give support to an eventual challenge of the agreement must be addressed, too: the third party's damage by the indicated resignation (cf. art. 6.2 CC), the foreseeable precariousness post-crisis which can be an argument to challenge the resignation based on public order, etc.

14   The *rebus sic stantibus* doctrine ("things standing thus") is a typical civil law doctrine similar to the common law *frustration* test and *termination*. It's applicable when, without intervention of the contract parties, there is a great change of the circumstances they took in account at the moment of the perfection of the contract, and this change makes the fulfilment to one of them unbearable and unfair.

a corollary of such reasoning, the Supreme Court has declared the termination of alimony once the obligee's negligence in searching for a job or autonomous support is proven.[15] Partly because of the above, there are many cases where the High Court has admitted the conversion of a lifetime alimony to a temporary one due to the change of personal circumstances;[16] the mere passage of time cannot be considered as such, unless initially it was so configured (cf. SCJ of 27 June 2011 [RJ 2011, 4890]).[17]

Child Support

As with the figures examined in the previous section, child support is another issue which in recent years has reached the Supreme Court with unusual frequency – logical consequence of the aforementioned increase of family crises.

From the outset, it is necessary to distinguish support for minors and referred to children of legal age; both receive a different treatment. Regarding minor's support, the Supreme Court declared that "more than a proper support obligation, what exists are inescapable duties inherent to filiation, which at first are unconditional regardless of the greater or lesser difficulty to comply with it or the degree

---

15   In this regard, the SCJ of 24 September 2018 [RJ 2018, 3856] emphasizes "the impossibility to consider the loss of the right to alimony as a kind of sanction for the fact of not having accessed a job, unless it is proven that the concurrent circumstances in which it turns out to be a beneficiary of the pension show a real lack of interest and disinterest regarding access to the labor market." After the aforementioned statement, the solution to that case is surprising, since it seems to focus only on the impossibility of conceiving the termination of alimony as a sanction and maintains it in that case. Previously, SCJ of 23 January 2012 [RJ 2012, 1900] and 15 June 2011 [RJ 2011, 4634] have already declared that "passivity, insufficient interest shown by the wife with her conduct in order to get an employment that would allow her to reach a situation of economic independence, it is decisive when assessing the objective situation of overcoming the imbalance or being able to do so, since it is not legally acceptable to refer to the pension payer the negative consequences derived from the lack of access to a job based on the wife's passivity in her search and obtaining."

16   Vid., in this regard, the SCJ of 27 October 2011 [RJ 2012, 1131] and 20 June 2013 [RJ 2013, 4377] where it was stated that "the person obligated to pay the pension may request the modification of this measure, but for this he must prove that the causes that gave rise to its existence have ceased to exist, totally or partially. It is the change of circumstances that determined the imbalance which motivated its recognition, which can also make temporary a lifetime pension, because it is authorized by article 100 CC, and because the legal regulations do not configure, with a necessary character, the pension as a right of indefinite duration." As an example, SCJ of 17 March 2014 [RJ 2014, 1501] establishes the termination of alimony based on the perception of an inheritance.

17   In a similar way, vid. SCJ of 3 October 2008 [RJ 2008, 7123] and SCJ of 19 February 2016 [RJ 2016, 554].

of reprehensibility in father's lack of attention" (SCJ of 12 February 2015 [RJ 2015, 338]).[18]

Be that as it may, on several occasions the jurisprudence has recognized that the matter now mentioned is a *ius cogens* issue and, consequently, the court can set up the support *ex officio* – the proportionality is of the prudent discretion of the instance, not susceptible to be appealed. And while it is not possible to waive the future support, it is valid if it is referred to what was not perceived in the past, including that one earned in favor of minors (cf. SCJ of 27 September 2017 [RJ 2017, 4110] and 10 November 1987 [RJ 1987, 8344]). This does not impede to affirm that, from a procedural point of view, the 'open' lawsuits are more accurate in order to leave the court freedom to set up, where appropriate, the corresponding child support and the amount.

Another consequence of the aforementioned is the maintenance of a very strict line with respect to the "minimum vital" necessary to cover the most essential expenses in child care by the Supreme Court: it must be paid in any case, relegating to second place the obligor's needs. According to the Supreme Court, such minimum does not disappear because the obligor has entered prison (cf. SCJ of 14 October 2014 [RJ 2014, 4754]), because article 93 CC is not solely based on 'pocket money' but on obligor's economic capacity, on his resources, and not only on his income. Therefore, immediate liquidity is not required, because the estate amount is also taken into account and the payment of the minimum is only suspended in certain exceptional cases (cf. among others, SCJ of 10 July 2015 [RJ 2015, 2563] and of 21 November 2016 [RJ 2016, 6304]).[19] In fact, the Supreme Court notes that only with a "very exceptional character, with restrictive and temporary criteria" the "suspension of the obligation" should be admitted and, accordingly, "in the face of the slightest presumption of income, whatever its origin and circumstances may be, it would be necessary to recur to what is considered the normal solution, even at

---

18   In recent years there has been a change in the Supreme Court doctrine according to which children with disabilities are no longer automatically identified for support purposes with minors, especially in relation to family house. Vid., in this regard, SCJ of 13 December 2017 [RJ 2017, 5406]. Similarly, vid. SCJ of 19 January 2017 [RJ 2017, 924], of 8 March 2017 [RJ 2017, 1633], or of 4 April 2018 [RJ 2018, 1185], all of them in relation to the use of family house. As an example of the traditional thesis, which made the aforementioned identification, vid., among all, SCJ of 7 July 2014 [RJ 2014, 3540] and 17 July 2015 [RJ 2015, 3020].

19   Proof of the "minimum vital" importance is that articles 607 and 608 Spanish Civil Procedure Act (hereinafter CPA), regarding the non-seizure of the minimum wage, are not applied when there are breaches of the support obligation, unless otherwise established by the judge in the judgement. On the other hand, the terms used in the judgements that exempt the aforementioned obligation clearly show its extraordinary nature: "absolute poverty" (SC) of 2 March 2015, [RJ 2015, 601]), "in case of proved insolvency of the obligor parent" (SCJ of 18 March 2016 [RJ 2016, 1136]), or "absolute poverty" (SC) of 20 July 2017 [RJ 2017, 3385]).

the cost of an obligor's great sacrifice" (SCJ of 2 March 2015 [RJ 2015, 601] and of 12 February 2015 [RJ 2015, 338]).

Notwithstanding the foregoing, and in accordance with article 147 CC, the child support can be modified when circumstances change and the obligor's patrimonial availability demands a modification of the amount; for example, and among others, because the custody of the children varies (cf. SCJ of 14 February 2018 [RJ 2018, 459]), or due to the birth of a new child (cf. SCJ of 30 April 2013 [RJ 2013, 4607] and 1 February 2017 [RJ 2017, 370]).[20] In any case, child support is owed from the date of filing the suit which claims it, if the resolution declares the obligation to pay the support (arg. *ex* art. 138 CC);[21] in case of subsequent modification of the amount, the support will be owed just since the date in which the change is established by the judgement, without retroactive effects to the moment of the filing of the claim (arg. *ex* art. 106 CC and 774.5 CPA).[22] Likewise, support must not to be paid if it is proven that filiation relationship which gives sense to it did not exist (cf. SCJ of 24 April 2015 [RJ 2015, 1915]).[23]

In relation to the children of legal age support, it is worth mentioning several Supreme Court judgments in which its extinction is addressed. According to the doctrine held in them, living together and economic dependence do not guarantee that right to support – it can also be voluntarily paid – and, if it is in existence, it will be extinguished if the child leaves the family home or is economically independent. However, there is a right to support when there is a lack of consolidated professional training without fault, and, consequently, it is excluded or extinguished when the obligee has a passive attitude to conclude his studies (cf. SCJ of 28 October 2015 [RJ 2015, 4785], 21 September 2016 [RJ 2016, 4443], 22 June 2017 [RJ 2017, 3040], 24 May 2018 [RJ 2018, 2130] or 14 February 2019 [RJ 2019, 562]). Finally, the support is also extinguished if there is a distancing relationship with the obligor parent attributable to the obligee or he incurs in an ingratitude cause.[24]

---

20   Another issue that has raised a big debate in courts is the determination of whether an expense is of ordinary or extraordinary character. Some cases of extraordinary expenses, subject to both parents or to the judicial agreement, are extracurricular activities, those derived from stays and language courses abroad, or those resulting from obtaining the driver's license.

21   Vid. also SCJ of 6 October 2016 [R] 2016, 4737] where the retroactive effects are explained, as well as the specific case included in SCJ of 18 July 2018 [RJ 2018, 2952].

22   Cf. SCJ of 26 March 2014 [R] 2014, 2035], of 15 June 2015 [R] 2015, 2289], of 2 February 2018 [R] 2018, 291], of 19 June 2018 [R] 2018, 2667] and of 17 January 2019 [R] 2019, 105].

23   In the case mentioned in the text, the obligor claimed unduly paid pensions, and the Supreme Court, with, in my opinion, a poor and inadequate criterion, denied it. A similar criterion was maintained in SCJ of 29 September 2016 [RJ 2016, 4457].

24   Regarding this, vid. SCJ of 19 February 2019 [R] 2019, 497].

Conclusion

In the preceding pages the difficulty to determine from a legal perspective whether the family as such is in crisis has been pointed out. At the same time, it has also been stated that the legal system can establish – as it actually does – suitable tools to solve the problems that arise from the frequent family crises; among others, alimony and child support. In this context, the difficulty of a constant updating of the laws as well as people's greater autonomy in order to configure some of the family relationships – i.e. prenuptial agreements – give both judges and family members an important role in the search for fair solutions to the problems which emerge from the application of family law.

Bibliography

Asociación Española de Abogados de Familia. *I Observatorio del Derecho de Familia*, 2019, www.aeafa.es. Accessed 20 Feb. 2020.

Espinosa de Soto, José Luis. "Nuevas tendencias en el Derecho de familia." *Escritura Pública*, vol. 73, July-August, 2016, p. 73.

García Rubio, María Paz. "Acuerdos prematrimoniales. De nuevo la libertad y sus límites en el Derecho de Familia." *Nuevos retos de Derecho de Familia*. Documentia Universitaria, 2005, pp. 95-122.

Glendon, Mary Ann. "Foreword." *Reconceiving the Family* edited by Robin Fretwell Wilson, Cambridge UP, 2006, pp. xiii-xv.

Martínez de Aguirre, Carlos. "Familia, sociedad y Derecho." *Curso de Derecho civil*, IV, 5th edition. Edisofer, 2016, pp. 21-36.

Quicios Molina, Susana. "Liberalidades acordadas en previsión de una hipotética ruptura conyugal." *Tratado de las liberalidades*, Thomson Reuters Aranzadi, 2017, pp. 999-1021.

Rodríguez Guitián, Alma María. "Los pactos en previsión de crisis y los límites de su validez." *Cuadernos Civitas de Jurisprudencia Civil*, no. 109, 2019, pp. 261-77.

Scherpe, Jens. *The Present and Future of European Family Law*, IV. Edward Elgar Publishing Limited, 2016.

Spanish Constitution. https://www.boe.es/biblioteca_juridica/index.php?tipo=C &modo=2. Accessed 20 Feb. 2020.

Spanish Supreme Court Judgements

SCJ of 3 October 2008 [RJ 2008, 7123]

SCJ of 31 March 2011 [RJ 2011, 3137]

SCJ of 15 June 2011 [RJ 2011, 4634]
SCJ of 27 October 2011 [RJ 2012, 1131]
SCJ of 23 January 2012 [RJ 2012, 1900]
SCJ of 20 June 2013 [RJ 2013, 4377]
SCJ of 17 March 2014 [RJ 2014, 1501]
SCJ of 26 March 2014 [RJ 2014, 2035]
SCJ of 7 July 2014 [RJ 2014, 3540]
SCJ of 2 March 2015 [RJ 2015, 601]
SCJ of 15 June 2015 [RJ 2015, 2289]
SCJ of 24 June 2015 [RJ 2015, 2657]
SCJ of 17 July 2015 [RJ 2015, 3020]
SCJ of 19 February 2016 [RJ 2016, 554]
SCJ of 18 March 2016 [RJ 2016, 1136]
SCJ of 29 September 2016 [RJ 2016, 4457]
SCJ of 6 October 2016 [RJ 2016, 4737]
SCJ of 19 January 2017 [RJ 2017, 924]
SCJ of 8 March 2017 [RJ 2017, 1633]
SCJ of 20 July 2017 [RJ 2017, 3385]
SCJ of 13 December 2017 [RJ 2017, 5406]
SCJ of 2 February 2018 [RJ 2018, 291]
SCJ of 4 April 2018 [RJ 2018, 1185]
SCJ of 30 May 2018 [RJ 2018, 2358]
SCJ of 19 June 2018 [RJ 2018, 2667]
SCJ of 18 July 2018 [RJ 2018, 2952]
SCJ of 24 September 2018 [RJ 2018, 3856]
SCJ of 17 January 2019 [RJ 2019, 105]
SCJ of 19 February 2019 [RJ 2019, 497]

II.
FAMILY – (MULTI)PARENTALITY – BELONGING:
"It Takes a Village"

Multiparentality and New Structures of Family Relationship[1]

Josep Ferrer-Riba, Universitat Pompeu Fabra

I. Introduction

A remarkable feature of contemporary family law is the way in which traditional family statuses – the status of spouse, based on marriage, and the statuses of father, mother, or child, based on the legal establishment of parenthood – are becoming blurred. These statuses have of course survived, but their essential elements and inherited rules are constantly being eroded and they have to co-exist with new personal and family statuses and roles. New and more complex structures have appeared as a result of the process of societal change. This is a characteristic dynamic of pluralist societies, which prohibit discrimination, respect sexual orientation and gender identity, and protect the free development of personality, and therefore provide room for the thriving of private autonomy.

This phenomenon is quite obvious in marital relationships. Marital status, which was the only way of articulating a couple's relationship in traditional law, has surrendered its exclusive position in western societies and been overwhelmed by statutory or judicial recognition of other patterns of living together, whether on a purely *de facto* basis, or formalized through registration or the issuance of a public deed.[2] The marriage relationship itself has undergone profound changes, both, as a result of being opened up to same-sex couples[3] and the growing liberalization of

---

1   This work has been funded by the Spanish Ministry of Economy, Industry and Competitiveness (MINECO), under the project DER 2014-5575-R on "Reproductive freedom and formation of family links." It is a revised and abridged version of the paper "Familias y pluriparentalidad en Derecho español," published in *Derecho de Familia (Revista Interdisciplinaria de Doctrina y Jurisprudencia) AbeledoPerrot* 85 (2018).

2   On the different types of legal recognition of cohabitation or partnership relationships other than marriage, see, in the European context, Miles 92-113; Scherpe, "The Past, Present and Future…," 566-76.

3   As of July 2018, 15 European countries had legally recognised same-sex marriage; see Curry-Sumner 118-26. In Spanish law, see Art. 44 II CC, as introduced by Act 13/2005 of 1 July, which modified the Civil Code concerning the right to contract marriage.

divorce, which in some countries has become available on demand.[4] The traditional family status of marriage is now viewed more as a contract, in which spouses or future spouses can not only reach agreements on the ancillary consequences of the dissolution of the marital bond, when this comes about, by signing a separation agreement, but can also do so in advance in anticipation of a future break-up.[5] As a result, a growing number of jurisdictions have accepted that the dissolution of a marriage may take place privately without judicial involvement, if the spouses agree to it and have no minor or dependent children.[6]

The family statuses arising from a parental relationship have also undergone changes in their establishment, features, and content, partly as a consequence of the changes in the marital status. The opening up of marriage or registered partnerships to same-sex couples has had an impact on parental relationships, which can now consist of two fathers or two mothers in a growing number of European countries.[7] Divorce, in turn, has contributed to the proliferation of blended families and this has made evident that new spouses or partners can take on parental roles of a greater or lesser extent with respect to their partner's children from previous relationships. The transformation of parental status can also be explained by specific legal developments and technological advances that have a direct impact on the relationships between parents and children. Protecting the child's best interests transcends the content of parental functions and legitimizes intervention of public authorities into the way these are exercised, leaving parents aside and replacing them with other carers. The spread of assisted reproductive techniques (ARTs) and the fact that they can be carried out with genetic material from donors, is changing the basis of legal fatherhood and motherhood to some extent, diversi-

---

4   European jurisdictions range from basing divorce in the irretrievable breakdown of marriage to embracing divorce on demand (as in Sweden, Norway and Spain). See an overview of the main European legal systems in Antokolskaia 46-65.

5   On the wide recognition of pre-nuptial and post-nuptial agreements in both civil and common law jurisdictions and the variety of systems in place, see Scherpe, "Marital Agreements and Private Autonomy...," 483-511.

6   For a comparative analysis of divorce procedures and the acceptance of administrative divorce, see Antokolskaia 72-79, and especially with respect to the gradual admission of private proceedings, see Dutta et al., eds. In Spanish law, see Art. 87 CC, following its modification by Law 15/2015, dated 2 July, on Voluntary Jurisdiction.

7   The acceptance of same-sex marriage has largely been accompanied by the acceptance of the adoption of a partner's children either by both spouses or by one of them: see the evolution in Fenton-Glynn 328-30. The next step was to regulate the dual motherhood of children born to lesbian couples through assisted reproduction, without the need for adoption.

fying forms of parentality and opening a highly significant space for the principle of consent as the basis for qualifying as father or mother.[8]

Private autonomy has less impact on the shaping of parental statuses than it does on the shaping of marriage and partnerships, but its relevance is now increasing. While it is common for the law to allow the conclusion of private agreements, subject to court approval, dealing with the exercise of parental responsibilities, custody and personal contact with children after the parents' separation or divorce,[9] it is less inclined to accept this autonomy if it is aimed at building father- or mother-child relationships. Hence, child adoption is always established on the basis of a public authority decision.[10] In legal systems allowing heterologous ARTs, the mother's husband or partner's fatherhood and the mother's partner's co-motherhood are ultimately based on consent, but this consent is not normally conceived as contractual consent but as a unilateral act.[11] Nonetheless, the introduction of the principle of consent to establish fatherhood and co-motherhood in such cases prompts legal analysts to consider its binding force, even as contractual consent, in different settings as well as for building parental relationships and defining their effects.

II. Parentality and Its Different Expressions

The developments described here, noted for the diversification of parental positions, have spurred the debate on multiparentality. Two concepts or notions of multiparentality need to be dealt with.[12] A first notion, narrower in scope, refers to the possibility of extending the legal condition of father or mother of a child to more than two persons at the same time, thus breaking the two-parent paradigm. A second notion, much broader, refers to the possibility of recognizing a number of

---

8   See the contributions by Gloria Álvarez Bernardo (on Assisted Reproductive Technologies and Lesbian Families in Spain) and by Eva-Sabine Zehelein (on the American MTV docu-diary *Generation Cryo*).

9   See the relevant comparative law data in Boele-Woelki et al. *European Family Law...*, 299-312, 379-84. The possibility of reaching agreements concerning the exercise of parental responsibilities has become a European principle: see Principle 3:13 (Agreement on Exercise) of the *Principles of European Family Law Regarding Parental Responsibilities* (hereafter, PEFLPR) and the comparative overview in Boele-Woelki et al. *Principles of European Family Law...*, 91-94.

10   See Art. 3 *European Convention on the Adoption of Children (revised)*, done in Strasbourg on 27.11.2008, Council of Europe Treaty Series – No. 202.

11   In Spanish law, this is an express formal act preceding the practice of a reproductive technique carried out in accordance with the law, or formalised at the Civil Registry after the child's birth (Art. 8, Sections 1 and 3 of Law 14/2006, dated 26 May, on assisted human reproduction techniques, BOE No. 126, dated 27 May; hereafter, LTRHA).

12   German scholarship highlights this distinction; see Helms, "Wie viele Eltern....".

parental positions with respect to the same child, even though with different ratio-nales, characteristics, and degrees of importance. This second notion undoubtedly provides the most fruitful way into the topic and will be followed here.

The conjunction of social changes and technological advances noted above have enabled positions with different degrees of parental quality to multiply. Taking a conceptual distinction developed by Andrew Bainham (Bainham 25-31) and widely referred to in subsequent legal literature,[13] the positions of biological or genetic progenitor (parentage), father or mother in a legal sense (parenthood) and individ-uals exercising parental responsibilities (parenting) have to be distinguished.

– Genetic or biological parentage, which could be described as the condition of male or female progenitor, refers to the man and woman whose gametes engen-dered the child, and also, appropriate distinctions notwithstanding, to the woman who carried and gave birth to the child, whether or not she contributed her genetic material. The current possibility of using third party mitochondrial donations to replace the mother's damaged mitochondria and prevent the transmission of ge-netic illnesses could add yet another layer of genetic contribution to the child's generation, bringing a further complexity to this type of parentality with it.

– Under the heading of parenting, we refer to the position occupied by persons which take on typical parental functions with respect to a minor. This functional or socio-affective parental position normally falls to the legal parents, to whom the law attributes parental responsibilities.[14] However, as is well-known, these functions can also be exercised by other persons in the parents' place, either because they are absent or cannot assume them, or because the child has been the victim of ill treatment or neglect and has been placed in someone else's care.[15] Apart from this, the emergence of blended families has also made it necessary to address cases in which an individual takes on typical parental functions with respect to their spouse or partner's minor children because they are living in the same family household. A wide range of approaches are currently used to deal with these situations, which legally materialize in very different ways (Ferrer-Riba 297-99).

– The legal condition of father or mother comes about via the application of different rules for establishing parenthood. Laws generally recognize three pos-sible types of parenthood (by natural reproduction, by adoption, and by assisted reproduction),[16] and apply a wide range of criteria to assign fatherhood or moth-

---

13   See e.g. Scherpe, "Breaking the existing paradigms" 350-51; in Spain, Verdera 117.

14   See PEFLPR 3:8 (Parent): "Parents, whose legal parentage has been established, should have parental responsibilities for the child."

15   See PEFLPR 3:9 (Third persons): "Parental responsibilities may in whole or in part also be attributed to a person other than a parent."

16   In reality, many legal systems do not recognise ARTs as an autonomous form of parenthood and restrict themselves to transferring the rules for natural reproduction over to it, along with the necessary specialities. Legal doctrine is critical of this approach and mainly prefers to

erhood, such as biological contribution (gestation and childbirth), genetic contribution (providing gametes), the marital relationship with the pregnant woman, the decision to begin a medically-assisted reproductive process, and the decision to take on parental responsibilities, either through acknowledging a child or via adoption. In most family law systems, the legal condition of father or mother is subject to the "two-parent paradigm:" an individual cannot simultaneously have more than one father and one mother, or two fathers, or two mothers. Legal parenthood produces broadly speaking three types of legal consequences: (i) it affects the personal status of the child, to the extent that it confers an essential identification element (surname) and is a criterion for attributing citizenship; (ii) it imposes duties of care and protection (parental responsibilities) while the child is a minor; (iii) it creates family bonds and thus kinship ties, between the child and his or her legal parents and other relatives, including some maintenance rights and duties, and some succession rights.[17]

The application of legal criteria to establish fatherhood and motherhood and the restrictions arising from the dual paradigm can at times undermine or relegate to irrelevance some parental positions. The opening of contemporary family law to multiparentality has several implications. On the one hand, in view of the legal rules for establishing parenthood and attributing parental responsibilities, it entails re-assessing the legal treatment of all positions that include elements of parentality, whether biological, genetic, social, or intent-based. On the other hand, it is then necessary to address proactively the issue of whether, in view of the interests of the parties involved and especially the minor child, it is advisable or necessary to accommodate the coexistence of different forms of parentality in different terms from those laid down in existing law, and eventually open up legal parenthood to more than two persons.

III. Rethinking Parentality in Societies with Complex Family Structures

The existing rules for establishing parenthood and attributing parental responsibilities causes major difficulties for accommodating different forms of parentality in any reasonable sense. These difficulties can partly be explained by the adherence to the two-parent paradigm, but they are also a consequence of legal policy decisions whose conformity with the child's best interests is questionable. The entrenchment

---

understand parenthood resulting from heterologous ARTs as a different type of parenthood: in recent Spanish literature see, e.g., with further references, Farnós 49-51; Benavente, 6, 32.

17   See e.g. paragraph 63 of the *Report on Principles concerning the establishment and legal consequences of parentage ("the White Paper")*, drafted by the committee of experts on family law (CJ-FA) of the Council of Europe and published in 2006 [CJ-FA (2006) 4 e] (hereafter, *White Paper*).

of new family structures and the spread of ARTs, in a context of greater appreciation for personal freedom and the free development of personality, are an invitation
to rethink the legal techniques for recognizing parentality. A recent project, *Adults
and Children in Postmodern Societies*, which was mainly devoted to this end, describes
three possible techniques to deal with this type of challenges, giving rise to four
different regulatory models (Sosson et al. 855-64):

– The flexibility model proposes retaining legal fatherhood and motherhood as
the fundamental legal relationships between adults and minors, while introducing greater flexibility into their establishment and reassignment and thus making
them more sensitive to changes in family structures. Flexibilization of legal parenthood would include, in particular, overcoming the two-parent paradigm and
opening up parenthood to more than two persons, should this be justified by circumstances.

– The diversification model proposes developing alternatives to legal parenthood with the aim of reflecting current changes in the way family relationships are
built. Diversification would involve shaping other parental statuses, in addition to
those of legal father or mother, and endowing them with a predefined bundle of
effects, rights, and duties. This type of approach would allow a more satisfactory
accommodation of the relationship between a child and their biological or social
parents in cases in which these positions do not bring with them the condition of
legal father or mother.

– The diffraction model proposes assigning the rights, duties, and legal consequences associated to parenthood without making this conditional on predefined
statuses; that is, on an *ad hoc* or case by case analysis subject to the child's best interests. This proposal would therefore entail the possibility of breaking up the set of
legal consequences of parenthood currently associated to the legal status of father
or mother (surname, kinship, succession rights, maintenance duties, parental responsibility, custody, personal contact), and assigning them, notwithstanding the
traditional statuses, according to the circumstances.

– Hybrid models: the project also acknowledges that the wide range of parental
relationships that can take shape in postmodern societies, and the speed with
which they develop, could require combining elements from two or all three of
the models outlined above, giving rise to hybrid models.

The last approach would seem to be the most suitable. Accounting for the different parental positions that may concur in personal relationships between adults
and children requires combining various regulatory techniques. Legal parenthood
needs to become more flexible so that new family structures can be recognized in
law. However, it is also necessary to formulate and reframe other parental statuses
which accommodate certain parentality bonds that must not produce the effects
of legal fatherhood and motherhood. Finally, some situations require diffracting

legal effects, attaching to them specific consequences, even if their generalization might not be advisable.

IV. The Legal Establishment of Parenthood and Its Shortcomings

1. Parenthood by Natural Reproduction

In respect of the mother, the clear and simple *mater semper certa est* principle is used to establish parenthood by natural reproduction: motherhood is determined by the fact of giving birth, so that legal motherhood always matches biological and genetic maternity, except in highly exceptional cases involving a mistake in registering the birth.[18]

Establishing parenthood by natural reproduction is far more complex where the father is concerned. The law ultimately makes provision for legal parenthood to be matched with genetic parentage through the availability of claims to establish and challenge it in court proceedings where DNA tests can be carried out. However, fatherhood is normally established in the first place through other channels: it is usually established in favor of the mother's husband or partner by virtue of legal presumptions, or in favor of the man that acknowledges parenthood in the forms provided for by laws. These mechanisms of parenthood determination give weight to the mother's family relationship with her partner, which is the setting in which the child will usually be brought up, and to the voluntary decision to take on parental responsibilities on the part of the man who acknowledges his paternity. In such cases, while fatherhood is established on the assumption of having procreated the child, it can also end up being established for a man who was not the child's begetter (e.g., if the acknowledgment of paternity was wrong or false). The law allows these discrepancies to be corrected bringing a claim in court to challenge fatherhood, but it also imposes both legal standing requirements and time limits.[19] The outcome is that a man other than the progenitor can sometimes have his condition as legal father reinforced, because the child has become part of the mother and her husband's or partner's family and the law protects this family setting (the so-called "family peace").

---

18   On the widespread application of this principle in Europe, with the exception of French law, (because of its recognition of *accouchement sous X*), see Schwenzer, 3-4. See also Principle 1 (*White Paper*): "The woman who gives birth to the child shall be considered as the mother."

19   As stated by Principle 8.3 *White Paper*: "States may specify time limits to institute legal proceedings aiming to establish paternal affiliation." National legal systems frequently resort to this technique; thus, in Spanish law, for instance, the father has a one-year period to claim fatherhood beginning from the date on which he became aware of the facts on which the claim has to be based (Art. 133.2 CC).

The traditional system of establishing legal fatherhood in cases of natural reproduction is thus torn between two purposes: on the one hand, it is aimed at acknowledging that a child's biological father is the legal father – in which case parenthood is natural in the real sense of the word – and on the other, it is also aimed at respecting the position of the person that normally undertakes the functions and responsibilities of fatherhood, either because of his relationship with the mother or because he has deliberately chosen to accept them. In most legal systems, there can be no compromise between both aims: only one can prevail, because only one person can be invested with legal fatherhood. Hence, if both dimensions of being a father do not correspond to the same person and a successful paternity claim is brought in court, applying the legal rules can lead to biological parentage prevailing over socio-affective paternity. By the same token, should there be legal barriers to the judicial challenge of paternity, the reverse can happen; i.e., paternity exercised in a family context or taken on voluntarily overrides biological parentage.[20]

The main problem in these cases is that the law does not usually provide mechanisms able to accommodate both forms of parentality. The unicity of the condition of legal father means that all the legal consequences of fatherhood fall on the person that has prevailed and assumed the legal condition, while the other party and his parental status are overshadowed or completely dislodged.[21] These consequences should be revised. There are many circumstances that can lead to clashes between social and biological paternity in the parentage by natural reproduction framework, and these can be neither addressed nor resolved uniformly. One way of overcoming the problem is to resort to multiparentality and accept that a child can have two legal fathers.[22] In my opinion, however, the best way to approach these situations is not to adopt a forced multiparentality solution in a narrow sense, that is, to permit the coexistence of two legal fathers, but rather to diversify parental roles or statuses, respecting whatever is worthwhile in the paternal position that has to be relegated and excluded as legal fatherhood. If the natural father finds that access to establishing legal fatherhood is denied to him (e.g. because the statutory deadline for claiming fatherhood has elapsed, or because he is lacking legal standing), he should at least be able to establish his condition of biological father, if he so

---

20   Comparative law shows a wide range of approaches here. See Schwenzer 1-8; Henrich; Helms, *Rechtliche, biologische und soziale Elternschaft*, F41-44.

21   As stated by Verdera 105, the law generally assigns the effects of parentage to the holder of the legal condition of father, without allowing undue nuances.

22   In situations of competing parentage claims, the *Uniform Parentage Act* (2017) in the US admits that a court adjudicates a child to have more than two parents "if the court finds that failure to recognize more than two parents would be detrimental to the child" (Section 613, Alternative B).

wishes, for the purpose of satisfying his interest in knowing the biological truth.[23] The same right should be assigned to the child. On the contrary, should biological paternity prevail in court proceedings as legal fatherhood, as is becoming increasingly common, the laws should safeguard the position of the person that has taken on parental functions and has created psychological, family and social bonds with the child.[24] This could result in the judicial recognition of parental responsibilities or custody and personal contact rights in favor of whoever had satisfactorily undertaken these responsibilities prior to the dispute.[25]

2. Parenthood by Adoption

National legal systems and international instruments conceive adoption as a formal legal act through which a parent-child relationship is formed between the adopter or adopters and the adopted person on the basis of a voluntary undertaking. In spite of this voluntary basis, adoption is not a manifestation of private autonomy: it has to be granted by order of a public authority, and its legal effects are also shaped by the law.[26]

The establishment of a parent-child relationship by adoption entails an adoptive parent or two adoptive parents being superimposed over one or two pre-existing parents (usually birth parents). The concurrence of two sets of parents requires delimiting their respective positions vis à vis the adopted child. Comparative law shows that two types of adoption with different legal requirements and effects need to be distinguished: what is known as full or plenary adoption on one hand, and simple adoption on the other.

a) Plenary or Full Adoption

The most widespread type of adoption – and the only type in many countries - is full or plenary adoption. Full adoption produces substitution effects: the adopter or

---

23   In Spanish legal literature, discussing the possibility of introducing purely declarative fatherhood claims, without the typical effects of legal parentage, see Barber, "Nuevos retos..." 37-38 (although rather critical); Barber, "Autonomía de la voluntad..." 1127.

24   The ECtHR (*Nazarenko v. Russia*, 16 July 2015) has protected the position of the person who has taken on the father's role for a significant time period but has been defeated in a parentage claim; the relationship between this person and the minor may amount to family life within the meaning of Article 8.1 ECHR. See para. 44-46 of the *Nazarenko* decision for comparative law information on this issue.

25   In the same vein, see Arts. 331 and 337 of the French Civil Code, which allow the courts to set the forms of the child's relationship with the person who has been established as the legal father or mother and also with the person who brought them up until the challenge of paternity succeeded.

26   See Sonia Di Loreto's contribution on adoption for a literary and historical (American) perspective.

adopters replace the birth father or mother or both, either because they are non-existent, absent, have decided to abandon their parental responsibilities or have proved unable of exercising them. In this form of adoption, all legal links with the birth parents come to an end and are replaced by links with the adopters and their families.[27] The extinguishing of all effects with respect to the biological parents includes kinship bonds and usually extends to the entire birth family.

This extreme approach is increasingly being questioned. While it is reasonable for adoption to lead to a change in parental responsibility and kinship, the relationship with the birth parents and family (grandparents, siblings) can retain a certain value for the child in the formation of personal identity. Therefore, some legal systems qualify the principle of completely cutting all ties with the birth family, at least in two ways:

– Recognizing the right of adopted persons to have access to information about their origins (Fenton-Glynn 331-35). The right to know focuses on the birth parents' personal identities and may extend to other personal background data, including family and social environment, medical history and childhood experiences. Individuals' interest in receiving "the information necessary to know and understand their childhood and early development" is protected by Art. 8 ECHR.[28] However, in some jurisdictions (e.g. France) this right clashes with the birth parents' right to remain anonymous.[29]

– The possibility of setting up open or semi-open adoption. The legal framework in which child adoption is set up in most western legal systems is still based on the model of closed or secret adoption, but a certain evolution can be observed in both adoption praxis and in legal settings.[30] Open adoptions allow varying degrees of contact, or at least regular exchanges of information between the adopted child and members of his or her birth family, depending on an assessment of the circumstances of the case made by the court or administrative authority that grants the adoption.

These exceptions are an example of the use of diversification and diffraction techniques to give legal relevance to birth parentality when it ceases to be treated

---

27   As the heading preceding Principle 15 of the *White Paper* states, adoption brings about "change of parentage."

28   See *Gaskin v. the United Kingdom* (ECtHR 7 July 1989): the child's right to have access to information imposes on the authorities intervening in the adoption the duty to collect and retain relevant information concerning his or her origins.

29   Taking this into consideration, Art 22(1) of the *European Convention* of 2008 still authorizes states to keep adopters' identities a secret.

30   See, e.g., in Spanish law, Art. 178.4 CC. Setting up an open adoption requires a court decision and the adoptive family's consent. Contact with the birth family has to be subject to conditions set by the court and supervised by the public body responsible for child protection.

as legal parenthood as a consequence of the birth parents' replacement by adoptive parents. Where the birth parents are concerned, the law does not establish a statute of rights and duties, but simply their passive subjection to the adopted child's eventual exercise of the right to know his or her origins. The regulating of open and semi-open adoption is a good example of the use of diffraction techniques, insofar as personal contact rights are not recognized in a general sense but on a case by case basis and in the light of circumstances.

b) Simple Adoption

Unlike full adoption, simple adoption produces additional rather than replacing effects *vis à vis* the holder or holders of legal parenthood. Setting up a simple adoption establishes legal parenthood between the adopter or adopters and the adoptee, but it does not remove legal parenthood with the birth parents nor kinship with their families. Simple adoption is suitable for the adoption of adults and in general for cases in which maintaining personal, family or inheritance ties with the original paternal and/or maternal families is considered beneficial for the adoptee. This typically occurs, for example, in adoption by relatives or step-parents.[31] In these statistically common cases, breaking all ties with the birth family is not always advisable, and some legal systems make specific provisions to this end.

The fact that simple adoption continues to exist, is an interesting case of legal parenthood's increased flexibility. It is an undisputed case of acceptance of legal multiparentality and highlights that there are no insurmountable technical barriers to overcome the dual parents paradigm and recognizing three or four legal parenthood bonds with reference to the one and the same person. Nevertheless, it is important to take into account the fact that simple adoption is normally used to adopt adults, and therefore the concurrence of legal parenthoods is only projected onto kinship, and not onto parental responsibilities.

Simple adoption is currently being advocated as a technique for establishing legal multi-parenthood relationships in other contexts. It is considered particularly useful in cases in which, following a child's birth, the legal parents and a third party who is involved in the parental project (e.g. the surrogate mother, or a genetic contributor of the opposite sex) agree to extend the legal condition of father or mother to this person in equal terms.[32]

---

31 On the suitability of simple adoption as a tool for formalising the relationship between a step-parent and his or her spouse's child, with essentially inheritance-related goals, see Mignot 532-42.

32 See, in this vein, the report drafted in the Netherlands by a government committee to propose legal reforms in the area of parenthood, *Child and Parents in the 21st Century (Government Committee on the Reassessment of Parenthood)*, 69-72.

3. Parenthood by Medically Assisted Procreation (ARTs)

Conjunction of parental positions of different kinds abound in the ARTs sphere, as long as the legal system in question accepts the practice of heterologous techniques; that is, the use of gametes or embryos from donors. The law applies a range of criteria to establish legal parenthood:

– Where women are concerned, legal parenthood is established via pregnancy and childbirth according to the same rule (*mater semper certa est*) applied in natural reproduction, with the only exception of the surrogate mother in legal systems that allow and enforce surrogacy agreements. In addition to it, if the woman that gives birth takes the parental project forward with a lesbian partner, the latter also generally qualifies for the condition of co-mother. Legal systems address the assignment of co-motherhood among lesbian couples in different ways: at times it is directly established on the basis of marital status, if the birth-giving mother is married to her partner;[33] in other cases, it is grounded in consent to the practice of ARTs,[34] and in yet others it is based on consent to co-motherhood, even if consent is given after the child's birth.[35]

– Where men are concerned, national legal systems also present a range of legal approaches. The laws usually resort to the criteria for establishing parenthood in natural reproduction cases, but block the possibility of challenging paternity on the basis that this does not match biological truth, and also enable the possibility of claiming it with respect to the man who consented to the practice of ARTs if he does not recognize the child voluntarily. Ultimately, aside from specific techniques to establish paternity, in cases involving the practice of heterologous artificial insemination legal fatherhood can be said to be based on consent.[36]

Applying the consent criterion for establishing legal fatherhood and co-motherhood, and for assuming parental responsibilities, brings the problem of the genetic contribution's legal relevance, if any, to the forefront. There is a clear dividing line between jurisdictions whose ARTs systems legally sanction donor anonymity and those that recognize the right of children to know the donor's identity and thus their own genetic backgrounds.[37]

---

33   See e.g. Art. 42 *Human Fertilization and Embryology Act* 2008 (United Kingdom); Art. 325.2 *CC* (Belgium); Art. 198 *BW* (Netherlands); Chapter 2, Section 3, 4a *Children Act* (Norway).

34   See e.g. Arts. 235-8.1, 235-13.1 *CC* (Catalonia); Section 3a, 3 c *Children Act* (Denmark); Arts. 562, 569 *CC* (Argentina).

35   See Art. 7.3 *LTRHA* (Spain).

36   Principle 10.2 of the *White Paper* states that "(t)he mother's husband or companion who gave his consent to the treatment cannot oppose the establishment of his paternity, unless the court finds that the child was not born as a result of the treatment he consented to."

37   See Gloria Álvarez Bernardo's contribution on lesbian parenthood via sperm donation in Spain.

The child's interest in learning such a significant fact about personal identity as his or her begetters' identities should not be overridden by the donors' right to privacy and,[38] on a practical level, the convenience of guaranteeing enough donations to meet the demand for reproductive services at a reasonable cost. National lawmakers should define the legal status of genetic contributors with no parental responsibilities, where assisted reproduction processes are concerned, in terms that allow children to know that they were conceived via ARTs and access information about their genetic origins. In Europe, they are under no obligation to do so under ECtHR case law, which has not had the occasion to decide on this issue yet, but comparative law shows a quick evolution towards more transparency, *"double track"* policies, guarantee of universal access to biological origins and an increased sensitivity to the importance of knowing one's background in the shaping of personal identity (see e.g. Alkorta and Farnós 158-64).

The voluntary basis of parenthood arising from ARTs, on the other hand, is increasingly putting pressure on parentage law to recognize the legal relevance of consent in other reproductive contexts (surrogate motherhood, home insemination), also as expression of acts of private autonomy aimed at establishing parental relationships or modulating them according to personal preferences. The possibility of moving to other countries to fulfil some of these aspirations (especially in the case of surrogate motherhood) and the birth of children whose best interests are paramount, irrespective of how they were conceived, reinforce this trend.[39]

The establishing of legal parenthood arising from ARTs normally presupposes that the techniques are carried out in licensed clinics and within the legal framework. In view of this, there is an increasingly urgent need to elucidate which effects derive from do-it-yourself (DIY) practices, i.e., the undertakings of a small but growing number of women, whether single or in a couple, that opt for home insemination with sperm from a man known to them or an international sperm bank, with or without donor anonymity. The best interests of any children born should imply that the family law effects of these practices are equated with those carried out in authorized clinics, if the aim is to establish the same type of relationship and the person involved in the parental project as spouse or partner of the pregnant woman, should there be one, has given consent. The most critical point in this scenario arises when the person contributing the sperm is a friend or acquaintance, in which case problems surround both the issue of his immunity *vis à*

---

38   See Eva-Sabine Zehelein's article on *Generation Cryo*'s thematization of this conflict of interest
      – between the donor conceived children and their right to know 'where they come from', and
      the donor's right to stay anonymous.

39   The need to take into account the possibility of carrying out these reproductive practices
      abroad and to protect children's best interests in cases of surrogate motherhood was under-
      scored by ECtHR judgments in *Mennesson vs. France* and *Labassee vs. France*, both on 26 June
      2014.

vis claims for establishing paternity, whether brought by the mother or the child, and the way in which the resulting multiparentality situation should be addressed if the mother shares her parental project with her spouse or partner.

In our opinion, the law should respect the sperm donor's immunity if his contribution was made and accepted under this premise, thus achieving the same outcome as when gametes of an anonymous donor are used in a licensed clinic, without involving anyone else, in legal systems that allow single women access to ARTs.[40] By the same token, the law should respect any agreements made between the pregnant woman and her partner, should there be one, and the man that contributes his gametes to the reproductive process, if these include the establishment of paternity with all its effects – leading to a multiparentality situation in the narrow sense – or the full or limited attribution of parental responsibilities or other rights and duties with respect to the child (information, personal contact, visits, etc.). This approach should also be extended to the two male partners that agree to form a multiparental relationship with a woman who contributes to the parental project by bearing the child.

Although these are minority models, recognizing this type of relationship satisfies homosexual couples' idiosyncratic personal and family aspirations (*rainbow families*). In some European countries, there is statistical evidence to show that a significant number of gay and lesbian couples wish to involve individuals or couples of the opposite sex in their reproductive and parenting decisions.[41] What kind of institutional framework should be created to channel these aspirations is debatable. It could be based on a flexibility model of legal parenthood, directly allowing the attribution of fatherhood or motherhood to more than two persons; on a diversification of statuses model, based on extending parental responsibilities (but not legal parenthood) to some of the participants in the parental project, or on a diffraction model, recognizing effects with greater or lesser scope (legal parent-

---

40   This position has already found a place in comparative law: see in Ontario the *Children's Law Reform Act* [R.S.O. 1990, Chapter C.12, Section 7 (4)], following its 2016 reform, which excludes the paternity of any male that has a written agreement with the prospective parents not to assume paternity, including both cases of artificial insemination and sexual intercourse. In general, in relation to legal systems that are beginning to accept multiparentality agreements, see Scherpe, "Breaking the existing paradigms" 353-56.

41   Cf. Haag 418-22. According to the author, in a large-scale survey carried out in Germany with homosexual persons who were considering to be parents, 24.8% of men and 31.6% of women stated that they expected their reproductive wishes to be fulfilled via the participation of a friend or friends, be it either a single person or a homosexual couple of the opposite sex. Where the form of this "cooperative parenthood" was concerned, gay couples were more inclined to approach this on equal terms, while lesbian couples showed a preference for limiting the man or men's role far more.

hood, parenting, or personal contact), according to the agreement made in each case.[42]

IV. The Attribution and Exercise of Parental Responsibilities

For a full assessment of all dimensions of multiparentality, it is also necessary to examine the rules for attributing and exercising parental responsibilities. As a general rule, the duties and powers comprising parental responsibility are attributed to the parents simply because they are the parents, and legal parenthood and exercised parenthood match: it is the legally established parents that have to take on parental responsibilities and exercise them according to the law. This match is reinforced because, in most legal systems, parental powers are conceived as a set of exclusive and privileged powers and duties, only attributable in full to legal mothers and fathers.

The parental responsibility's exclusive nature means that parental functions cannot be shared with third parties cumulatively. Third parties cannot be included in the exercise of parental responsibility or any of its functions, even if its powers and duties fall on one person, i.e., a single father or mother. This feature of parental responsibility manifests itself in the disregard with which the legal system treats the father or mother's spouses and partners, which are frequently involved in exercising the parental functions of care, custody, maintenance and decision-making – especially concerning daily or urgent decisions – with regard to their partner's children. The *de facto* exercise of these functions is not reflected in law, whether the child has another legal father or mother who retains his or her responsibility (in which case the refusal to acknowledge the step-parent's position could be justified by the idea of not involving more than two persons in the exercise of parental functions), or does not (in which case there is no such limitation and the law's refusal thus seems far less justifiable).

The only way to overcome these restrictions – and always within the two-parent paradigm – is to transform the exercise of parental roles into legal parenthood, through adoption. Although adoption will certainly be a reasonable step if the length, strength, and permanence of the bonds created with the child are analogous with those of paternity or maternity, there are cases in which adoption can

---

42   See a detailed proposal for a multiparentality contract in the Dutch report *Child and Parents in the 21st Century*, 62-69. The proposed model requires the contract to be formalised, validated by a legal authority and signed by the parties before the birth. Other than this, simple adoption would be an alternative route. Appointing a guardian *ad litem* would ensure that the best interests of the *concepturus* were taken into account.

be either impossible (because of the opposition from the biological parents) or excessive. In societies with high rates of divorce, a child's adoption by the biological parent's spouse or partner can be advantageously replaced by the attribution of parental responsibility. The acknowledging of parental responsibility can confer symbolic and emotional legitimacy which denotes commitment to the child and his or her family and could eventually operate as a preliminary step towards subsequent adoption.

Although legal systems in mainland Europe do not currently provide for parental responsibility to be attributed either to more than two persons or to anyone other than the legal parents (except by substitute or shared delegation), its extension to third parties could be a suitable tool for acknowledging the exercise of parental roles that do not necessarily require the features of full legal parenthood. English law provides the best example of this technique, which is characteristic of a diversification model and permits the accommodating of parentalities over minor children (e.g., foster parents, *de facto* guardians, step-parents) without having any impact on legal parenthood status (Scherpe, "Breaking" 356-58). Recent studies and reports on the accommodation of new forms of parentality, arising either from assisted reproduction with genetic or gestational contribution from a third party, or from blended families, do not hesitate to propose introducing multiple-parenting formulas.[43]

V. Conclusion

In today's societies, the free development of personality, which is protected as a constitutional value, respect for individuals' identity and sexual orientation, and technological progress lead to people making family and reproductive choices increasingly tailored to personal preferences, and consequently to building interpersonal relationships that are diverse, mutable, and complex. A marked feature of this complexity is the multiplying of parental positions that can come together around the same individual. Multiparentality questions the *statu quo* of legal systems that are still tethered to the unicity of legal parenthood, the two-parent paradigm and the exclusive attribution of parental responsibility to them, and raises challenges for the acknowledgment of the biological or genetic element in the forming of personal identity, the recognition of emotional, social, and intentional parentalities, and the role of private autonomy in the forming of parental relationships.

---

43   See also the Dutch *Child and Parents* report (78-81). In German law, along similar lines, proposing the extension of "elterliche Sorge" to third parties in blended families, but with the legal parents' consent, see Helms, *Rechtliche,...*, F66-F70.

Contemporary family law tends to emphasize the genetic link as the predominant criterion in legally establishing parenthood by natural reproduction and as an element making up personal identity. The law should therefore recognize the status of begetter, setting up mechanisms to facilitate the disclosure of this condition whenever his or her recognition as legal parent is blocked, and always allow children, in any type of parentage relationship (including by adoption or by ARTs) to be able to learn their origin story.

Genetic parentage's predominant position in establishing legal parenthood should go hand in hand with measures to preserve the personal bond and the exercise of the socio-emotional parental role by the person who had been previously acting as parent, if this is consistent with the child's best interest. The law should also allow persons other than the legal parents to exercise full or limited parental responsibilities, even cumulatively, according to the concurring circumstances. This approach should apply to the father or mother's spouse or partner in a blended family, whether by defining a specific status or the individualized attribution of powers and duties on the basis of what is justified by the situation and family practice.

The widespread use of ARTs and its implementation with genetic material provided by donors has brought the principle of consent to the forefront in the law of parent-child relationships. Basing parentage arising from ARTs on consent pushes family law to give legal force to other expressions of private autonomy in the reproductive field. The legal recognition of consent given for purposes of procreation should not depend on whether the reproductive technique is practiced in a licensed clinic or in the private sphere. Among the expressions of private autonomy that are beginning to become prominent among certain social groups, those aiming to create parental relationships which would include more than two individuals (two fathers or mothers of intent and another individual who can contribute to the birth by providing gametes or carrying the child) stand out. This entails the agreeing with the third party that he or she will participate in the child's care and upbringing on an equal footing as legal parent or by exercising parental responsibilities, depending on the preferences of the parties involved. Family law has to respond to these aspirations, inasmuch as they are consistent with the child's best interests, by means of legal regimes of parentality that are more flexible, diversified and adjusted to each case.

Bibliography

Alkorta, Itziar, and Esther Farnós Amorós. "Anonimato del Donante y Derecho a Conocer: un Dificil Equilibrio." *Oñati Socio-Legal Series*, vol. 1, no. 1, 2017, pp. 148-78.

Antokolskaia, Masha. "Divorce law in a European perspective." *European Family Law, Vol. III (Family Law in a European Perspective)*, edited by Jens M. Scherpe, Elgar, 2016, pp. 41-81.

Bainham, Andrew. "Parentage, Parenthood and Parental Responsibility: Subtle, Elusive Yet Important Distinctions." *What is a Parent? A Socio-Legal Analysis*, edited by Andrew Bainham et al., Hart, 1999, pp. 25-46.

Barber Cárcamo, Roncesvalles. "Nuevos retos ante el Derecho Español de Filiación." *Revista de Derecho Privado*, vol. 93, no. 4, 2009, pp. 3-47.

—. "Autonomía de la voluntad y derecho de filiación." *Estudios de derecho civil en homenaje al profesor Joaquín José Rams Albesa*, edited by Matilde Cuena Casas et al., Dykinson, 2013, pp. 1111-30.

Benavente Moreda, Pilar. "Los Errores de Legislar en Paralelo: La Problemática Aplicación de las Reglas sobre Filiación (Determinación, Acciones de Reclamación e Impugnación) en la Filiación Derivada del Uso de Técnicas de Reproducción Humana Asistida." *Oñati Socio-Legal Series*, vol. 7, no. 1, 2017, pp. 1-36.

Boele-Woelki, Katharina, et al., eds. *European Family Law in Action. Vol. III: Parental Responsibilities*. Intersentia, 2005.

Boele-Woelki, Katharina, et al. *Principles of European Family Law Regarding Parental Responsibilities*. Intersentia, 2007.

Committee of Experts on Family Law. *Report on Principles Concerning the Establishment and Legal Consequences of Parentage – "The White Paper."* Council of Europe, CJ-FA, 2006, 4e.

Curry-Sumner, Ian. "Same-sex relationships in a European perspective." *European Family Law, Vol. III (Family Law in a European Perspective)*, edited by Jens M. Scherpe, Elgar, 2016, pp. 116-45.

Dutta, Anatol, et al., editors. *Scheidung ohne Gericht? (Neue Entwicklungen im europäischen Scheidungsrecht)*. Gieseking, 2017.

Farnós Amorós, Esther. "La filiación derivada de reproducción asistida: voluntad y biología." *Anuario de Derecho Civil*, vol. 68, no. 1, 2015, pp. 5-61.

Fenton-Glynn, Claire. "Adoption in a European perspective." *European Family Law, Vol. III (Family Law in a European Perspective)*, edited by Jens M. Scherpe, Elgar, 2016, pp. 311-40.

Ferrer-Riba, Josep. "Parental responsibility in a European perspective." *European Family Law, Vol. III (Family Law in a European Perspective)*, edited by Jens M. Scherpe, Elgar, 2016, pp. 284-310.

—. "Familias y pluriparentalidad en Derecho español." *Derecho de Familia (Revista Interdisciplinaria de Doctrina y Jurisprudencia) AbeledoPerrot*, vol. 85, 2018, 163-77.

Government Committee on the Reassessment of Parenthood. *Child and Parents in the 21st Century*. Xerox/OBT, The Hague, 2016.

Haag, Christian. "Zum Kinderwunsch homosexueller Männer und Frauen." *Kinderwunsch und Reproduktionsmedizin – Ethische Herausforderungen der technischen Fortpflanzung*, edited by Giovanni Maio et al., Karl Alber, 2013, pp. 400-25.

Helms, Tobias. *Rechtliche, biologische und soziale Elternschaft – Herausforderungen durch neue Familienformen (Gutachten F zum 71. Deutschen Juristentag)*. Beck, 2016.

—. "Wieviele Eltern verträgt ein Kind? Mehr-Elternfamilien aus rechtlicher Sicht." *Moderne Familienformen (Symposium zum 75. Geburtstag von Michael Coester)*, edited by Katharina Hilbig-Lugani and Peter M. Huber, De Gruyter, 2018, pp. 125-28.

Henrich, Dieter. "Streit um die Abstammung – Europäische Perspektiven." *Streit um die Abstammung – ein europäischer Vergleich*, edited by Andreas Spickhoff et al., Gieseking, 2007, pp. 403-12.

Miles, Joanna. "Unmarried cohabitation in a European perspective." *European Family Law, Vol. III (Family Law in a European Perspective)*, edited by Jens M. Scherpe, Elgar, 2016, pp. 82-115.

Mignot, Jean-Francois. "L'adoption simple en France: le renouveau d'une institution ancienne (1804-2007)." *Revue française de sociologie*, vol. 56, no. 3, 2015, pp. 525-60.

Scherpe, Jens. "Marital Agreements and Private Autonomy in Comparative Perspective." *Marital Agreements and Private Autonomy in Comparative Perspective*, edited by Jens M. Scherpe, Hart, 2012, pp. 443-518.

—. "The Past, Present and Future of Registered Partnerships." *The Future of Registered Partnerships (Family recognition beyond marriage?)*, edited by Jens Scherpe and Andy Hayward, Intersentia, 2017, pp. 561-86.

—. "Breaking the existing paradigms of parent-child relationships." *International and National Perspectives on Child and Family Law (Essays in Honour of Nigel Lowe)*, edited by Gillian Douglas et al., Intersentia, 2018, 343-59.

Schwenzer, Ingeborg. "Tensions between legal, biological and social conceptions of parentage." *Tensions between legal, biological and social conceptions of parentage*, edited by Ingeborg Schwenzer, Intersentia, 2007, pp. 1-26.

Sosson, Jehanne, et al., editors. *Adults and Children in Postmodern Societies (A Comparative Law Multidisciplinary Handbook)*. Intersentia, 2019.

Verdera, Rafael. "Ser padre." *Derecho Privado y Constitución*, vol. 30, 2016, pp. 75-126.

Court decisions

Gaskin v. the United Kingdom, ECtHR, 7 July 1989.

Mennesson v. France, ECtHR, 26 June 2014.

Labassee v. France, ECtHR, 26 June 2014.

Nazarenko v. Russia, ECtHR, 16 July 2015.

Assisted Reproductive Technologies and Lesbian Families

Gloria Álvarez Bernardo, Universidad de Granada

Introduction

Human reproduction is a central aspect in kinship relations. Its importance is made evident in the different mechanisms and measures that regulate and control reproduction (González Echevarría et al. 104; Stone 546). In western societies, the heterosexual family occupies a privileged position (Pichardo 341). This family model is based on two principles: priority is given first to there being continuity between the conjugal and filial bond (Beck-Gernsheim), and second, between sexuality and reproduction (Cutas and Chan 4).

The social, political, and cultural transformations that have been taking place in the last few decades have called into question the hegemony of this family model. As Rivas states, there have been four main transformations. First, a breaking of the conjugal and filial connection, which has resulted in different family formations in which the figures of spouse and biological parent are not the same (e.g. blended or step-families) (13). Another transformation concerns the break in the sexuality-reproduction continuity. In this regard, sexuality should not be thought of exclusively in reproductive terms, which leads to questioning the hegemony of heterosexuality (14). A third change is connected to the dissociation between conjugal partner/couple, parental partner/couple and progenitorial partner/couple. Thus, the very "biparental" model, which defends the existence of a father and a mother in a monogamous and reproductive relationship, is called into question (14). Lastly, Rivas states that the advance of assisted reproductive techniques has played an important role in this process of transformation of parenthood. The possibilities offered by these technologies are multiple, which is made manifest in, among other things, the plurality of the people, roles, and functions that are involved. The parental fragmentation that is associated with these techniques shows that, after their application, there is a complex process of negotiation in which certain aspects of kinship are emphasized at the cost of others (15). Because of this, the laws that each particular country has in order to regulate these treatments exemplify the family ideology that prevails there.[1] Other authors have analyzed the impact that the introduction of reproductive technologies has brought about. Specifically, one of these changes has been connected with the resignification of biology. When reproduction passes into the hands of technology, progenitors occupy ambivalent positions that break from the natural sequence of human reproduction (Mamo 92). We are witnessing, as Stone (549) and Thompson (183) state, a construction of kinship on the basis of the strategic meanings that are attributed to the biological and genetic elements involved in reproduction. In short, biology is subject to the cultural framework.

The Involvement of Assisted Reproductive Treatments in the Gestation Process

Access to assisted reproductive treatments varies from country to country, depending on the legislation that regulates this matter. In some places, recommendations, regulations and laws have been passed that can become very restrictive with regard to the criteria and conditions controlling this access (Bergmann 56). On occasion, these limitations mean that non-heterosexual women cannot benefit from these technological/medical interventions and, therefore, find that one of the routes to attaining maternity is cut off (Mezey 67).

In matters of assisted reproduction, Peramato (180) states that a classification of countries can be made according to the degree of restrictiveness of access to this type of treatment. The author shows that, broadly speaking, there are two types of countries: those that do not limit access because of sexual orientation and/or civil status, and those that consider assisted reproduction a right restricted to heterosexual couples. Among these latter countries, some can go so far as to require that the couple be married and, even, prohibit the involvement of donors in the insemination process.

Following this classification, Spanish Law 14/2006, of 26 May, on human assisted reproductive techniques, guarantees that all women, independent of their sexual orientation and/or civil status, can have access to assisted reproductive treatments. Specifically, Article 6.1 recognizes that: "Every woman above the age of 18 and with full capacity to act, can receive or use the techniques regulated in this Law, provided that she has given her free, conscious and express written consent to their use. She may use or receive said regulated techniques in this Law independent of her civil status and sexual orientation."

Despite this apparently favorable legislation, different developments have been occurring that hinder the access of female couples to assisted reproductive treatments in Spain. In 2014, Order SSI/2065/2014 was passed, which establishes that

---

1   See Josep Ferrer-Riba in this volume for a discussion of multiparentality and (Spanish) law.

the access requirement to assisted reproductive treatments in the public health system is a woman's infertility. One of the clauses of the regulation establishes this as: "Inability to achieve pregnancy after a minimum of 12 months of sexual relations with vaginal intercourse without the use of contraceptive methods." With this requirement, lesbian women can be excluded from public coverage of this type of treatment. Faced with this situation, many couples are compelled to pay for their own treatment in private clinics. This can end up causing unequal access to maternity, which, ultimately, is determined by the purchasing power of individuals to afford this type of reproduction (Mezey 67).

At times, this legal discrimination has been accompanied by smear campaigns that have reinforced some of the postulates upon which such laws are based. In this regard, in the 1990s, the Ethics Committee of the American Fertility Society showed that there was a preference toward heterosexual couples in reproductive treatments (Johnson 395). In some American states, heterosexual couples are still being given precedence over same-sex couples (ibid. 395). In Europe, the results are similar to North America. The study by Záchia et al. with European healthcare professionals concluded that these professionals believe that heterosexual couples should have preferential access to these types of treatment. The reason for this preference, the healthcare professionals argued, was based on preserving the welfare of the children born by means of these treatments: to avoid the rejection or conflicts arising out of the absence of a paternal figure (7). Lastly, in Spain, different professionals associated with the field of assisted reproduction drew up a document that concluded that "reproduction forms part of the life project of a couple and this is the fundamental reason for it and for society" (13). Despite this statement, and based on the cost of healthcare resources, they opined that these treatments should be for "members of a couple affected by sterility/infertility" (13).

Exclusion on the legal and medical level is also considered with other discriminations that emerge from the socio-political discourse. Internationally, different campaigns have asserted that assisted reproduction should be the exclusive right of heterosexual couples. Thus, as Bryld (308) shows, as a result of these campaigns, maternity in female couples is held in certain disrepute, and the centrality of the paternal figure has been reasserted. This discourse holds the belief that for the development of children there needs to be a male figure represented in the father. Once again, this argument for the development and well-being of children has been used in many other countries to justify the exclusion of lesbians from assisted reproduction (Robinson 220). According to Julien Murphy, heterosexual couples are seen as the legitimate beneficiaries and, simultaneously, the reproductive capacity of lesbians is denied. Thus, Murphy concludes, "the standard assumption is that only heterosexuals *can* reproduce, which comes to mean that only heterosexuals *should* reproduce" (186, author's italics).

Furthermore, female couples who are considering accessing motherhood through assisted reproduction also have to negotiate a whole other series of difficulties. One of them, closely related to the very conceptualization of kinship and the biological, is donor selection. Donors, both of eggs and sperm, play a decisive role in the reproductive process. The literature on egg donation is scant when compared to the studies that have analyzed sperm donation (Álvarez 60). Research on the sperm donor is more prolific and the most noteworthy aspects concern the revealing of donor identity (anonymous or public) and the donor's phenotypical characteristics. In Spain, the current legislation makes it impossible for the recipient to learn the identity of the donor, who, excluding exceptional situations, remains anonymous. However, in other countries there is greater flexibility in this regard, and women can decide whether to know the donor's identity or not. Even when this possibility exists, choosing an unknown donor is guarantee that he does not become involved in the education and raising of the children, nor in the family life of the couple (Mamo 99). Being an independent family project, it is not necessary that there be either a male or paternal figure. Including the donor might be considered as artificial and unnecessary and could result in more drawbacks than advantages (Ben-Ari and Livni 528). Therefore, the anonymity of the donor entails a dissociation regarding the family project, which is demonstrated by the fact that, among other issues, the donor is neither designated nor considered the father of the children (Herrera 48). With this formula, the possibility of claiming custody and/or paternity rights is avoided (Mamo 101). Even though there is a biogenetic connection between donor and child, on the social level there is no type of recognition. Consequently, the donor is neither considered as nor is equivalent to the father figure (Herrera 49).[2]

Those couples that opt for knowing the identity of the donor – when the relevant legislation guarantees it – seek a more active role in the raising and education of their children (Ryan-Flood 224). In other cases, there is a desire to be alike to the "ideal" family model and enjoy greater social recognition (Cadoret 55) or for the children to be able to have a "male role model" (Lewin 154). It should be emphasized that the research (Golombok and Tasker 9; González et al. 340) has not found differences in the development of children raised without this paternal role.

Along with identity, another important element in choosing the donor are the phenotypical traits of the donor. In Spain, the law regarding assisted reproduction establishes clear limits in this matter. The recipient women's margin of decision is fairly reduced and is based on the criteria established by the medical team. When the law allows, some studies (Hayden 637) show that what is sought is that the donor have similar phenotypical traits to the non-gestational mother. Along with

---

2   On a discussion of father figures in sperm donor families see Eva-Sabine Zehelein in this volume.

the physical traits, some couples also value other aspects relating to personality (Jones 222). A third aspect regarding donor selection is that of returning to the same person when more than one treatment is carried out. This reiteration in the selection is explained as an attempt to recreate a bond that is not only social but also biogenetic between descendants (Hayden 637). Authors such as Jones (230) indicate that repeating with the same donor is a guarantee of giving continuity to their biogenetic material, independent of whatever their identity is.

Methodology and Results

The results shown here are part of a wider research project (Álvarez), the aim of which is to examine the implications of paternity and maternity in Spanish same-sex couples. To achieve this, an ethnographic study was carried out with 21 same-sex couples during the period 2013-2015. In this article, I present the results on the perception that the female couples (n=11) interviewed have had regarding their access and experience in undergoing assisted reproductive treatment.

One of the most noteworthy results concerns the preference for the private rather than the public system for undertaking assisted reproductive treatment. The absence of a favorable legal framework toward their situation was one of the determining factors of this option. Some couples had attained motherhood at a time when in Spain marriage was still not legal between people of the same sex, which meant that their family situation lacked official recognition. Opting for a private clinic was one way of avoiding questions or having to give explanations about the situation in which these couples found themselves.

On other occasions, the decision was based on the negative experiences of friends or acquaintances in the public health system. Resorting to a trustworthy private clinic was a formula that gave them guarantees for carrying out the treatment. In these clinics, with the exception of one couple, lesbian women felt no differentiated treatment compared to their heterosexual peers.

Regarding parental capacity, the interviews showed that the "absence" of a father – one of the arguments used to deny female couples access to assisted reproduction – had had no influence on the raising of their children. The women interviewed stated that both mothers were capable of providing the care and satisfying the needs of their children without the involvement of a male figure. The idea of "father" was not present in their discourses and, at all times, they spoke of the donor as an anonymous subject that had contributed to the successful endeavor of their maternal project. When they were asked about the possibility of knowing the identity of this person, all the women were alike in saying that Spanish law did not permit it. Nevertheless, they continued, if it were legal, they still would not choose to discover his identity. The reasons given for this opinion concerned the rejection of that person being involved in family life and, therefore, in the raising and educa-tion of the children. The family project of these couples had been planned without the need or desire for a third active parental role, so the donor had no significant role in their family life stories whatsoever. The opinions of the women interviewed all coincided in that paternity was to be found beyond the biological and includes practices and concerns that donors do not undertake.

Despite being sure that the donor should be anonymous, some couples ex-pressed fear that this decision could affect their children. In particular, it worried them that, when they grew up to be adolescents, they would reproach them for not knowing who the donor had been. Nevertheless, they thought that they could ne-gotiate this difficulty by instilling in their children values other than their descen-dance and, principally, the meaning and socio-cultural construction of kinship. In particular, this involved addressing their origins through teaching and not hiding information about the process nor concealing details that could prove of interest to the children. They believed, moreover, that they should manage this issue from a young age, from the moment that their children were old enough to have sufficient reasoning to be able to understand the information.

With regard to the phenotypical characteristics of the donor, differences can be observed between those who achieved motherhood using the public system and those who used private clinics. Those couples who opted for treatment in the public sphere stated that the phenotypical characteristics of both partners were requested and, from this information, the medical team selected the donor according to their physical traits. In contrast, those who resorted to a private clinic had a wider mar-gin of selection. These couples based their decision on two criteria: physical simi-larity with the non-gestational mother and the application of the dominant models of beauty, the former being the most common criterion. Regarding donor reselec-tion, the only couple that had repeated an insemination process had selected the same donor as in their initial treatment.

The couples asserted that their motherhood was whole and complete, that they saw no need for a father figure for the appropriate development of their children. Through the model they adopted for the upbringing of their children, they con-sidered that their children were capable of having a broader and less biased view of gender roles. Equality between women and men was one of the pedagogical premises in which most of the interviewed couples took refuge. Two couples did consider it important that their children interact with male figures, but not father figures. For this reason, the interviewees commented that they encouraged their children to have direct contact with some of the men from their families of ori-gin. However, other couples interviewed did not give particular importance to the necessity of providing differentiated gender models. They considered that as they lived in a pluralistic society, there are many times and settings in which one can interact with different and diverse people without the need to actively search for those differentiated gender models.

Lastly, the couples who formed part of this study valued their maternal-filial relationship positively, attaching great importance to their internal relationships independent of their composition and structure. In this regard, they emphasized love and affection as the most important values that should be present in the upbringing and education of their children. For these women, these values were not exclusive to one family model or structure, but were within the reach of all people. Thus, they countered the many criticisms from certain sectors that have been cast upon this type of family.

Conclusions

The families formed by female couples have to negotiate the obstacles of a society that privileges the heterosexual family model. This results in discourses and practices that discriminate those other family models that move away from that "ideal." One of these expressions of discrimination is the unequal access to assisted reproductive treatments, in which it is argued that the lack of a father figure can influence a child's development. The results of this study reveal that among some female couples, fears prevail of suffering discrimination in the processes of assisted reproduction. Similarly, faced with the criticism, the families interviewed state that a father figure is not necessary for cementing a solid family project. Love, affection and care are the keys to legitimizing these families, both in their own eyes and in the eyes of society.

Bibliography

Álvarez, Gloria. *Etnografía de las relaciones de parentesco en familias encabezadas por parejas del mismo sexo*. U de Granada P, 2016.

Beck-Gernsheim, Elisabeth. *Reinventing the family: In search of new lifestyles*. Polity, 2002.

Ben-Ari, Adital, and Tali Livni. "Motherhood is not a given thing: experiences and constructed meanings of biological and nonbiological lesbian mothers." *Sex Roles*, vol. 54, no. 7, 2006, pp. 521-31.

Bergmann, Sven. "Cambiar el óvulo manteniendo el fenotipo: la búsqueda de semejanza en la FIV con donación de óvulos transnacional." *Cuerpos y diferencias*, edited by Eulalia Pérez and Rebeca Ibáñez, Plaza y Valdés, 2012, pp. 55-78.

Bryld, Mette. "The infertility clinic and the birth of the lesbian: the political debate on assisted reproduction in Denmark." *European Journal of Women's Studies*, vol. 8, no. 3, 2001, pp. 299-312.

Cadoret, Anne. *Padres como los demás. Parejas gays y lesbianas con hijos*. Editorial Gedisa, 2013.

Cutas, Daniela, and Sarah Chan. "Introduction. Perspectives on private and family life." *Families. Beyond the nuclear ideal*, edited by Daniela Cutas and Sarah Chan, Bloomsbury, 2012, pp. 1-12.

Golombok, Susan, and Fiona Tasker. "Do parents influence the sexual orientation of their children? Findings from a longitudinal study of lesbian families." *Developmental Psychology*, vol. 32, no. 1, 1996, pp. 3-11.

González, María del Mar, et al. "Ajuste psicológico e integración social en hijos e hijas de familias homoparentales." *Infancia y aprendizaje: Journal for the Study of Education and Development*, vol. 27, no. 3, 2004, pp. 327-43.

González Echevarría, Aurora, et al. "Sobre la definición de los dominios transculturales. La antropología del parentesco como teoría sociocultural de la reproducción." *Alteridades*, vol. 20, no. 39, 2010, pp. 93-106.

Hayden, Corinne. "Género, genética y generación: reformulación de la biología en el parentesco lésbico." *Antropología del parentesco y de la familia*, edited by Robert Parkin and Linda Stone, Editorial Universitaria Ramón Areces, 2008, pp. 621-46.

Herrera, Florencia. "Tradition and transgression: lesbian motherhood in Chile." *Sexuality research and social policy*, vol. 6, no. 2, 2009, pp. 35-51.

Johnson, Katherine. "Excluding lesbian and single women? An analysis of US fertility clinic websites." *Women's Studies International Forum*, vol. 35, no. 5, 2012, pp. 394-402.

Jones, Carolina. "Looking like a family: Negotiating bio-genetic continuity in British lesbian families using licensed donor insemination." *Sexualities*, vol. 8, no. 2, 2005, pp. 221-37.

Lewin, Ellen. *Lesbian mothers. Accounts of gender in American culture*. Cornell UP, 1993.

Mamo, Laura. *Queering reproduction*. Duke UP, 2007.

Mezey, Nancy. "How lesbian and gay men decide to become parents or remain childfree." *LGBT-Parent families. Innovations in research and implications for practice*, edited by Abbie Goldberg and Katherine Allen, Springer, 2013, pp. 59-70.

Murphy, Julien. "Should lesbians count as infertile couples? Antilesbian discrimination in assisted reproduction." *Queer families. Queer politics. Challenging culture and the state*, edited by Mary Bernstein and Renate Reimann, Columbia UP, 2001, pp. 182-200.

Peramato, Teresa. *Desigualdad por razón de orientación sexual e identidad de género, homofobia y transfobia*. Aranzadi, 2013.

Pichardo, José Ignacio. *Opciones sexuales y nuevos modelos familiares.* U Complutense P, 2008.

Rivas, Ana María. "Pluriparentalidades y parentescos electivos. Presentación del volumen monográfico." *Revista de Antropología Social*, vol. 18, 2009, pp. 7-19.

Robinson, Bambi. "Birds do it. Bees do it. So why not single women and lesbians?" *Bioethics*, vol. 11, no. 3, 2002, pp. 217-27.

Ryan-Flood, Róisín. "Queering representation: Ethics and visibility in research." *Journal of Lesbian Studies*, vol. 13, no. 2, 2003, pp. 216-28.

Stone, Linda. "Introducción." *Antropología del parentesco y de la familia*, edited by Robert Parkin and Linda Stone, Editorial Universitaria Ramón Areces, 2008, pp. 545-58.

Thompson, Charis. "Strategic naturalizing: kinship in an infertility clinic." *Relative Values. Reconfiguring kinship studies*, edited by Sarah Franklin and Susan McKinnon, Duke UP, 2001, pp. 175-202.

Záchia, Suzana, et al. "Assisted reproduction: What factors interfere in the professional's decisions? Are single women an issue?" *BMC Women's Health*, vol. 11, no. 21, 2011, pp. 2-10.

"He's Not Family"[1]
Family Between Genetic Essentialism and Social Parenthood in MTV's Docu-Diary *Generation Cryo* (2013)

Eva-Sabine Zehelein, Goethe Universität Frankfurt / Brandeis University WSRC

Generation Cryo is a 2013 MTV show packaged as a reality docu-diary.[2] Serialized in six 40-minute episodes, it portrays 17-year old Breeanna Speicher from Reno, Nevada, who sets out to meet as many of her 15 half-siblings (conceived with sperm from the same donor) as possible. And with their help, she is determined to find the donor, the guy who "did his thing in a cup" ("Trailer") and whose sperm her two mums, Sherry and Debra, had chosen from a cryo bank. The show is filmed to suggest that Bree records her trip with her own hand-held camera as a video diary. There are sections where she speaks into her camera, addressing the donor directly, and this is also, programmatically, how the show opens:

> It's all for you, my sperm donor, so hi. For so long it hasn't even felt like reality that this mystery man brought me into the world and I am so appreciative of my life and where it's going and I just wanna know who you are. Hopefully one day, if you are willing, I would love to meet you, so I'm gonna try to find you and if I do, my diaries will tell you my whole story. ("Who's Your Daddy?")

Over the summer of 2013, Bree travels the country – Atlanta, Boston, and California – to meet with ten of the siblings and their families: Jonah and Hilit Jacobson (and their parents Eric and Terri), Jesse Bogdan (and his parents Jim and Laurie and his sister Emily, who is not donor conceived), Jesse and Jayme Clapoff (and their single mum by choice Janis), Molly, Paige, and Will Chaifetz (and their parents Perry Chaifetz, who doesn't feature in the show, and Laura Schofield), as well as Julian (whose single mum is not part of the show) and Maddi Walker (with her mum Mara, who conceived Maddi when she was single, and her dad Phil). With

---

1 Heartfelt thanks to Rosanna Hertz (Wellesley College), as well as to the members of the Brandeis Women's Studies Research Center, especially to Karen V. Hansen, for their input and support. The larger research project is funded by the Fritz Thyssen Stiftung.

2 For analysis of Hollywood films or TV series dealing with sperm donation see e.g. Akass et al.; Gupta; Kennedy; Maher; Tropp.

the help of some donor siblings, Bree tries to contact the anonymous donor via the sperm bank. While waiting for a response, they manage to discover enough information about him that they can identify his name, find his current address in Oakland, CA., a picture from a high school yearbook, and even get his birth certificate. Bree writes him a letter. He responds via email and promises to also write to those other siblings who wish to establish contact. All of them will see where these conversations will take them – and their families – in the future.

Since all cultural artefacts are constructed by, but also co-construct, reflect, yet also create their socio-cultural and political milieu, they are central epistemological media, and their analysis via an intersectional practice can attempt to perform a richer and more complex reading. Thus, rooted in cultural studies, the following analysis of *Generation Cryo* draws primarily on sociology (new kinship studies) and (medical) anthropology as well as media and gender studies. First, I position the show briefly in the context of reality TV and the "docu-diary," focusing on the tricky claim to facticity, authenticity and truth that accompanies such an, as I argue, essentially (auto)biographical narrative form (Smith and Watson). In a second step, I highlight in two sections how *Generation Cryo* as (auto)biographical text (re)presents (re)negotiations of families created with sperm by the same anonymous donor, what Hertz and Nelson have called "Random Families." For one, *Generation Cryo* illustrates the complex internal as well as external family dynamics brought about by sperm donation, and illustrates the rewriting of nuclear family narratives as constant ongoing processes, also of in- and exclusion. As I will illustrate, these narratives of belonging constantly oscillate between genetic essentialism and social parenthood. Secondly, the show allows an intimate glance at what it means for each family member to be confronted with the looming presence of the donor. One of the fundamental questions all ask is what role a sperm donor could have for them as families, as individual family members, and as children conceived with his sperm; for Eric, an infertile father, it's clear: "He's not family" ("The Reunion").[3]

Really *Auto-Bios-Graphe*: *Generation Cryo*

Reality TV "as a textual, social and cultural formation" (Kavka 4) is a highly hybrid form, characterized primarily by its "generic haziness" – "there is probably not a single feature that is shared by all of the programmes which fall under the rubric of 'reality TV'" (Kavka 1, 8). Its single primary characteristic and selling point is that it presents (facets of) the authentic lives of ordinary people, challenging the private-

---

3   Throughout and as a fundamental tenet, I conceptualize family as a network characterized also, but not exclusively, by genetic belonging (genetic essentialism), yet first and foremost by the longing to belong (relatedness).

public and 'fact-fiction' divides, opening opportunities to address social discourses in quasi documentary ways, no matter how scripted and selective the shows ultimately may be (Cummings), while aiming for high entertainment value with limited production costs (Murray and Ouellette 4).

Generation Cryo finds itself at the opposite end of the Reality TV spectrum from, say, *Big Brother, Temptation Island* or *Survivor* (Feasey). This show is not about exhibitionism, celebrity culture, voyeurism, and surveillance. It aims to introduce to a younger audience (MTV) a lived reality which is very much and increasingly so part and parcel of younger generations' lives and identities with wide reaching ramifications, and might thus warrant not only some informed thought, but also lots of de-stigmatization. Far from showing men who survive on a desert island, restore a motorbike, or try to find their perfect female match, this show presents people who live the ordinary family life – diverse family constellations which try to do right and good to their members and to each other; young adults who search for their identities as donor siblings; two men, genetically not related to their children, who strive for masculine authenticity as family dads, struggle with the stigma and hardship of infertility, and are confronted with the absent presence of a hypermasculine, virile, and fertile donor who, although anonymous, shakes up all families, their lives, and the fathers' (masculine) self-identifications.

Whereas many Hollywood movies thematizing reproductive technologies (say, *Baby Mama* and *The Switch* (both 2008), or *Starbuck* (2011) in essence reaffirm the traditional nuclear family model, despite the depictions of neo-liberal reproductive freedom and nearly unlimited possibility and opportunity (Maher; also Bruzzi; Tropp), *Generation Cryo* presents different forms of doing and narrating family. The show supports the call for both, open identity or identity release donation, as well as for family openness and inclusiveness, and acceptance of new families and extended networks of care and compassion.

It might be particularly fruitful to focus on the show's use of the video diary format, suggesting that the story comes 'straight from the heart' of the protagonist and narrator, transforming the audience into sneaky witnesses to this quasi-confessional and intimate autobiographical narrative. What Carsten ("Knowing" 689) and then also Klotz have described as a lack of agency, the lack of constitutive knowledge about genetic origins, be that in cases of adoption or sperm donation, might better be understood through the lens of self (*auto*) life (*bios*) writing (*graphe*). No matter whether we see relatedness on the basis of genetics immediately as geneticization (e.g. Mamo) or not – a desire to explore origins and construct a self life narrative (Smith and Watson 2001) as fundamental part of a self and identity is at the heart of *Generation Cryo*, and for all involved – every self is conceived "not as an essence, but as a subject, a moving target, which provisionally conjoins memory, identity, experience, relationality, embodiment, affect and limited agency" (Smith and Watson, "Virtually Me" 71).

Bree says in the trailer: "I am trying to piece together my history," accompanied by a photographic portrait of Bree being put together from many building blocks or pieces illustrating transtextually the idea of an autobiographical project. The self feels incomplete and hopes for or expects closure through finding the missing pieces. And the show as video diary supports this theme structurally as well: Bree tells her story, in words and images, with the help of her donor siblings who accompany her on her geographical as well as spiritual quest and autobiographical journey to find the donor and thus also (a part of) her self. At the same time, with every family we visit with Bree, *Generation Cryo* introduces us also to fundamental challenges to the individual identity constructions of all family members. The project is thus autobiographical as well as biographical; it straddles the 'fact-fiction divide', entertains through the presentation of a topical human interest story told by 'real people', and in its formula also mirrors how public private decisions can become – the super private act of human procreation becomes a public issue when it comes to medical intervention or assistance and the ensuing legal as well as socio-cultural ramifications.[4]

Rewriting Nuclear Scripts

Generation Cryo's trailer features a drawn family tree; at the stem, there is a black silhouette of a generic male head, of donor #1096, and the families with the donor kids are the 'fruit' hanging in the tree's foliage in clusters with their individual real-life portraits and names. The imagery invokes notions of dependence and scale of importance – the stem of the tree being decisive for (bringing forth) the fruit. The family tree here seems to suggest notions of natural pedigree, blood relations, heredity, purity and transmission (Weil 3). It thus symbolically represents the fundamental conflict at the heart of the story – genetics *vs* social parenthood, a definition of family based on shared genetics or shared emotional bonds of belonging. For the children, the extended family exists only because of the genetic connection, and they say they feel strong bonds between each other and act as sisters and brothers. At the same time, though, the donor is not considered a family member, since the provision of sperm does not establish the right to fatherhood. The encounters between the sibling families and Bree illustrate that it is sociability that glues the extended family network together – a "productive paradox" (cf. Hertz and Nelson; McKinnon). The use of the family tree seems to aim at naturalizing this family constellation (Zehelein), to open the concept and term 'family' in view of the existing realities of belonging, the plethora of family constellations we live today and have

---

4   See Zehelein, "Mothers, ART, …", as well as "'India is our twins' motherland'…" and "'Sara, Bill, Kristine, ..'" on surrogacy and "IP Memoirs."

lived for centuries – be they mono- or pluripaternal, hetero- or homonormative, with genetically related children or not.

The family narratives presented through Bree's road trips oscillate between on the one hand deeply ingrained notions of heteropatriarchy and the nuclear family model with clearly defined templates for the performances of family roles (the Jacobsons, Bogdans and Chaifetz), and on the other hand lived realities of rainbow families or new families (the Speichers and Clapoffs) in which individual roles have to be and are renegotiated or/and reframed – what Carsten, referencing Charis Thompson, has nicely called "a complex 'choreography' between social and biological factors" (*After Kinship* 179; also Weston; Hertz; or Nordqvist and Smart). Both fundamental parameters which we usually associate first and foremost with kinship and family formation are present here at the same time: social parent-/fatherhood is discursively emphasized within heterosexual two parent families in which male infertility necessitated the use of donor sperm in order to have children; genetic parent-/fatherhood comes into play once the reality of the donor is brought into focus. Just as e.g. Hertz and Nelson have shown in their field research, here, too, the two in essence co-exist and challenge the narrative family fabrics as well as individual identity constructions. For the heterosexual parents the nuclear family ideal looms large, maybe as a reactionary reflex to confirm their intra-familial positions and bonds. It is important to note, that, interestingly enough, the ideal, so often decried for its conservatism, heteronormativity and cementation of patriarchal structures, is here rather experienced as a reassuring matrix in which all find their space and scripts and thus reassurance of their respective identities.

To have the donor appear on the scene – with a name and a photo and an address and an email – brings back on the family dinner tables a fundamental epistemic fracture. Many iconic scenes at family dinner tables à la Norman Rockwell illustrate that old wounds are opened up, that threatened masculinities necessitate the re-affirmation and the re-assertion of adapted and negotiated notions of doing masculinities defying certain assumptions deeply ingrained in dominant cultural narratives / hegemonic masculinities that deny fatherhood and essentially also manhood to infertile men (Griffin). Molly's mum Laura thought she had bought all the donor's sperm and thus 'kept it in the family' and protected her husband and his role as man and father. For Eric, too, it is deeply disturbing and unsettling that the borders of his family are becoming porous, that new members are added. Although he loves them, is welcoming to Bree and includes her in the deeply symbolic family celebration of shabbat, the potential appearance of the donor, in the flesh, and no longer as a vial, seriously upsets him: "Maybe it's about who my family is. And adding others to it, adding sibling, adding the donor, is not my definition of family" ("Who's Your Daddy?").

Men - Women - Children

At the center of the 'nuclear families' and their stories are the husbands and fathers, Eric Jacobson and Jim Bogdan, who struggle with their self-worth and masculine identities. To them, these appear as diminished because they cannot fulfil
the hegemonic masculinity template (Kimmel) that includes 'fathering' their own
genetic offspring. The men are willing to confront their pain about not being the
genetic fathers to their children, and make sense of infertility and of what it means
for them as individuals and as members of the collectives in which they perform.
After all, certain cultural scripts are not attainable or performable in social practice,
and thus the *habitus* (Bourdieu) needs discursive or narrative reframing or re-artic-
ulation. Eric is the show's most deeply hurt and threatened man and his divergent
views and desires from those of his wife lead to a serious marital crisis. For Eric,
it's traumatic to the day that he "couldn't do that one manly thing a man is expected
to do." Eric even says that his wife "didn't lose anything, I lost everything" and that
he had to undergo a process of grieving, of accepting that he cannot produce kids
("Who's Your Daddy?"). When Jonah tells his father: "It's about the raising of the
kids and keeping your name going," he reassures Eric of his position as *pater familias* which he has always performed well and which goes unchallenged, also with a
redefinition of patriliny or patrilineal continuity ("Who's Your Daddy?").

However, *Generation Cryo* also highlights the women and the partners who have
to conceptualize the donor and to define their roles – as non-biological co-parents in the case of lesbian couples, as single mothers, or as biological mothers of
a child not related genetically to their husbands. When Bree asks her mum Sherry
whether it "bums her out" that she is not biologically related to her, and that it
bums her out, Sherry says that from the moment Bree was born she was her child.
"You know, when you were born, the minute you came into my arms, I started
singing this song, This Old Man, and you stopped crying. You have a bond with me
that will never go away. Nothing can take that away. Nothing." Sherry fought for
visitation rights when she and her partner Debra, Bree's biological mother, broke
up. Bree lives with Sherry and it is she who supports Bree most on her journey.
Sherry expresses gratefulness towards the donor, but she warns Bree, jokingly, but
maybe with some kernel of significance, that if the guy wanted to take her place, she
would probably have to shoot him ("The Reunion"). Emotional bonding and shared
experiences since minute 1, care, and affection constitute the fundamental core of
parenthood and trump genetics.

Barnes has pointed out that women's experiences with male infertility and
women's roles in men's reproductive health are still "relatively unexplored fields of
social inquiry. Within marriage, women are highly influential in their husbands'
medical treatment decisions and reserve the right to control their own bodies"
(Barnes 164). *Generation Cryo* presents a rare glimpse at some women's responses,

attitudes, and narrative frames to intellectualize what their partner's infertility and the use of donor sperm meant then and means today. Laura feels physically sick when she sees the donor picture, and is afraid of feeling that she 'betrayed' her husband – as if the use of donor sperm had been an act of adultery. She also says that the existence of a donor is very difficult to accept for her husband, who, maybe tellingly, doesn't feature in the show ("The Reunion"). But she understands that this search for the donor is also, and maybe mostly, about the kids, and she vows to Bree to help her and be there for her and her own three children. Terri is adamant to know "the science, the biology" of it ("The Reunion"). She wants to know who is genetically related to her children, and has little understanding for her husband's fears and deep-seated anxieties concerning the impact of his infertility. In the story of Terri and Eric it becomes very clear that couples have to frame their parental identities and performances. The donor is a silent presence, a third person in a couple relationship, an unknown other who wedges himself into the partnership and questions some fundamental tenets of self-same. Eric says: "Twenty years ago you said to me we will never meet this guy. And now you want to! It deeply hurts me. It seems to me that the vow we took has been negated. I feel as if we have gone past the line of no return and it hurts me" ("The Reunion").

Donor conceived children have to work out their sense of self and their autobiographical narratives, including what it means to be donor conceived and whether or not – and if, how – the donor plays any role for this narrative and for their lives. This also goes for the inclusion of additional "genetic strangers" (Hertz and Nelson) to the family narratives. All children portrayed have known for as long as they can remember that they are donor conceived. For some, this fact remained largely insignificant to their identities and feelings of belonging, because of the presence of their social father. Some children would like to see a picture of the donor to check for physical resemblances,[5] but not do more; some would like to talk to him, over a coffee (not lunch); some would like to get to know him better. The fear of upsetting the family tectonics, of hurting the parents (Molly), the wish to protect the parents, the worry "that dad and you are both going to feel we're not yours" (Molly) ("The Reunion"), the fear that "it's going to mess up my family relationship" (Jonah, "The Reunion"), makes the siblings hesitate to help Bree on her journey, despite their "natural curiosity" to know who he is. Molly says: "I have my own dad. Why should I think about this other guy?" ("The Reunion"). And for Jesse, who has a younger sister conceived with his father's sperm, there is a constant feeling of being a second-class child; to be a sperm donor kid is shameful and exclusionary/stigmatizing/othering. He wants to be "a Bogdan," yet this definition

---

5   Physical resemblances are a huge topic in the show. The half-siblings check each other and also eagerly peruse the donor's high school picture. For what role physical resemblances with the donor play for heterosexual parents, cf. Isaksson et al.

of belonging is characterized by a "grammar of blood" (Payne) which does not apply to him. For a long time, he denies any physical resemblance to the donor and does not want to talk about him or the half-siblings, because "it's embarrassing for my dad" ("Come To Grips"). Only the interaction with the other half-siblings gradually makes him realize how good it is to have this extended family, triggers his interest in the donor, and boosts his self-worth ("One Last Trip").

Bree argues that meeting the donor will not change the siblings, and that the door they are about to open with their search "doesn't open on hell" ("We're Your Family"), yet deep seated insecurities and unstable family and identity tectonics cannot be denied, since the donor is, in the end, not just a sperm.

Conclusion: Belonging and Longing to Belong

When Eric says that for him, the donor will never be family, he draws a clear line around his circled wagons and most other families and siblings do the same. Some consider meeting the donor, yet all will have to figure out individually "where to put him in [their] lives." As Hilit says: "We don't want him to think we are his kids" ("The Reunion"). The infertile men in heterosexual family settings as well as the lesbian non-biological mum try hard to be open about the situation, yet struggle with feelings of insecurity and potential loss – loss of the role of father to the donor conceived children, loss of paternal authority or position within the family setting, loss of love and affection by the children and/or their wives.

Generation Cryo normalizes and inscribes into the cultural imaginary or narrative a family form which is still frequently either unknown or often marginalized or invalidated because not-normative. The format draws on narrative tropes and established cultural practices such as the family tree image (Weil; Zehelein, "Family Trees...") to illustrate the complex family relationships, but also to close the gap between the known and sanctioned and the new and (often) censured. It welcomes networks of belonging as support structures with flexible practices of masculinities and femininities, and understands those not as a threat, but an enrichment to a family's individual members and societies at large (cf. Kramer and Cahn). *Generation Cryo* is primarily the (auto)biographical story of Bree and her genetic siblings setting out on a journey to find their donor and to find and accept themselves, to rethink and reconfirm their family ties and autobiographical narratives. It is, in the end, a story of finding family, of experiencing new forms of family belonging, based on genetics, yet flourishing on emotional bonds and mutual support.

Bibliography

Akass, Kim, et al., editors. *Reading the L word: Outing Contemporary Television*. Palgrave Macmillan, 2006.

Alexander, Susan M., and Katie Woods. "Reality Television and the Doing of Hyperauthentic Masculinities." *Journal of Men's Studies*, vol. 27, no. 2, 2019, pp. 149-68.

Barnes, Liberty W. *Conceiving Masculinity: Male Infertility, Medicine, and Identity*. Temple UP, 2014.

Bell, Ann V. "'I don't consider a cup performance; I consider it a test': masculinity and the medicalization of infertility." *Sociology of Health & Illness*, vol. 38, no. 5, 2016, pp. 706-20.

Bruzzi, Stella. *Bringing Up Daddy: Fatherhood and Masculinity in Post-War Hollywood*. British Film Institute Publishing, 2005.

Bourdieu, Pierre. *Masculine Domination*. Stanford UP, 2002.

Carsten, Janet. *After Kinship*. Cambridge UP, 2004.

—. "Knowing where you've come from: Ruptures and continuities of time and kinship in narratives of adoption reunions." *Journal of the Royal Anthropological Institute*, vol. 6, no. 4, 2000, pp. 687-703.

Connell, R.W. *Masculinities*, 2nd edition. Polity, 2015.

—. "Masculinities: The Field of Knowledge." *Configuring Masculinity in Theory and Literary Practice*, edited by Stefan Horlacher, Brill Rodopi, 2015, pp. 39-51.

Cummings, Dolan, editor. *Reality TV: how real is real?* Hodder & Stoughton, 2002.

Dudgeon Matthew R., and Marcia C. Inhorn. "Gender, Masculinity, and Reproduction: Anthropological Perspectives." *Reconceiving the Second Sex. Men, Masculinity, and Reproduction*, edited by Marcia C. Inhorn, et al., Berghahn Books, 2009, pp. 72-102.

Feasey, Rebecca. *Masculinity and Popular Television*. Edinburgh UP, 2008.

Forhan, Betsy, et al., executive producers. *Generation Cryo*. MTV, 2013.

Franklin, Sarah, and Susan McKinnon, editors. *Relative Values: Reconfiguring Kinship Studies*. Duke UP, 2001.

Franklin, Sarah. "From Blood to Genes? Rethinking Consanguinity in the Context of Geneticization." *Blood and Kinship: Matter for Metaphor from Ancient Rome to the Present*, edited by Christopher H. Johnson, et al., Berghahn Books, 2013, pp. 285-306.

Golombok, Susan. *Modern Families: Parents and Children in New Family Forms*. Cambridge UP, 2015.

Griffin, Ben. "Hegemonic Masculinity as a Historical Problem." *Gender & History*, vol. 30, no. 2, 2018, pp. 377-400.

Gupta, Kristina. "Picturing space for lesbian nonsexualities: Rethinking sex-normative commitments through *The Kids Are All Right* (2010)." *Journal of Lesbian Studies*, vol. 17, no. 1, 2013, pp. 103-18.

Halberstam, Jack. *Female Masculinity*. Duke UP, 1998.

Harper, Joyce C., et al. "The End of Donor Anonymity: How Genetic Testing Is Likely To Drive Anonymous Gamete Donation out of Business." *Human Reproduction*, vol. 31, no. 6, 2016, pp. 1135-40.

Hertz, Rosanna. *Single by Chance, Mothers by Choice*. Oxford UP, 2006.

Hertz, Rosanna, and Margaret K. Nelson. *Random Families: Genetic Strangers, Sperm Donor Siblings, and the Creation of New Kin*. Oxford UP, 2019.

Horlacher, Stefan. "Configuring Masculinity." *Configuring Masculinity in Theory and Literary Practice*, edited by Stefan Horlacher, Brill Rodopi, 2015, pp. 1-10.

Inhorn, Marcia C., et al., editors. *Reconceiving the Second Sex. Men, Masculinity, and Reproduction*. Berghahn Books, 2009.

Inhorn, Marcia C. *The New Arab Man: Emergent Masculinities, Technologies, and Islam in the Middle East*. Princeton UP, 2012.

Isaksson, Stina, et al. "Managing absence and presence of child-parent resemblance: a challenge for heterosexual couples following sperm donation." *Reproductive BioMedicine and Society Online*, vol. 8, 2019, pp. 38-46.

Kavka, Misha. *Reality TV*. Edinburgh UP, 2012.

Keith, Thomas. *Masculinities in Contemporary American Culture – An Intersectional Approach to the Complexities and Challenges of Male Identity*. Routledge, 2017.

Kennedy, Tammie M. "Sustaining White Homonormativity: *The Kids Are All Right* as Public Pedagogy." *Journal of Lesbian Studies*, vol. 18, no. 2, 2014, pp. 118-32.

Kimmel, Michael. *Manhood in America. A Cultural History*. 3rd edition. Oxford UP, 2012.

Klotz, Maren. "Wayward Relations: Novel Searches of the Donor-Conceived for Genetic Kinship." *Medical Anthropology*, vol. 35, no. 1, 2016, pp. 45-57.

Kramer, Wendy, and Naomi Cahn. *Finding Our Families: A First-of-Its Kind Book for Donor-Conceived People and Their Families*. Avery, 2013.

Mamo, Laura. "Biomedicalizing Kinship. Sperm Banks and the Creation of Affinity-ties." *Science as Culture*, vol. 14, no. 3, 2005, pp. 237-64.

Maher, Jennifer. "Something Else Besides a Father. Reproductive technology in recent Hollywood film." *Feminist Media Studies*, vol. 14, no. 5, 2014, pp. 853-67.

McKinnon, Susan. "Productive Paradoxes of the Assisted Reproductive Technologies in the Context of New Kinship Studies." *Journal of Family Issues*, vol. 36, no. 4, 2015, pp. 461-79.

Moore, Lisa J. "Killer Sperm: Masculinity and the Essence of Male Hierarchies." *Reconceiving the Second Sex. Men, Masculinity, and Reproduction*, edited by Marcia C. Inhorn, et al., Berghahn Books, 2009, pp. 45-71.

Murray, Susan, and Laurie Ouellette, editors. *Reality TV: Remaking Television Culture*. New York UP, 2004.

Nordqvist, Petra, and Carol Smart. *Relative Strangers: Family Life, Genes and Donor Conception*. Palgrave Macmillan, 2014.

Payne, Jenny Gunnarsson. "Grammars of Kinship: Biological Motherhood and Assisted Reproduction in the Age of Epigenetics." *Signs*, vol. 41, no. 3, 2016, pp. 483-506.

Smith, Sidonie, and Julia Watson. *Reading autobiography: a guide for interpreting life narratives*. U of Minnesota P, 2001.

—. "Virtually me: a toolbox about online self-presentation." *Identity Technologies: Constructing the Self Online*, edited by Anna Poletti and Julie Rak, U of Wisconsin P, 2014, pp. 70-96.

Thompson, Charis. *Making Parents: The Ontological Choreography of Reproductive Technologies*. MIT P, 2005.

Tober, Diane. *Romancing the Sperm. Shifting Biopolitics and the Making of Modern Families*. Rutgers UP, 2019.

Tropp, Laura. "Who's Your Daddy: Sperm Donation and the Cultural Construction of Fatherhood." *Deconstructing Dads – Changing Images of Fathers in Popular Culture*, edited by Laura Tropp et al., Lexington Books, 2016, pp. 31-49.

Weil, Francois. *Family Trees. A History of Genealogy in America*. Harvard UP, 2013.

Weston, Kath. *Families We Choose: Lesbians, Gays, Kinship (Between Men-Between Women)*. Revised and with a new Preface. Columbia UP, 1997.

Zehelein, Eva-Sabine. "'Sara, Bill, Kristine, …you're pregnant!' Gestational surrogacy, biomedicalized bodies and reconceptualizations of motherhood." *Hektoen International. A Journal of Medical Humanities*. Fall 2017, http://hekint. org/2017/11/20/sara-bill-kristine-youre-pregnant-gestational-surrogacy-biomedicalized-bodies-reconceptualizations-motherhood/. Accessed 20 March 2020.

—. "Reproductive Justice and (the Politics of) Transnational Gestational Surrogacy: Pande, *Wombs in Labor: Transnational Commercial Surrogacy in India*, Rudrappa, *Discounted Life: The Price of Global Surrogacy in India*, Jacobson, *Labor of Love: Gestational Surrogacy and the Work of Making Babies*, Solinger/Ross, *Reproductive Justice*, Briggs, *How All Politics Became Reproductive Politics*." *American Quarterly*, vol. 70, no. 4, 2018, pp. 889-901.

—. "Mothers, ART and Narratives of (Be)longing." *CoSMo*, vol. 12, Spring 2018, pp. 74-91, http://www.ojs.unito.it/index.php/COSMO/issue/view/272. Accessed 20 March 2020.

—. "Family Matters in Contemporary Literature – an introduction." *CoSMo*, vol. 12, Spring 2018, pp. 7-10, http://www.ojs.unito.it/index.php/COSMO/issue/view/ 272. Accessed 20 March 2020.

—. "Mummy, me, and her podcast – feminist and gender discourses in contemporary podcast culture." *International Journal of Media & Cultural Politics* vol. 15, no. 2, 2019, pp. 143-61, https://www.ingentaconnect.com/content/intellect/mcp/ 2019/00000015/00000002;jsessionid=3pmsd9rs5b2jh.x-ic-live-01. Accessed 20 March 2020.

—. "'India is our twins' motherland': Transnational Cross-Racial Gestational Surrogacy and the Maternal Body in 'IP Memoirs'." *Feminist Encounters – Journal of Critical Studies in Culture and Politics*, vol. 3, no. 1-2, 2019, article number 11, pp. 1-12.

—. "Love, Marriage and Family in the 21st Century: *All We Had* (Annie Weatherwax), *The Nest* (Cynthia D'Aprix Sweeney)." *The American Novel in the 21st Century: Cultural Contexts – Literary Developments – Critical Analyses*, edited by Michael Basseler and Ansgar Nünning, EVT, 2019, pp. 215-30.

—. "Family Trees: Mnemonics, Identity and Cultural Memory." *Trees in Literatures and the Arts: Humanarboreal Perspectives in the Anthropocene*, edited by Daniela Fargione and Carmen Concilio, Lexington Books, 2020, pp. tba.

Narrative Ethics in HBO's *Big Little Lies*[1]
Reframing Motherhood

Virginia Pignagnoli, Universidad de Zaragoza

The idea that representation matters, albeit perhaps not very original, easily applies to the analysis of HBO's *Big Little Lies* (2017), a television narrative that engages with issues of domestic abuse and intimate partner violence. Indeed, as Diane Shoos remarks, "our individual and collective stake in popular representations of violence against women is extremely high," because of the role mainstream media assume "in shaping attitudes towards abuse" (Shoos 161). Even today, domestic abuse and intimate partner violence are social issues of considerable concern in the United States. According to The National Intimate Partner and Sexual Violence Survey (NISVS), an average of 20 people is physically abused by intimate partners every minute (Black et al.). This adds up to more than 10 million abuse victims annually (ibid.). According to the US Department of Justice, intimate partner violence accounts for 15% of all violent crime (Truman and Morgan), and 1 in 15 children is exposed to intimate partner violence each year (Hamby et al.). These are only a few data on domestic abuse and violence, but they give us an idea of the magnitude of the problem and the lack of adequate responses from institutions.

Through a non-stereotypical depiction of an abusive relationship, the first season of *Big Little Lies*[2] expresses a critique of such deficient responses from American institutions and asks: how does violence spread in today's society and family dynamics? And, given the lack of adequate policies to prevent domestic violence, is there something members of society can do to address such an endemic problem? Seeking answers to these questions, the series conveys an ethics of motherhood as collective agent of change. In other words, *Big Little Lies* addresses the social

1   The research carried out for the writing of this article is part of a project financed by the Spanish Ministry of Economy, Industry and Competitiveness (MINECO, Juan de la Cierva-Formación) in collaboration with the European Regional Development Fund (DGI/ERDF) (code FFI2017-84258-P). The author is also thankful for the support of the Government of Aragón and the European Social Fund (ESF) (code H03_17R).
2   The second season of *Big Little Lies* aired in June and July 2019. Because of space limitations, this article will focus only on the first season. Unless otherwise specified, "*Big Little Lies*" is employed throughout the essay to refer to the first season.

issues of domestic violence and intimate partner rape presenting mothers as the agents able to act collectively and stop violence from spreading into their children's worlds. Thus, this essay explores "the intersections between the domain of stories and storytelling and that of moral values," namely narrative ethics, as James Phelan defines it (par. 1).

Focusing on how the plot signals its stance on the ethical issues faced by its characters and, more generally, on the ethics of its rhetorical purpose (cf. Phelan), this essay argues that *Big Little Lies* conveys an ethics of motherhood as a collective experience, despite the general belief that motherhood is an individual achievement.[3] For the most part, this ethics emerges from the intersection of two main storylines. One revolves around a bullying episode in a primary school; the other tells the story of a mother who, despite initial appearances, is trapped in an abusive marriage. When the violence spreads from the adults to the children's worlds, the mothers take action, first individually, but later collectively. Thus, contrarily to what happens in many Hollywood films where abuse "begins and ends as a private matter, a problem of the individual solved by personal agency" (Shoos 158), *Big Little Lies* frames abuse as an issue of the "larger society that must be addressed through *collective* political action aimed at systemic change" (ibid.; emphasis added). This collectivity is represented by mothers who become agents of change and undertake a political act.

Despite their active role in opposing domestic violence, however, these mothers align with traditional gendered domestic roles and, in particular, with the clichés of current ideologies such as the "motherhood mystique" and the "new momism" (cf. Douglas and Michaels; O'Reilly). The "new momism," as Douglas and Michaels highlight, supports the idea that "no woman is truly complete or fulfilled unless she has kids," while promoting "a highly romanticized view of motherhood in which the standards for success are impossible to meet," because, in order to be a "remotely decent mother, a woman has to devote her entire physical, psychological, emotional, intellectual being 24/7, to her children" (4). By juxtaposing a view of motherhood as a site for producing societal change with another that highlights the impossible standards today's mothers need to meet, the series offers a nuanced, and at times contradictory portrayal of contemporary motherhood.

---

3   See, for instance, Rosalind Gill's remark on postfeminism: "In these iterations of popular feminism, the solution to injustice is to work *on the self* rather than to work with others for social and political transformation" (617; emphasis added).

Gender Violence and Contemporary Motherhood

The seven episodes composing the first season of *Big Little Lies* (created and written by David E. Kelley and directed by Jean-Marc Vallée), each about one hour long, are based on Australian writer Liane Moriarty's novel of the same title (2014). Set in the city of Monterey on California's central coast (unlike the novel, which was set on the northern beaches of Sydney), the miniseries orbits around the life of five women, Madeline Mackenzie, Bonnie Carlson, Celeste Wright, Renata Klein and Jane Chapman, whose young children are classmates. The setting resonates with O'Reilly's idea that

> under the patriarchal institution and ideology of motherhood, the definition of mother is limited to heterosexual women who have biological children, while the concept of good motherhood is further restricted to a selected group of women who are white, heterosexual, middle-class, able-bodied, married, thirty-something, in a nuclear family with usually one to two children, and, ideally, full-time mothers. (O'Reilly 7)

Madeline is married to Ed and has two daughters: Chloe and Abigail. Abigail's father is Nathan Carlson, Madeline's ex-husband, now re-married to Bonnie (the only biracial character in the series), mother of Skye. Madeline is a part-time employee at the local community theater, but she describes herself as a stay-at-home mom. Celeste, once a successful lawyer, left her job to marry Perry Wright and stay at home while he is pursuing his career and very often travels for work. Celeste and Perry have twins, Josh and Max. Renata, married to Gordon, is the mother of Amabella. She is not only a working mom, but a very successful professional. Jane Chapman, the single mother of Ziggy, contrasts nicely with Celeste, Madeline, and Renata. Young, single, and indifferent to her looks, she hardly fits in with Monterey's flaunting display of personal perfection.

The two storylines – the bullying and the domestic violence – whose intersection signals the narrative stance on the ethical issues faced by its characters, are presented as parallel sub-plots. On the first day of school, six-year-old Amabella Klein shows marks of violence on her body. Urged to reveal her aggressor, she accuses Ziggy Chapman who, in turn, claims to be innocent. Jane believes him, but, as the bullying continues, she is afraid that "violence can be in his DNA" ("You Get What You Need"). Indeed, her pregnancy was the result of rape, as will be revealed in the third episode ("Living the Dream"). Jane's rape is not a "dark-man-in-a-park" story. Rather, the narrative portrays the way sexual abuse is often perpetuated in many distinctive ways. One night, the audience is told through Jane's confession to Madeline, she met a man in a bar: "He said his name was Saxon Banks. Mr. Banks, like the dad in 'Mary Poppins.' But I Googled him after, and … We met in a bar. He was funny, and sexy… we were both… pleasantly drunk" ("Living the Dream").

Blurred images of the night alternate with the present time of Jane's narration: "We got a room at a hotel, it overlooked the ocean. It was… romantic […] But then he changed" (ibid.). The man suddenly became "extremely aggressive" and eventually raped Jane, who was paralyzed by fear. Many years later, Jane is still traumatized: hunted by the images of the man and that night, she secretly hopes that it "was just a big misunderstanding, or a night gone wrong, or he'd had a bad day, or his parents got in a car crash," because she is "so desperate to believe that Ziggy's father might actually be a good person" ("Burning Love"). Ziggy's family history hardly fits in with the apparent perfection of his classmates' families. But the bully, it will be revealed at the end of the season, is Max, one of Celeste's twins.

Jane, in the attempt to console Celeste about it, tries to downplay the episode. She tells her: "Look, kids sometimes bully, it's human nature. They grow out of it." But Celeste replies: "Sometimes they don't" ("You Get What You Need"). Celeste knows that the cause of Max's violent behavior is that he has witnessed his father being abusive with her. This revelation triggers the intersection of the two storylines: violence, the narrative tells us, is *not* something people inherit in their genes. Rather, it is learned behavior. Max, having being exposed to his father's abuse of his mother, reproduces the violence on his classmates. Perry, the audience will start discovering from the first episode, is violent and abusive. He is also controlling and manipulative: he seems aware of being violent and suggests to Celeste to go to therapy together. He keeps promising her he is going to change and asks her not to give up on him. Celeste, as many victims of domestic abuse, is extremely vulnerable. As Marylin Friedman notices:

> It is not too much of an exaggeration to say that a battered or abused woman shares a limited space with an "animal" that "perpetually hunts for her." She must use all her resources to avoid his wrath. She may have to think all the time about how to survive. Not only is an abused woman vulnerable to being harmed directly, physically or psychologically, by her abuser. She is also vulnerable to his coercive influence on her moral agency. The fear of physical injury or psychological attack by her abuser can lead an abused woman to do things that are wrong, things she might not otherwise do. (223)

Despite her vulnerability, Celeste eventually decides to leave Perry, and this decision is rooted in her greatest fear that her husband's violence might affect her children. That is, the realization that one of her children is not only aware of the acts of violence Perry commits against her, but repeats them, at school, with other children, is what makes Celeste regain control and agency.

From the outside, the couple is the quintessential symbol of romantic love, thus slightly at odds with the "new momism" that sees children at the top of the priorities list (cf. Macdonald). In fact, romantic love provides the foundation to justify gender inequality, i.e. Celeste giving up her career to be with Perry. But Celeste and

Perry's relationship only appears to be romantic. Celeste's character, while on the surface the archetypal mother of "new momism," conceals a reality suffused with domestic violence. Vulnerable, trapped, scared for her life, Celeste keeps pursuing an idealization of motherhood by compulsively taking pictures of her family to later arrange, rearrange, edit and post online. It is clear that, through this, Celeste is 'lying' to herself, in the attempt to build an alternative reality, with no room for domestic violence.

Pursuing Unattainable Standards: *Big Little Lies* and "New Momism"

The pursuing of an idealized version of motherhood is not surprising. The lives of Celeste, Madeline, and Renata, all to a different extent, conform to mainstream family patterns and reinforce gender roles. Wealthy, white, educated, they account for a privileged model of motherhood, complying with current beliefs and practices known as "intensive mothering," "the motherhood mystique" and "new momism" (cf. O'Reilly; Macdonald; Warner). Celeste and her friend Madeline attend to an ideal of motherhood according to which working and parenting are mutually exclusive. Their lives are meant to be completely devoted to the upbringing of their children, as they embody what Susan Douglas and Meredith Michaels call "the mythology of the new momism" (23). This mythology suggests that:

> the enlightened mother chooses to stay at home with the kids. Back in the 1950s, mothers stayed at home because they had no choice. Today having been to the office, having tried a career, women supposedly have seen the inside of the male working world and found it to be the inferior choice to staying at home, especially when her kid's future is at stake. It's not that mothers can't hack it (1950s thinking). It's that progressive mothers refuse to hack it. The June Cleaver model, if taken as a *choice*, as opposed to a requirement, is the truly modern fulfilling forward-thinking version of motherhood. (Douglas and Michaels 23).

Celeste and Madeline act as if they actually had a choice – to work or stay at home – while they fail to recognize the role society has assumed in such choice.

Renata represents the other side of the coin of such mythology: mothers who do choose to have a career and then perceive it as a mistake, a selfish act that negatively affects their mothering. Renata, like Celeste and Madeline, fails to understand that the anxiety and pressure ensuing from the difficulty in balancing work and family life do not result from a "wrong choice" she made, but from a dominant view that, on the surface, seems to celebrate motherhood, but instead "promulgate[s] standards of perfection that are beyond [women's] reach" (Douglas and Michaels 5). In one revealing scene, Renata looks at the ocean while sipping wine on her deck and she tells her husband Gordon: "It's one thing to be demonized to have the temerity of a career, but look at this, look at our life. Which kind of person chooses to work? Certainly not a mother by any acceptable standards" ("Somebody's Dead"). These acceptable standards, however, are the current idealized standards of perfection that characterize the "new momism." By definition, these standards can never be reached, so they induce feelings of guilt or even shame.

While these characters obliviously have internalized the ideals of the new momism, the narrative is meant to deconstruct its mythology by portraying the defectiveness and contradictions of such beliefs. That is, the narrative trusts the audience's ability to judge the standards the characters aspire to as impossible, as well as the gender inequality they experience as unjust. In the dialogue between Renata and Gordon referred to above, the core of Renata's self-critique is not mutually applicable to her husband, because the childrearing of their daughter Amabella is done primarily by her. It is she who, for instance, worries when she discovers that Amabella has been bullied at school and who considers consulting a therapist specialized in children's psychology, a request that her husband ridicules and then shuts off by seducing her. In this scene, instead of being supportive, Gordon tells Renata she overthinks and this makes her doubt herself: "Have I become tragically unfun?" she asks ("Leaving the Dream"). When, in the same episode, Madeline reveals to Ed that she is terrified seeing their daughters grow up, she complains about how her "enlightened" (Douglas and Michaels 23) choice of staying at home produces inequality between them as partners: "I just feel they are going to grow up and be gone and it's gonna be you and I and we're gonna begin another chapter in our life but you have another chapter, you have a business and I don't. I'm a mom. This is my universe" ("Somebody's Dead"). This universe, however, is not enough, as Celeste and Madeline manage to confess to each other in another revealing scene ("Push Comes to Shove"). Again, the two friends display feelings of shame for not being able to comply with current assumptions of motherhood. But, as neither Ed nor Gordon are portrayed as living within the same set of impossible standards for fatherhood, the audience is cued to judge these assumptions as unequal and defective.

The mothers in *Big Little Lies* ostensibly comply with the ideology of the "new momism," that is, they cannot but attend to its mainstream beliefs and patterns. When confronted with the violence spreading from the adults to the children's world, however, they depart from it, replace the individualism the new momism requires, and reframe motherhood as a collective experience.

Motherhood as Collective Agent of Change

As is often the case, the ending is revealing of the narrative's ethics, i.e. of the way the narrative has guided the audience's judgments. Thanks to her therapist's advice, Celeste has bought a house and has started to move some of her children's belongings over. But, on the night of the school's fundraising party – whose faded images appear at times throughout the series – Perry discovers Celeste's plan to leave him. Progressing towards the series' climax, Perry and Celeste have a final confrontation on their way to the party. Perry once again tells Celeste he is going to change and when she replies that it is too late for that, revealing that it was Max hurting Amabella, he switches to denial, saying he would talk to him. And Celeste, trapped in a car with locked doors, replies: "Really, and what will you say? That it's not the way to treat a woman? That men should never hit women?" ("You Get What You Need"). Renata and Gordon Klein, also on their way to the party, knock on the car's window, involuntarily offering Celeste a chance to run out and reach the fundraiser. Once there, Celeste looks for her friends, Madeline and Jane, knowing Perry is after her. She finds Renata and reveals to her that it had been Max who had been hurting Amabella and that she had pointed at Ziggy only because she was frightened of him.

Perry reaches Celeste at the party and violently grabs her arm. Bonnie, up until that moment only a supporting character on the sidelines of the plot, sees the scene from afar. Celeste manages to reach Madeline, Jane, and Renata, who are talking on a terrace close to a steep staircase. Perry follows her, but Celeste tells him she is not coming back with him. In that moment, Jane recognizes in Perry her rapist. Perry grabs, then hits Celeste, while the other women try to stop him. The scene is framed through the point of view of Bonnie who, concerned for what she has just seen, has followed Celeste on the terrace. The following scene shows the five women, Madeline, Jane, Renata, Bonnie, and Celeste in an interrogation room. Through Celeste's voice saying that "he took a step back, lost his balance and fell," the audience understands that Perry is dead ("You Get What You Need"). Interrogated, all of the mothers offer the same version of the incident, with the same choice of words. This leads one of the detectives to infer that they are lying. The question that then her partner asks – "It'd be self-defense, why bother lying?" ("You Get What You Need") – is the question that brings the narrative to a resolution and guides the audience's ethical readings. Indeed, the blurred images of the fundraising scene revealed that Perry did not fall; it was Bonnie who, seeing the fight from a distance, defended Celeste by pushing him down the stairs. Yet, why bother lying by testifying it was an accidental fall?

Certainly, victims of abuse may act unwisely. And these women's vulnerability is further exemplified by their inability to tell their stories of abuse: Jane has never reported her rape, never tried to track her abuser down, Madeline is the first person she tells about it because "What could anybody say? Or do?" ("Living the Dream"). Likewise, Celeste spends years concealing her bruises and tells no one about Perry's violence except her therapist. In showing this inability to speak the truth, *Big Little Lies* hints at the widespread practice of victim-blaming, which induces the victims

of abuse to think it was their mistake: they could have avoided the violence perpe-
trated against them. Indeed, in the car, Celeste tells Perry she should have left him
years before, i.e. blaming herself. The ethics conveyed by the narrative, however,
works on the assumption that the audience recognizes the widespread practice of
victim-blaming and understands Celeste's and Jane's lack of accountability: male
violence and domestic violence are not separate issues. These women's vulnerability, moreover, is not only the result of violence, but of the impossible standards the
"new momism" imposes on them, fostering gender inequality.

Not only does the narrative call attention to the failure of institutions in their
response to these social issues, but it also suggests that mothers should regain collective agency and act. The last five minutes of the series show scenes from Perry's
funeral, the fighting on the terrace on the night of the school's fundraising and the
five women with their children on the beach, playing, and looking ahead. The images of Perry beating Celeste, of her friends trying to defend her, and of Bonnie's
intervention are blurred as if to blur the specificity of the single actions; the five
women repeat the same words to the detective and they all look together into the
future. This collective act is thus symbolized not so much by the accidental killing
of the perpetrator, but by the lie the group of mothers will use to cover it. And while
this final lie puzzles the detective investigating the perpetrator's death, the narrative cues the audience's judgments towards an understanding of such a *big* lie as
an acceptable reaction: a *little* lie. If the problem is not only that of two women, but
systemic, then it requires collective action. In a society that fails to protect women
from violence and abuse, where women are afraid to speak up, the only way to
change is by acting collectively.

Bibliography

Black, Michele C., et al. "The National Intimate Partner and Sexual Violence Survey
(NISVS): 2010 Summary Report." Center for Disease Control and Prevention,
2011, https://www.cdc.gov/violenceprevention/pdf/nisvs_report2010-a.pdf. Accessed 10 Feb. 2020.
Douglas, Susan, and Meredith Michaels. *The Mommy Myth: The Idealization of Moth-
erhood and How It Has Undermined All Women.* Simon and Schuster, 2004.
Friedman, Marilyn. "Moral Responsibility for Coerced Wrongdoing: The Case of
Abused Women Who 'Fail to Protect' Their Children." *Vulnerability: new essays in
ethics and feminist philosophy,* edited by Catriona Mackenzie et al., Oxford UP,
2014, pp. 222-41.
Gill, Rosalind. "Post-Postfeminism? New Feminist Visibilities in Postfeminist
Times." *Feminist Media Studies,* vol. 16, no. 4, 2016, pp. 610-30.

Hamby, Sherry, et al. "Children's Exposure to Intimate Partner Violence and Other Family Violence." U.S. Department of Justice, Office of Justice Programs Office of Juvenile Justice and Delinquency Prevention, 2011, https://www.ncjrs.gov/pdffiles1/ojjdp/232272.pdf. Accessed 10 Feb. 2020.

Kelley, David E., creator. *Big Little Lies*. Hello Sunshine and Blossom Films, 2017.

Macdonald, Cameron. "The Rise of the 'Motherhood Mystique'." Council on Contemporary Families, 2013, https://contemporaryfamilies.org/the-rise-of-motherhood-mystique/. Accessed 10 Feb. 2020.

O'Reilly, Andrea. *Twenty-first Century Motherhood: Experience, Identity, Policy, Agency*. Columbia UP, 2010.

Phelan, James. "Narrative Ethics." *the living handbook of narratology*, edited by Peter Hühn et al., Hamburg UP, 2014, http://www.lhn.uni-hamburg.de/article/narrative-ethics. Accessed 10 Feb. 2020.

Shoos, Diane L. "Conclusion: *Safe Haven* and Ideological Gaslighting." *Domestic Violence in Hollywood Film*, by Shoos, Palgrave Macmillan, 2017, pp. 153-75.

Truman, Jennifer L., and Rachel E. Morgan. "Nonfatal Domestic Violence." US Department of Justice, Bureau of Justice Statistics, 2014, https://www.bjs.gov/content/pub/pdf/ndv0312.pdf. Accessed 10 Feb. 2020.

Warner, Judith. *Perfect Madness: Motherhood in the Age of Anxiety*. Riverhead Books, 2005.

(De)Constructing Gender and Family Roles in Helen Simpson's Short Stories

Margarita Navarro Pérez, Universidad de Murcia

In the present article a thorough analysis of Helen Simpson's short story "Erewhon" will be carried out from the point of view of identity and gender studies, understanding both as not only a social construction, but also a personal choice, whether it is conscious or unconscious, or both. In doing so, de Beauvoir's, Butler's, Althusser's and Foucault's ideas will be considered as the theoretical basis for the analysis. Together with this, I will resort to Russian formalist theories on estrangement, a technique that proves to be very (a)/(e)ffective on readers, in so far as it has the power to call readers' attention, something that in turn invites reflection on some of the taken-for-granted and accepted aspects of gender performativity and understanding in our society.

Erewhon – the Novel and the Short Story

The short story "Erewhon" is part of the collection *Cockfoster* (2015), a total of nine short stories which compound to a very critical and powerful collection of stories, where womanhood is presented as subject to unavoidable decay, where the passing of time and aging are presented as the inevitable downfall of women. However, "Erewhon" seems to be especially poignant in its social criticism.

The first noticeable aspect about the short story is the title, which it shares with Samuel Butler's novel *Erewhon*,[1] and as this article will show, there are many more parallels that can be established between both literary works. A comparison may enlighten the reader towards the understanding of the criticisms put forth in both literary works, and also suggest that, although neither in the collection itself, nor

---

1   The novel *Erewhon* was first published anonymously in 1872, after Butler had been advised not to publish it. Thus, the novel became popular with many readers believing that the author was Edward Bulwer-Lytton. It was only two months later, on 25 May 1872, that Butler's authorship was announced in several journals, namely *The Athenaeum* and *The Drawing Room Gazette* (Holt 147).

in the author's statements any explicit reference has been made (Crown; Lindsay), the title of the short story is far from coincidental.

To begin with, "erewhon" is clearly an anagram of 'nowhere', which could be understood as the authors' intent of associating their stories with a place that does not exist anywhere, not to be found on earth.[2] Nonetheless, after a thorough analysis of both stories, it is possible to argue, that despite their fictionality, they are clearly inspired by the contemporary society of their respective times, which is in turn harshly exposed and criticized. That is, on the one hand, the place they describe does not exist as such, neither the Erewhon to be found in Butler's novel, nor the society Simpson describes in her short story; however, and despite the clear and apparent fictionality of the societies portrayed, the descriptions given by the narrators in both seem curiously recognizable, too familiar in many ways. It is precisely these familiar aspects which often end up being the object of criticism in both, the short story and the novel, as this article argues.

Simpson's short story develops around the unnamed narrator's thoughts as he is finding it hard to sleep from 3:29 a.m. to 7:10 a.m., when, after falling asleep for less than an hour, he finally wakes up. The narrator takes readers through his thoughts in a stream-of-consciousness manner, orderly structured around the 17 times he looks at his digital clock. Consequently, and as can be seen from the citations of the book included below, the language used is simple and direct. On the other hand, the novel is written as a Victorian travel-writing novel, in the style of a traveler's diary, typical of the colonial tradition of the time. This novel deals with the adventures of an also unnamed male settler who finds a place called Erewhon, where very unexpected, but at the same time seemingly familiar things take place. In the novel, the protagonist finds himself in a place where everything seems different to the known European flora, fauna, people, and customs he is familiar with,[3] but at the same time, everything bears a strange resemblance and familiarity to Europe. This being something the narrator explicitly alludes to throughout the novel, as can be seen in the example below, when he describes the houses he sees as he is being transported to be presented to the authorities:

It was here hitherto: all things were generically the same as in Europe, the differences being of species only; and I was amused at seeing in a window some bottles with barley-sugar and sweetmeats for children, as at home; but the barley-sugar was in plates, not in twisted sticks, and was coloured blue. Glass was plentiful in the better houses. (Butler 34-35)

---

2   It is worthy of mention that the collection itself, as well as the rest of the short stories in this collection have been named after real places, "Erewhon" being the only one that is titled after and deals with a non-existent place.

3   It is believed that Butler took the inspiration for this novel from his time in New Zealand (Jones; Smithies; Roger Robinson; Fox).

In Erewhon, he clearly identifies similarities with Europe, nonetheless, there are some differences he records in his traveler's diary. Not only is he surprised at the familiarity of the place, but also, he is bewildered by the beauty of its people as he clearly states in the following, where again, a reference to Europe is made when mentioning Italian features:

> [...] the people were of a physical beauty which was simply amazing. I never saw anything in the least comparable to them. The women were vigorous, and had a most majestic gait, their heads being set upon their shoulders with grace beyond all power of expression. Each feature was finished, eyelids, eyelashes, and ears being almost invariably perfect. Their colour was equal to that of the finest Italian paintings; being of the clearest olive, and yet ruddy with a glow of perfect health [...] Even in middle age they were still comely, and the old grey-haired women at their cottage doors had a dignity, not to say majesty, of their own. (35)

However, and despite the narrator's first impression of the seeming attractiveness and goodness of the place he is in, with its seemingly good intentioned citizens and extremely beautiful women, he soon finds out that the apparent utopia is in fact a dystopia, where people are heavily punished for not keeping healthy – the worst crime to be committed in Erewhon.

It is worthy of consideration that the novel has often been described as a harsh criticism of Victorian judicial systems and self-righteousness (Knoepflmacher in Breuer 317), especially if we consider the fact that Butler himself wrote "An Erewhonian Trial" as an almost exact copy of a newspaper account of how a judge addressed a convicted criminal on trial, only in the novel, the offence was no other than suffering of ill health (Zemka; Breuer). Butler's could then be said to be a satire of a non-existent upside-down society, which is used to present readers with the reproachable attitudes of his contemporary society, something Simpson herself also does. The short story, too, describes a non-existent society, shows actual contemporary issues, and depicts various social incongruities and flaws, in order to criticize the underlying conceptual constructions as flawed and outright wrong.

Both present readers with very unjust societies where power supremacy is exercised in order to oppress the weak. In the novel, we are presented with a society whose members are extremely beautiful and healthy, since those who have had the misfortune of having unsuitable breading and have not been nurtured appropriately – which has led to ill health in later life – are inexorably punished and blamed for their illness. Thus, anybody suffering from any kind of physical ailment was liable to be severely punished, as the narrator clarifies:

> [...] in that country if a man falls into ill health, or catches any disorder, or fails bodily in any way before he is seventy years old, he is tried before a jury of his countrymen, and if convicted is held up to public scorn and sentenced more or

less severely as the case may be. There are subdivisions of illnesses into crimes and misdemeanours as with offences amongst ourselves – a man being punished very heavily for serious illness, while failure of eyes or hearing in one over sixty-five, who has had good health hitherto, is dealt with by fine only, or imprisonment in default of payment. (54)

Erewhon is a place where having bad health is punishable by prison and hard labor. Furthermore, this is an unfairness, which in the novel Butler clearly shows is something that must be and is in fact accepted by erewhonians, in the knowledge that not doing so would entail much harsher punishment.

Helen Simpson, too, presents us with a main character, victim to a harsh, unfair and much suffered situation of disadvantage and discrimination, in a fictional society, but where the ailments endured by the narrator are widely known and familiar to our contemporary world. The narrator is tormented and stressed about issues that present a clear criticism of our contemporary society's expectations imposed on individuals in relation to their gender, which are nonetheless presented in an unusual context. The 'weaker sex' finds itself juggling a full-time teaching job and trying to do all the household chores, combined with the feeling of insufficiently looking after the family. Listening to a confession of physical abuse is followed by the compromise of not saying anything to anyone and the feeling of guilt that this silence entails. Ageing and a deteriorating physical appearance are added worries which are magnified thanks to a partner who constantly jokes about the less than attractive consequences of the unavoidable ageing of the narrator, which compounds with the partner's delight in porn and the "impersonal demands for sex" (21), that make the narrator feel uneasy and even more insecure. Approaching the partner in order to suggest going part time, so as to be able to adequately do the household chores and look after the family properly, implies being tactful, so as not to provoke an angry reaction from the spouse, since money would be the reason not to. And the list goes on. Perhaps against all expectations, the narrator is a man. This is what guarantees the fictionality of the story, the 'unreal' society, where power relations discriminate men, turning them into the 'weaker sex'. Even new vocabulary is invented to better fit the otherness of the story, and we find that "MascuNazi" (21) is a term Ella, the protagonist's wife, uses to attack him, when he suggests it is necessary to fight to "get more men out of prostitution" (21) and more men into Parliament (22) – an unfair situation, which Ella sometimes recognizes, but which she is undoubtedly not willing to change: "[w]hy would she when it worked so well for her?" (22).

This transposition of gender roles and therefore of gender relations is what leads us to the literary technique of estrangement, that will be further explained in relation to the short story below, and which is also to be found in Butler's novel.

Both unnamed characters are framed within a society which, to readers of their time, can be said to be both, uncannily familiar and strangely alien at the same time. In both cases, the familiar and the strange are combined in a way that alerts readers to the fictionality of the written works, but that also invites reflection on the real social issues dealt with and exposed in fictional form. Both works can be described as satirical descriptions of the societies they depict, where injustices are being pointed out and denounced, exposing the random nature behind all accepted social norms. Hence, estrangement is not merely a literary technique, but one that, I will argue, creates awareness of the social issues being put under the spotlight.

The following sets out to analyze how estrangement, combined with assumptions on gender construction and gender performativity expectations are used in order to expose the very damaging assumptions that tend to inform our society's construction of femininity as opposed to its – also normative, non-inclusive – binary opposite, masculinity. However, and as I will argue, due to the use of estrangement, readers will be exposed to an unusual way of looking at these constructions, making them linger in the realms of the unreal, and question the foundations of such assumptions, exposing their purely socially accepted patterns in its creation, and therefore focusing the readers' attention on their social constructedness.

Gender Issues

Throughout the collection, Simpson is clearly concerned with the construction of femininity in society, and how this affects and impinges directly on women's experiences of life. These short stories deal openly with the understanding of gender as a social construct, as defined by feminist and poststructuralist scholars, where the human body does not only carry a political dimension, but is a political statement itself, formed from the assumptions a patriarchal society has about womanhood (de Beauvoir; Butler). In this sense, feminists' theorization combined with the Foucauldian forms of critical analysis focus on the assumptions that inform texts (Foucault 2002; 2005), and in the creation and social construction of culture, which at the same time establish certain hierarchies that influence discourses and societies in general (McNeil 158; Bordo 181; McLaren, "Foucault;" McLaren *Feminism*). These assumptions materialize in the form of personal identity and are expressed through language, which, as Althusser explained in 1971 in his "Ideology and Ideological Apparatuses," in turn transpires into the creation of cultural, social, and political structures and frameworks which individuals live in and with (Sharp 2). These socially created apparatuses establish and maintain hegemonic plays which favor one side to the detriment of the other, by establishing what Gramsci referred to as a cultural common sense, that naturalizes and seems to make the situation acceptable (Hennessy 21).

In the case of "Erewhon," Simpson takes all these well-known and widely ac-cepted assumptions about a femininity constructed on the basis of the male phys-ical superiority and alters the roles by making the man the weaker, docile, senti-mental carer, the servile individual forever concerned about the family's well-being. This image contrasts directly with that of the strong, abusive, hard drinking and smoking, bread-winning woman. By doing this, readers are, on the one hand, rec-ognizing the strategies used in order to create a position of superiority and benefit for one of the sexes, but on the other hand, this alteration of roles estranges and procures a sensation of certain surprise, thus, putting into practice what Somerville refers to as a "key theoretical and political strategy for feminist theorists" (48), that of "disturbing the taken-for-granted relationships between biological sexual differ-ence and women's oppression" (Somerville 47).

By using such an unlikely suspect to become the victim of gender oppression, due to physical and emotional weakness (something history and society have made us believe falls on women as the 'weaker sex'), Simpson resorts to estrangement, a literary resource believed by many to be more than a literary device. In fact, es-trangement has been argued to be a way to practice a special kind of existential art, which encourages dissent and with it, promotes the practice of freedom (Boym; Ti-hanov).

In order to understand this term, it is necessary to go back to Russian for-malism and to Victor Shklovsky's ideas, one of the most renowned authors on the topic,[4] who referred to *ostranenie*, translated into English as estrangement. Looking at Shklovsky's concept of estrangement, Douglas Robinson identifies it is a device which "works on readers: by dividing their entire emotional-becoming-mental per-ception of a thing into two parts, the familiar and the strange, and contaminating the former with the latter, perhaps also in cases the latter with the former" (120). This is to say, our perception of something which has been presented to us through estrangement will not be pure and uncontaminated any more, it will, from that mo-ment onwards, be altered by the new ideas and thoughts put into it by the literary work.

As Jameson explains, the term estrangement, if understood in its Brechtian sense, can be said to serve a purpose of social awareness in order to facilitate a vision of entrenched ways as somehow ephemeral and thus liable to change:

---

4   As Douglas Robinson explains in 2008, the concept of estrangement has had a long history: we hear about this concept in Wordsworth's advertisement for his *Lyrical Ballads*, when in 1798, he writes about "feelings of strangeness and awkwardness;" and with Shelley in his "Defence of Poetry," when he refers to the way in which poetry presents familiar known ob-jects as if they were not. However, one the main precursors of estrangement could be said to be Shklovsky, who got his inspiration from the Russian Futurists (and, more specifically, from Mayakovsky and Khlebnikov), as well as from the Russian Symbolists (Andrey Bely and mainly Tolstoy, whose literature Shklovsky found particularly estranging).

The purpose of the Brechtian estrangement-effect is therefore a political one in the most thoroughgoing sense of the word; it is, as Brecht insisted over and over, to make you aware that the objects and institutions you thought to be natural were really only historical: the result of change, they themselves henceforth become in their turn changeable. (58)

Estrangement is therefore a technique that pursues some distancing on the part of the reader, within the realm of literary analysis, in order to show the unnaturalness of what we perceive to be natural. So, in the same way, Judith Butler defends gender as a social construct, in an attempt to make us reflect on the way in which socio-historical evolutions are the basis of our constructions of gender, showing how these constructions are far from natural, so does estrangement in both the novel and the short story function as an attention caller in order to criticize the very object of our readerly attention, that which is made strange for us, but which at the same time has a familiar and seemingly natural form and tone to it.

Therefore, and using Shklovsky's and Brecht's ideas, estrangement, as a literary artifice, can be used in order to awaken society from the numb depersonalized attitudes individuals sometimes fall into when they embrace collective reality, to the point where they seem to stop questioning that accepted reality (Douglas Robinson 120). Therefore, estrangement as a literary device would be used as a technique to awaken individuals from their automatized, passive, and unquestioning lethargy, which, in the case of the short story under study here, is society's understanding of gender. Thus, Simpson's short story, by altering gender expectations, manages to challenge and undermine the wielding of a discourse of truth that delegitimizes the gender expectations our society seems to take almost for granted in relation to femininity, something feminist theorists have been doing for a long time, namely, and just to name one of the most influential feminist writers of our time, Butler way back in 1999 in her *Troubling Gender* (2002). By showing men as the 'weak sex', Simpson successfully exposes a situation where that inferiority is clearly imposed by society and does not derive from a weaker, natural, evolutionarily inferior physical capability, but from gender construction and an imposed expected performativity. Inferiority in this short story is enforced by a construction of gender which sets men in a position of inferiority, not by a physiological condition, but in order to grant superiority to the other, in this case, to women.

Estrangement and Its (A)/(E)ffect on Readers

In "Erewhon," Simpson resorts to estrangement as an attention calling technique, that, as I have already discussed, seems to be very effective in creating a certain uneasiness in the reader, affecting readers' responses, by combining both familiarity and societies' commonly tolerated/accepted assumptions on gender with a strong feeling of alienation and fictionality, in this case presented from the superposition of the aforementioned assumptions on an unlikely individual.

From the beginning, Simpson uses the subject pronouns and there is no mistake to be made in order to be aware the narrator is a *he*. In fact, she starts this short story as follows: "03:29. Foolishly he had opened his eyes" (16). From the very beginning, the reader finds there seems to be something odd in the narrator's thoughts and worries. It seems especially peculiar to read about the narrator and his anxiety about talking to his wife, Ella, to express his desire to go part time in his teaching job. We read about how he wants to do so in order to have more time to do the household chores properly, he also seems very concerned about the little time he has left for looking after his wife and the children. In this line of thought, the narrator confesses to his anxiety about how to approach his wife, his main worry being avoiding Ella screaming at him, for this, he had to make it seem as if it was Ella's idea, something he justifies by referring to "[f]eminine pride" (17). This paragraph certainly alerts the reader to some kind of alteration in gender roles.

Nonetheless, if there is any doubt about exactly what it is, or any hesitation in order to pinpoint exactly what it is that feels strange about the plot, it is pretty soon in the short story that the reader is aware of the fact that gender roles are reversed:

> Stop worrying. Count backwards from a thousand. Nine hundred and ninety-nine. That was another good worry, whether he'd done the right thing not to report what he'd been told at the last parents' evening. Timothy Tisdall's father had sat opposite him for the obligatory four minutes and with tear-filled eyes had whispered to him what he suffered at the hands of his wife; how his wife was a policewomen so knew not to hit him anywhere it would show; how he couldn't report it and was begging him not to report it but how he had to tell someone and thank you for listening, it made him feel less alone. (17-18)

This passage clearly depicts marital abuse from the stronger member of the relationship to a weaker more submissive one. Additionally, it is followed by the narrator's thoughts of an almost acceptance and normalization of such abuse, as the narrator of the story thinks about his own situation as a more advantageous and privileged one, as he's thinking that: "[t]here was a bit of pushing and shoving from Ella, but she didn't hit him [...] Not nice to think how the overwhelming majority of men who were murdered were murdered by their own wives" (18).[5]

This passage clearly alerts readers to some kind of strange and unexpected gender construction. Given that by looking at numbers, a study carried out in 2018 in

---

5   See also Pignagnoli's contribution on HBO's *Big Little Lies* for a discussion of domestic violence in that series.

England and Wales showed that in 2016-2017 out of the 95 recorded victims of domestic violence, 13 were men and 82 were women (Mankind Initiative 2018).

Considering the narrator's thoughts about how men were being killed at the hands of their wives, in the light of the Mankind Initiative data, clearly shows that the situation we are presented with is a reversal of what is actually happening in contemporary England and Wales. Notwithstanding the fact that more and more men seem to be reporting abuse at the hands of their wives, numbers show that nowadays, women amount to a considerably higher number of domestic violence abuse at the hands of their partners. According to a survey carried out by the BBC, this abuse is mainly non-physical and has more to do with financial/emotional issues, followed by force, threats, and stalking (indecent exposure or sexual abuse amount to less than 5% of the abuse) suffered by men.

The short story is full with these kinds of comments about how men are unjustifiably and unfairly discriminated and oppressed in all aspects of life: how they have to choose between wife, work, and family, having to always choose two out of the three, whereas women do not have to choose; how men are expected to take the pill given that women, as is the case with Ella, "couldn't tolerate condoms" since "[t]hey muffled things up" (20); how they agonize about not being good fathers and are constantly bereaved by the idea of not managing to properly care for and cater to the family's needs; how the media constantly put men under the spotlight making them feel anxious about ageing, constantly zooming in on "paunches," "spindle shanks" and "pendulous earlobes" (18), which exacerbates young men's "shaky self-esteem" (19), due to their impinging worry about their physical appearance, etc. All these are images which constantly challenge our society's gender expectations, thanks to estrangement.

Nonetheless, it is the ending of this short story which could be argued poses the feminist argument best, by summarizing the unfairness of male gender expectations in the following way:

> So it was generally agreed that men were nicer than women, less selfish, more caring; men had been awarded the moral high ground. Big deal! And was that supposed to make everything all right? He twisted in the dark, the acid reflux of injustice rising in him. The world wasn't going to change just because he wanted it to, though, was it. The world was woman-shaped – get over it! (24)

This is clearly a rather dooming prospect, with a disenchanted narrator, who proves to be resigned to the injustice with the last two lines of the short story: "This was the way things were. This was the natural order" (25). Thus, Simpson presents us with a very critical view of our patriarchal society, but from an upside-down society, where roles have been swapped in order to emphasize the unfairness and lack of justifiable basis for such discrimination.

The Dooming of Gender

The ending of the short story is far from optimistic; however, I would argue that Simpson successfully manages to dismantle our society's assumptions and expectations of gender through her estranged portrayal. Estrangement allows for the reader to distance him/herself from the text, thus procuring and facilitating a critical stance. Although the object of discrimination is a man, it is clear that it is presented as an alteration of the "natural order" of things. Thus, we are presented with a dooming construction of femininity, where womanhood seems to be inexorably linked with an inevitably looming and poignant downfall, where both, the passing of time, and with it, the loss of youth are linked with the idea of uselessness, physical decay, and unattractiveness. A femininity founded on the gift of nurture, which as the narrator clearly states, feels more like a burden than an endowment.

Additionally, it could be argued that this short story, by depicting such dystopian alteration of reality, by transposing fears, anxieties, injustices and sufferings often endured by women onto men, manages to successfully avoid the idealization of a world in reverse, by showing how the establishment of any hierarchy of one gender over another, is clearly a less than perfect and pretty undesirable situation to be in.

Bibliography

de Beauvoir, Simone. *The Second Sex*. Knopf, 2010 [1949].

Bordo, Susan. "Feminism, Foucault and the politics of the body." *Up against Foucault: Explorations of some tensions between Foucault and feminism*, edited by Caroline Ramazanglu, Routledge, 2003, pp. 179-202.

Boym, Svetlana. "Poetics and politics of estrangement: Victor Shklovsky and Hannah Arendt." *Poetics Today*, vol. 26, no. 4, 2005, pp. 581-611.

Breuer, Hans-Peter. "The Source of Morality in Butler's 'Erewhon'." *Victorian studies*, vol. 16, no. 3, 1973, pp. 317-28.

Butler, Judith. Gender trouble. Routledge, 2002.

—. "Performative agency." *Journal of cultural economy*, vol. 3, no. 2, 2010, pp. 147-61.

Crown, Sarah. "Helen Simpson interview: 'The great unspoken subject for couples is probably: whose job is more important?'." *The Guardian*, 24 Oct. 2015, https://www.theguardian.com/books/2015/oct/24/helen-simpson-interview-great-unspoken-subject-between-couples-is-probably-whose-job-is-more-import. Accessed 20 Feb. 2020.

Foucault, Michel. *The Archaeology of Knowledge*. Routledge, 2002.

—. *The Order of Things*. Routledge, 2005.

Fox, Alistair. "Inwardness, insularity, and the Man Alone: Postcolonial anxiety in the New Zealand novel." *Journal of Postcolonial Writing*, vol. 45, no. 3, 2009, pp. 263-73.

Hennessy, Rosemary. "Women's lives/feminist knowledge: Feminist standpoint as ideology critique." *Hypatia*, vol. 8, no. 1, 1993, pp. 14-34.

Holt, Lee Elbert. "Samuel Butler and his Victorian Critics." *ELH*, vol. 8, no. 2, 1941, pp. 146-59.

Jameson, Fredric. *The prison-house of language: A critical account of structuralism and Russian formalism*. Vol. 332. Princeton UP, 1974.

Jones, Joseph. *The Cradle of Erewhon: Samuel Butler in New Zealand*. U of Texas P, 2012.

Lindsay, Leslie A. "Wednesdays with writers: Helen Simpson talks about her collection of stories in Cockfosters, how a short story is really like a geological core sample, 'skipping the gossip and going for the jugular,' how an empty nest is invigorating, her to-read pile, and so much more." Leslielindsay, 23 Aug. 2017, https://leslielindsay.com/2017/08/23/wednesdays-with-writers-helen-simpson-talks-about-her-collection-of-stories-in-cockfosters-how-a-short-story-is-really-like-a-geological-core-sampleskipping-the-gossip-and-going-for-the-jugular/. Accessed 20 Feb. 2020.

Mankind Initiative. "Male victims of domestic and partner abuse 35 key facts, by Mark Brooks." 2018, https://www.mankind.org.uk/wp-content/uploads/2018/03/35-Key-Facts-Male-Victims-March-2018.pdf. Accessed 1 March 2020.

McLaren, Margaret A. "Foucault and the subject of feminism." Social Theory and Practice, vol. 23, no. 1, 1997, pp. 109-28.

—. Feminism, Foucault, and embodied subjectivity. Suny P, 2012.

McNeil, Maureen. "Dancing with Foucault: Feminism and power-knowledge." *Up Against Foucault: Explorations of some tensions between Foucault and feminism*, edited by Caroline Ramazanoglu, Routledge, 2003, pp. 157-86.

Robinson, Douglas. *Estrangement and the somatics of literature: Tolstoy, Shklovsky, Brecht*. JHU P, 2008.

Robinson, Roger. "Samuel Butler, 1835-1902." *Kōtare: New Zealand Notes & Queries*, vol. 7, no. 2, 2008, pp. 65-78.

Sharp, Hasana. "'Is it simple to be a feminist in philosophy?': Althusser and feminist theoretical practice." *Rethinking Marxism*, vol. 12, no. 2, 2000, pp. 18-34.

Somerville, Margaret. "Tracing bodylines: The body in feminist poststructural research." *International Journal of Qualitative Studies in Education*, vol. 17, no. 1, 2004, pp. 47-65.

Simpson, Helen. *Cockfosters: Stories*. Vintage, 2016.

Smithies, James. "Return Migration and the Mechanical Age: Samuel Butler in New Zealand 1860-1864." *Journal of Victorian Culture*, vol. 12, no. 2, 2007, pp. 203-24.

Tihanov, Galin. "The politics of estrangement': The case of the early Shklovsky." *Poetics Today*, vol. 26, no. 4, 2005, pp. 665-96.

Zemka, Sue. "'Erewhon' and the End of Utopian Humanism." *ELH*, vol. 69, no. 2, 2002, pp. 439-72.

Black Orphans, Adoption, and Labor in Antebellum American Literature

Sonia Di Loreto, Università di Torino

When discussing the plantation complex, the institution of slavery and their gradual abolition in the Atlantic world at large, Kris Manjapra observes that "during this age of abolition, new forms of forced and coerced labor arose on a global scale, and the plantation as an exploitative, racial, political-ecological complex began to expand and travel the face of the earth" (361). This assessment about the plantation complex invites us to ponder also what forms of household labor existed outside of the framework of the plantation system, and to what degrees they involved the black free population, and especially its youth. If we concentrate on the state of Massachusetts, for example, as a free state, void of the existing infrastructures regarding slavery, we learn that "in the eighteenth century and before, most children's work outside the household constituted a form of bound labor, not free labor. Formal indentures, either for apprenticeships or for simple service, exchanges labor in return for support and education" (Schmidt 317).[1] Only later, "over the course of the early nineteenth century, Massachusetts courts gradually abandoned this set of legal rules, replacing them with one that allowed minors to enter the world of free labor" (Schmidt 318).

As Schmidt explains, children, both white and black, could become indentured servants and work for a household until they reached their maturity. If bound labor was one of the ways in which children, especially destitute and orphaned children, could find themselves becoming part of a household, another one was adoption, as the formal and legal procedure of establishing a familial and parental relationship between an adult (or adults) and a child. I associate these two modes of household life because I wish to emphasize how they share some important elements, which

---

1   "Written and sealed, such agreements represented a bargain between a parent, usually a father, and a master, not between a child and an employer. Long-standing legal precedents, often referred to as the 'privilege of infancy,' prevented minors from making contracts for anything other than necessaries or education. In a second phase of judicial activity completed by the 1840s, a series of children's labor contract cases led the Massachusetts courts to produce a set of rules for children's work. The courts authorized minors to make wage contracts for themselves by fashioning the concept of implied parental consent" (Schmidt 317).

can more easily emerge, if studied together. What I believe is crucial to notice is that both these practices are regulated by norms regarding property and inheritance: in the case of bound labor the child is only afforded sustenance and in some cases education, therefore completely excluded from patrimonial privileges, while in the second case, the adopted child becomes part of the family and is eligible to acquire the family's estate.

The first law concerning adoption in the United States is the *Adoption of Children Act* (1851), when Massachusetts established adoption as a social and legal operation based on child welfare, rather than adult interests, expressing the conditions for adoption as follows: "If [...] the petitioners, are of sufficient ability to bring up the child, and furnish suitable nurture and education, having reference to the degree and condition of its parents, and that it is fit and proper that such adoption should take effect," then the child "shall be deemed, for the purposes of inheritance and succession by such child, custody of the person and right of obedience by such parent or parents by adoption, and all other legal consequences and incidents of the natural relation of parents and children, the same to all intents and purposes as if such child had been born in lawful wedlock of such parents or parent by adoption." This law does not explicitly name the race, or the status of the adoptee or the adoptive parents: "Any inhabitant of this Commonwealth may petition the judge of probate, in the county wherein he or she may reside, for leave to adopt a child not his or her own by birth." This Act is consistent with the cultural practices preceding it, when, in the absence of legal regulations, the custom for adopting a child was based on the guidance provided by the Bible, according to which the adopted child is compared to the community of Christians, that through adoption gains access to the kingdom of heaven.

This biblical foundation for adoption can be found, for instance, in a piece titled "Dialogue about Adoption," in *The Christian Sentinel* (Three Rivers, Quebec) and published on 8 July 1831, which demonstrates that the religious argument culturally circulated in the early decades of the 19th century, not only in the United States, but in Canada as well. In this piece, in fact, the theme of adoption is hermeneutically expounded in the section "Childrens' [sic] Department" through a conversation among three people, Charles, Thomas, and William. By using the reference to Dick Brown, "a poor orphan boy," and reminding the others how Mr. Johnson "told Dick, that if he behaved well, and became a good young man, when he came of age he would make him heir to his estate," Thomas invites the other two to view the church as God's family, where "all church members are his adopted children," thus becoming "inheritors of the kingdom of heaven."

In an article titled "The Spirit of Adoption," published in the weekly *The Presbyterian* (Philadelphia) on 6 September 1851, the writer mentions an exemplary parable in which "a rich man, having no son born of his body, and wishing to have one standing in that near relation to him, and on whom he may bestow his affection and his estate, picks up a poor child out the street, or out of the alms-house, and adopts him as his son." In reading this short anecdote two elements stand out, namely the question of property and the issue of class: the prospective father is a "rich man" and the "poor child" is going to receive "his affection and his estate." The article continues by suggesting that the sentiment that the child should feel is gratitude, once again reinforcing the idea that adoption is a favor bestowed by a powerful entity over a desperate creature: "If a great king should condescend to go to the poor-house, and adopt a child of wretchedness and poverty, and make him the heir of his riches and of his kingdom, what words could express the feeling of obligation which would be experienced by an ingenious mind?" After having prescribed the right affective relations between different classes, the author moves into the religious sphere, connecting the practice of adopting a child to the community of Christians, quoting from Romans 8: "For ye have not received the spirit of bondage again to fear, but ye have received the Spirit of adoption, whereby we cry Abba, Father. The Spirit itself beareth witness with our Spirit, that we are the children of God. And if children, then heirs; heirs of God, and joint-heirs with Christ," (*Holy Bible* 140) further commenting that "this spirit of adoption is the richest privilege vouchsafed by God to his children on earth." According to the Scriptures and to custom, therefore, the spirit of bondage is the opposite of the spirit of adoption. I would like to start with this distinction in mind in order to look at how these two cultural and legal practices are reflected in representations of childhood in 19th century American literature.

If the Bible provides a metaphorical language for the idea and the praxis of adoption, it likewise transfers into the social and legal spheres the strong sense of property and inheritance connected with this particular family union, as it becomes apparent when reading texts dealing with adoption in the antebellum era. So, while property is a crucial element, that travels through all the cultural systems, from legal language to the religious sphere, to literary representations, other aspects, like race and class, don't seem to be explicitly named: in the language of the law used in the *Adoption of Children Act*, and in that of religion drawn from the Bible, there are no references to race or the class status of the children, as if these two categories were irrelevant in the formation of families in the 19th century Northern states. But we have seen how at least class makes an appearance in print publications dealing with adoption. Therefore, it seems only logical and pertinent to wonder how 19th century culture at large, and literature more specifically, dealt with questions regarding the adoption of black children, or their lives in bondage. In this essay I propose to look at adoption and bound labor as two mutually exclusive cultural practices of family relations, because I believe that, couched in the conventional and popular vocabulary of sentimental literature, so popular in 19th century United States, there are interesting subtexts regarding economy and questions of property, which are especially evident when race enters the picture. Sentimental language, in fact, rather than obscuring economic issues, emphasizes them, in a sort of cultural bas-relief. Both, adoption and bound labor, are the means for transferring and accumulating property, but while in the case of adoption property remains within the family, ensuring in fact, a clear hereditary line of succession, bound labor is connected to the accumulation of property for the employers and the public (state), but certainly never for the child, whose welfare is distributed among a number of different agencies (asylum for the orphans or other benevolent institutions, employer, the public), thus diffusing all social responsibility while avoiding direct accountability. In both cases, though, children are requested to perform the sentimental work of experiencing the prescribed feelings necessary for them to be granted a role in society.

While I would agree with Cindy Weinstein's claim that "the cultural work of sentimental fictions is nothing less than an interrogation and reconfiguration of what constitutes a family" (9), I would revise the notion that "the generic goal is the substitution of freely given love, rather than blood, as the invincible tie that binds together individuals in a family, thereby loosening the hold that consanguinity has both as a mechanism for structuring the family and for organizing the feelings of the people in it" (9). I believe, in fact, that children, especially those who are considered the burden of the public and civil society, are requested to demonstrate their worth by performing the sentimental work that is often waivered for adults, especially white men, typically absent, ineffectual or dead in American sentimental literature.

By looking at Harriet Wilson's *Our Nig*, published in 1859, and other shorter texts appeared in periodical publications in the 1840s and 1850s, I will consider what the prospects imagined for black children, and especially black girls, are, in order to access the world of property and ownership, often in contrast to the sentimental rescue provided to white protagonists such as Estella in *Great Expectations* (1860), or Ellen in the *The Wide Wide World* (1850), and Gerty in *The Lamplighter* (1850).

Our Nig[2] is a work that has been read as a clear critique of the supposed benevolence of the white North, and it is certainly in conversation with the sentimental texts of the era, since, as Elizabeth Maddock Dillon remarks:

> while sentimental liberalism and domestic ideology may have disproportionately benefited the white middle class by consolidating the moral and economic authority of members of this group, the association of liberty with housekeeping formed an influential ideology that spurred a range of engagements – from aspiring imitation to critical revision – among African Americans, immigrants, and poor

---

2   The original title was: *Our Nig, or Sketches from the Life of a Free Black in a Two-Story White House, North. Showing that Slavery's Shadows Fall even There*. By "Our Nig" (Harriet E. Wilson), and it was published in 1859 for the author in Boston.

laborers who had little in the way of resources to maintain a home or to represent it as a space of 'leisure' for women and children (Dillon 204).

Far from showing reformable households, Harriet Wilson's *Our Nig* is a study in the utter impossibility for redemption, through adoption, or through bound and free labor, for at least three generations of African Americans in the early 19th century. This autobiographical novel describes the unhappy life of Frado, the protagonist, who is abandoned by her white mother, when she faces dire circumstances after the death of her black husband. Before leaving town, Mag, the mother, drops off her child in one of the better-off households, where six years old Frado is treated horribly by Mrs. Bellmont, who is depicted as a cruel, unsympathetic enforcer of a harsh indenture for the girl. As an interesting example of life of free blacks in the North, *Our Nig* has been extensively studied, and, in the words of Carol J. Singley, it "demonstrates the limits of adoption for a poor, racially marked Northern child deemed unfit for the middle class. In this, the first African American novel by a woman, child placement is not redeeming but tortuous, offering neither a connection to roots nor a future opportunity" (139). While I agree that this text shows "the limits of adoption," I believe that race and economy complicate in remarkable ways the white sentimental narrative of a girlhood's redemption through goodness and hard work, showing, instead, how a fair amount of sentimental work is requested of black children, without any profit provided in this exchange. While Frado certainly represents what Nazera Sadiq Wright has termed "the trope of the self-reliant black girl in the face of adversity in the writing of African American women in the antebellum era" (60), it seems to me that the promises made by the sentimental ideology – that through good feelings, religious beliefs, and the ethics of work young people could elevate themselves and acquire property – don't seem to have the same purchase for black children.

As Gretchen Short claims, "socially stigmatized by both her race and her destitution, Frado is forced into the dependence her mother feared, a dependence which only tightens the already strait bonds of communal censure. The unofficial indenture that is the charitable response to her abandonment gives Frado a 'place' that is essentially no place, that denies her full membership in a household, a community, or a nation" (2). Frado moves from different houses, not really belonging to any, and the only relevant contribution she can offer is work, as Mrs. Bellmont clearly states to her husband: "If you should go as you would like, it would not be six months before she would be leaving me; and that won't do. Just think how much profit she was to us last summer. We had no work hired out; she did the work of two girls –" (90). Not only does she provide profit to the white family, but she also doubles this profit, working for two, thus contributing even larger accumulation of capital for her white mistress. But this is not the only type of work she is asked to perform.

In the complex structure of the novel, the white woman from the North, Mrs. Bellmont, is the enforcer of the unofficial indenture. Her description is similar to those of women in the South, for which profit and property are of prime importance: like them, she does not hesitate to use torture to bring her servant to submission and despair. Her husband and the male children of the family are the sentimental figures with no direct power to intervene, nor cultural influence to change the course of action occurring within the household, but they are still exacting something. The husband is always afraid to contradict his wife, and prefers the attitude of not taking personal responsibility – notoriously chosen by Augustine St. Clare in *Uncle Tom's Cabin*[3] – while the two sons are either absent or dying the sentimental death made famous by Little Eva, proclaiming the existence of a "heavenly home together," as James does in the following passage:

> How poor you are, Frado! I want to tell you that I fear I shall never be able to talk with you again. It is the last time, perhaps, I shall ever talk with you. You are old enough to remember my dying words and profit by them. I have been sick a long time; I shall die pretty soon. My Heavenly Father is calling me home. Had it be his will to let me live I should take you to live with me; but, as it is, I shall go and leave you. But Frado, if you will be a good girl, and love and serve God, it will be but a short time before we are in a heavenly home together. There will never be any sickness or sorrow there (Wilson 95).

If for Mrs. Bellmont the profit provided by Frado is capitalistic accumulation for her household, the only profit granted to Frado is offered by James' dying words, and their characteristic sentimental lack of action. Because he will not live, she would not be able to leave, stuck once again in the rhetoric of the afterlife. What is more, James asks her to perform sentimental work ("if you will be a good girl, and love and serve God") for which she is promised the reward of another household, a "heavenly home together," but nothing to improve her current household situation. It seems that every time the sentimental tide rises, it crashes against economic and capitalist issues, without being able to produce a valid material alternative. In this exchange James is not helping Frado practically: by being removed from the earthly picture, he also does not exert any influence over his wife in order to take Frado with her, thus showing how the system of bondage is presiding over any other possible relations. After he dies, his wife Susan and his son leave, in what can be perceived as a missed opportunity of salvation for Frado, reinforced by the short and sharp sentence used in the novel. While Susan "wished [Frado] to attend his burial as one

---

3   In her *Racial Innocence. Performing American Childhood from Slavery to Civil Rights*, Robin Bernstein states that *Our Nig* "reimagined *Uncle Tom's Cabin*" in order to emphasize "black children's pain" (56) through "a narrative strategy of using racial flip-flops to decimate sentimental notions of childhood innocence" (58).

of the family" (Wilson 97), she does not seem to contemplate the prospect of taking the girl with her: "the family, gathered by James' decease, returned to their homes. Susan and Charles returned to Baltimore" (Wilson 102).

Once again Frado is left to her work, both material and sentimental, and her helplessness. When she turns eighteen, after years of abuse and violence, Frado finds herself weak, lame, and unable to take up work, hence having to resort to "the unpleasant charities of the public" (Wilson 124). The novel closes by showing how the protagonist, alone and with a baby to support, is left with only her written story, this book, which she prints as the only property she has, and through which she hopes, mistakenly, to profit from.

If for Frado the option of adoption is completely absent, and her life of bondage is the only possibility offered to her as a black child, in other texts, with white orphans as protagonists, the two paths are present and very clearly marked. An article titled "The Adopted Daughter" addresses the two options that orphans have in mid-19th century Boston: to be adopted or to be bound for work. In "The Adopted Daughter," published in the Youth's Companion on 16 October 1845, a couple in Boston, after having lost three children to sickness, is now looking for adoption. They visited the Orphan Asylum, and they chose Ellen, even though they also noticed another girl, Ellen's closest friend, Maria Day. Ellen is raised without any acknowledgements of her past, until the revelation comes. When another family moves in the neighborhood from the city, she learns about her origins:

> Mrs. Williams, to whose house she had been sent, had told her, with malice which can hardly be conceived, that she had no father or mother, but that she was a poor child, and come from the Asylum. And then […] she pointed to the little servant girl, who was cleaning knives in the room, and told her that she was no better than Maria there, and she need not be above speaking to her, for they both came from the same place, and they used to be very loving, then.

Ellen and Maria Day shared part of the same past, but they were offered two distinctive paths: Ellen, as her prospective father remarked, "ought to be raised above the station in which she was born, because she is by nature, above it," and therefore could be afforded the possibility of being adopted, whereas Maria Day, about whom we learn nothing, can only expect a life of bound labor. Interestingly enough the women here, Ellen's adoptive mother and Mrs. Williams, are the ones appointed to clarify and interpret the lives of the two girls, while at the same time obtaining from Ellen the sentimental work of 'feeling right', of "being grateful to her Heavenly Father:"

> She told Ellen that what Mrs. Williams had told her was quite true, but yet, instead of being angry and sinful when she thought of it, she must be more grateful to her Heavenly Father for her pleasant home and many blessings, when she child she

used to love was at hard service. This was indeed, a bitter lesson for poor Ellen; but her naturally strong character was capable of receiving it, and from that time, although perhaps not as light hearted, she became a more thoughtful and grateful child.

The last text I would like to discuss is a short story that appeared in the Boston publication *Olive Branch*, on 4 May 1844, and titled "The Orphan." This story is an excerpt from the novel *The Home, Family Cares and Family Joys* by the Swedish writer Fredrika Bremer, translated by Mary Howitt and published in 1843. The passage chosen from the novel is the act of adoption of a black girl by a white family and her arriving in her new home. Because the periodical does not provide any indication about the context of the story, or about its writer, and only the names of the characters are left to somewhat signal their foreignness, readers might assume that the story could be set somewhere, or anywhere in the United States.

The couple in question, Ernest and Elise Frank are parents to six children. The father is the sentimental engine here, the figure who suggests adopting the child who lives nearby and who has just lost her father. When Ernest and Elise go to take her, the girl reacts aggressively and the text describes her as "half-savage." This is how Elise entices her: "If you will come with me this evening to my little children, you shall have sweet milk and white bread with them, and then sleep in a nice little bed with a rose-colored coverlet. The white bread, the rose-colored coverlet, and Elise's gentle voice, seemed to influence the child's mind." The readers learn of her appearance when she enters her new home, and is observed by the Frank children: "a very nice thin girl of about nine years [...], with black hair, dark complexion, and a pair of uncommonly large black eyes, which looked almost threateningly on the white and bright-eyed little ones which surrounded her." This encounter is both a study in contrast, and an effort in finding some common ground: the orphan is dark (black hair, black eyes), and the other children are white, but they are surrounding her, as if they wanted to engulf her, and incorporate her into the family. We learn that her name is Sarah, while we also learn some of the other children's names: Henrik, Louise, Eva, Leonore and Petrea. This last one is the child who will accomplish the rites of welcoming:

> Petrea would so willingly give something with her whole heart. [...] Petrea really possessed nothing which was fit to make a gift of. She acknowledged this with a sigh; her heart was filled with sadness, and tears were just beginning to run down her cheeks, when she was consoled by a sudden thought. The girl and the rose-bush! [...] As the mother took Sara by the hand, to conduct her to rest, Petrea had the indiscribable [sic] delight of seeing that, from all the little presents which had been made to her, she only took with her the girl and the rose bush which she appeared to regard with pleasure.

Very clearly the act of adoption is performed by Petrea, who passes her most cherished possession to her new sister, thus marking her participation in the circulation of property in the family. Once again, the trajectory of the story tends toward the sentimental conversion of Sarah, who is transformed from being "half-savage" to be thoroughly domesticated. When the girl does not seem to be able to go to sleep ("The girl and the rose-bush hung over the bed, but still there seemed to be no rest in the snow-white couch for the 'little African'") the mother comes to the rescue by performing the ritual of sentimentally whitening the child, through the "Song of the Dove," which she herself composed :

> There sitteth a dove so white and fair,
> All on the lilly spray,
> And she listeneth how to Jesus Christ
> The little children pray.
>
> Lightly she spreads her friendly wings,
> And to heaven's gate hath sped,
> And unto the Father in heaven she bears
> The prayers which the children have said.
> And back she comes from heaven's gate,
> And brings that dove so mild—
> From the Father on heaven, who hears her speak,
> A blessing for every child.
>
> Then children, lift up a pious prayer,
> It hears whatever you say,
> That heavenly dove so white and fair,
> That sits on the lily spray.

This observant and controlling white dove is the symbol of the normativization of the young girl. The process of becoming part of the family involves therefore both her participation in the circulation of gifts and possessions, but also her complete acceptance of the constant motion of purifying, white, fair feelings of sentimental surveillance.

Bibliography

A.A. "The Spirit of Adoption," *The Presbyterian*, 6 Sept. 1851.

Bernstein, Robin. *Racial Innocence. Performing American Childhood from Slavery to Civil Rights.* New York UP, 2011.

"Dialogue about Adoption." *The Christian Sentinel*, 8 July 1831.

Dillon, Elizabeth Maddock. *The Gender of Freedom. Fictions of Liberalism and the Literary Public Sphere.* Stanford UP, 2004.

The Holy Bible. King James Version. Penguin, 1974.

Manjapra, Kris. "Plantation Dispossessions. The Global Travel of Agricultural Racial Capitalism." *American Capitalism. New Histories,* edited by Sven Beckert and Christine Desan, Columbia UP, 2018, pp. 361-87.

Massachusetts Adoption of Children Act. 1851, https://darkwing.uoregon.edu/~adoption/archive/MassACA.htm. Accessed 12 Feb. 2020.

M.L. "The Adopted Daughter." *Youth's Companion,* 16 Oct. 1845, p. 96.

"The Orphan." *Olive Branch,* 4 May 1844.

Schmidt, James D. "'Restless Movements Characteristic of Childhood': The Legal Construction of Child Labor in Nineteenth-Century Massachusetts." *Law and History Review,* vol. 23, no. 2, 2005, pp. 315-50.

Short, Gretchen. "Harriet Wilson's *Our Nig* and the Labor of Citizenship." *Arizona Quarterly: A Journal of American Literature, Culture, and Theory,* vol. 57, no. 3, 2001, pp. 1-27.

Singley, Carol J. *Adopting America. Childhood, Kinship, and National Identity in Literature.* Oxford UP, 2011.

Weinstein, Cindy. *Family, Kinship, and Sympathy in Nineteenth-Century American Literature.* Cambridge UP, 2004.

Wilson, Harriet E. *Our Nig; or Sketches from the Life of a Free Black.* Vintage, 1983.

Wright, Nazera Sadiq. *Black Girlhood in the Nineteenth Century.* U of Illinois P, 2016.

III.
FAMILY – SOCIETY – TOGETHERNESS:
Centrifugal and Centripetal Forces

Anne Frank, Franz Kafka and Charles Lindbergh "at the kitchen table in Newark"
Philip Roth's Autofictional Holocaust

Alice Balestrino, University of Illinois at Urbana-Champaign

In Philip Roth's *The Counterlife* (1986), Nathan Zuckerman has an argument with his brother Henry over the latter's fascination with a Jewish "gangster" living in Hebron. According to Nathan, Henry is captivated by this person because "the man is the embodiment of potency" (141); a quality that Nathan unmistakably associates with their father.

> "[T]ell me, who does he remind you of?" I asked. "Anyone we know?"
> "Oh, no, please, no – save the psychoanalysis for the great American public."
> Wearily he said, "Spare me."
> "Well, that's the way it sticks in my mind. Strip away the aggressive bully, strip away the hambone actor and the compulsive talker, and we could have been back at the kitchen table in Newark, with Dad lecturing us on the historical struggle between the goy and the Jew." "Tell me something, is it at all possible, at least outside of those books, for you to have *a frame of reference slightly larger than the kitchen table in Newark?*" (141-42; italics added)

The "kitchen table in Newark" is the synecdoche through which Nathan evokes the spatiotemporal and affective dimension of their family of origin. It recalls not only the figure of their Dad, but also the warm and genuine atmosphere of their family gathered for dinner; it stands for Nathan's first "world," his first and necessarily embryonic idea of community. Indeed, it seems to be the "frame of reference" backing Nathan's current views or, rather, the measure against which he analyzes the world, even though, as Henry contends, it is made "of things larger than the kitchen table! [...A] world defined by *action*, by *power*, where how you wanted to please Momma and Poppa *simply doesn't matter!*" (144; italics in original). To Nathan though, "the kitchen table in Newark happens to be the source of [their] Jewish memories, [...] the stuff [they] were raised on" (142); it is the essence of their ethnic roots, the inescapable scope of their formation.

Philip Roth grew up around a "kitchen table in Newark" too, and the source of his Jewish memories, as well as his "frame of reference," may well be the same. Roth asserts the simplicity yet exceptionality of the family as a paramount interest in his literary *oeuvre* on more than one occasion; in *The Facts: A Novelist's Autobiography* (1988), he summarizes his father's – and his own – "repertoire" as "never [...] large: family, family, family, Newark, Newark, Newark, Jew, Jew, Jew. Somewhat like mine" (16). This sequence identifies the cornerstones of Roth's epistemology and hermeneutics of human relationships and points to the family as the earliest and most essential instance of society; the milieu where one's mindset and value system become radical (in the sense of constitutional and powerful) and germinate in broader contexts (Newark, the Jewish American experience).

This essay focuses on Roth's *The Plot Against America* (2004) as an autofictional novel[1] in which the autobiographical depiction of Roth's actual family seems to clash with the counterfactual historical scenario of a US governed by Charles Lindbergh,[2] a fascist and anti-Semitic president, in the 1940s. By portraying the reality of his own family against the explicit fictionality of the historical setting, Roth succeeds in creating an autofiction merging the magnitude of history ("a world defined by *action*, by *power*") with the domestic dimension of the "kitchen table in Newark," eventually testing his own radical frame of reference against "the larger world."

I argue that the result of Roth's narrative choice is a synergetic rather than oppositional context through which he can address a number of authorial anxieties connected to the pressing presence of the Holocaust in (Jewish) American culture. In this respect, Roth seems to expose and stress his own view of the Holocaust as simultaneously remote and close by hypothesizing what would have happened if his own family had been an endangered Jewish family living in a fascist nation. He approximates the Holocaust in a narrative that aims to be faithful to reality (the autobiographical details) yet detached from it (the counterfactual apparatus); an enabling gesture for the exploration of an event that "from the 1970s on, [has] bec[ome] ever more central in American public discourse" so much so "on some

---

1   By autofiction, I mean a narrative based on "the inclusion of a characterized version of the author, usually as the protagonist," with an onomastic correspondence between the two. Also, "[u]nlike memoir or autobiography, autofiction often depicts its author-characters in clearly fictional situations, thus blurring the already hazy boundaries between fiction and nonfiction" (Worthington 2-3).

2   As Roth himself explains, *The Plot Against America* is a "uchronia:" a literary work "disarranging the historical past [...] by giving our twentieth century a twist that it had not taken" (Roth, "My Uchronia" 337; 339). Roth speculates on what might have happened if a Republican candidate had won the US presidential election in 1940 and he imagines this person to be Charles Lindbergh, a big name for the American public, as well as a supporter of the isolationist movement and an outspoken anti-Semite.

level, for all Americans [it] has become a moral reference point" (Novick 2; 13), despite its undeniable historical and geographical distance from the US.

With regard to Roth's relation to the Holocaust, I align my interpretation with Michael Rothberg's assertion that Roth focuses his attention on "the unbridgeable distance between the Holocaust and American life – and the inauthenticity of most attempts to lessen that distance" (Rothberg 53). This stance formulates the "central paradox" of Roth's Holocaust writings, because "the greater the significance accorded to the Holocaust as an event of modern history [cf. Novick], the more distant a role it [actually] plays in the lives of American Jews" (53). Ultimately, I contend that the autofictional breadth – that Roth deploys in a number of his Holocaust-related narratives – creates a hybrid narrative space of distant proximity particularly apt to convey this paradox and its complexities and ambiguities. In this sense, *The Plot* furthers and expands a literary thread that Roth explored as early as 1973 with the publication of the short story "'I Always Wanted You to Admire My Fasting' or, Looking at Kafka." This text is divided into one essayistic section recounting Franz Kafka's life, and a second part in which fiction supplants the biographical intent (a structure that is proposed again in *The Plot*, since the novel is followed by a postscript with "A True Chronology of the Major Figures"). In "Looking at Kafka," Roth imagines that the European writer, instead of dying in 1924, survives the Holocaust and arrives as "a refugee teacher" (17) in the Hebrew school the young "Philip Roth"[3] attends. Crucially, Kafka's fictional version dates "Philip's" Aunt Rhoda, thus becoming a familiar presence in the Roths' everyday life. Roth pursues this counterfactual intent connected to the reconfiguration of the extraordinariness of the Holocaust within ordinary family dynamics in *The Ghost Writer* (1979), in which Nathan Zuckerman fantasizes that the European refugee Amy Bellette may be Anne Frank, whom he imagines presenting to his parents as his girlfriend. Despite the non-autofictionality of this text (whose narrator is Zuckerman), *The Ghost Writer* can nonetheless be read as another instance of Roth's conceiving of the Holocaust through the mediation of the "kitchen table in Newark."

Moreover, through the inclusion of the family as key element of these stories, Roth seems to address and partially resolve the question of inauthenticity. In the particular case of *The Plot*, the realistic rendition of a history that never was interrogates the possibility and the narrative potentiality of a Holocaust in the US, while the choice of having it affect the "Roths" hints at its comprehension through the author's first idea of community. Paradoxically, the accurate description of autobiographical family relations within an explicitly counterfactual framework renders Roth's Holocaust novel more "authentic" by virtue of this very dichotomic juxtaposition. In turn, this autofictional and counterfactual approach allows a liminal

---

3   In line with autofiction theory, I distinguish the character-narrator with the same name as the author from the author himself by using quotation in the first case (cf. Worthington).

position to investigate the family dynamics around the kitchen table in Newark. Roth, indeed, restores the specificities of his own household and while discussing the main motivations and ambitions of this novel, clarifies:

> To tell the story of Lindbergh's presidency from the point of view of my own family was a spontaneous choice. [...] My book gave me an opportunity to bring my parents back from the grave and restore them to what they were at the height of their powers in their late 30's – my father, with all the vast energy he was able to pour into what I call his "reforming instincts," and my mother "performing each day in methodical opposition to life's unruly flux" – and then to go ahead to imagine how they might have conducted themselves under the enormous pressure of a Jewish crisis such as they never really had to encounter as native-born New Jerseyans, living all their lives, luckily enough, without an Aryan white supremacist in the White House. I've tried to portray them here as faithfully as I could – as though I were, in fact, writing nonfiction. My brother I've portrayed less faithfully. I had to manipulate him a bit for the sake of the story. When he read the finished manuscript, he slyly told me, "You've made me more interesting than I was." (Roth "The Story Behind")

As noted by several critics, *The Plot* represents a "return home" for Roth (Posnock 3), and it is his novel "most warmly appreciative of the family" (Hobbs 123). It has also been pointed out that the narrative "is unswerving in conveying the danger to the country through the danger to the family" (Cooper 251) and in it, "family matters forever expand and assume importance almost befitting community and national issues" (Neelakantan 128). The conflation of the familial and the national, the personal and the political, the real and the fictional constitutes Roth's conscious attempt to domesticate History[4] by having it intrude the everyday life of his family; a dimension that Roth masters and that exceptionalizes and contains "what we schoolchildren studied as 'History'" (Roth *The Plot*, 114). This downscaling of History from "epic" (114) to personal narrative does not undermine its momentousness because, as Herman Roth ("Philip's" father) observes in the novel: "'What's history?' he asked rhetorically when he was in his expansive dinnertime instructional mode. 'History is everything that happens everywhere. Even here in Newark. Even here on Summit Avenue. Even what happens in his house to an ordinary man – that'll be history too someday'" (180). In fact, family functions as a profitable way into history exactly because it opens up a space for negotiating the latter's supposedly monolithic narrative by turning it into a more relatable experience, both for the narrator and the reader.

---

4   The word "history" is capitalized in order to refer to the following quotation from the novel, where it is spelled like this.

The alternate history that transforms the autobiographical structure into an autofictional enterprise typically privileges private lives over the public sphere (Gallagher 8) and presents the possibility to speculate not only on the history that has been altered, but also on those who have lived through it and their potentially altered identities. In the case of *The Plot*, the counterfactual mode expands Roth's exploration of his family and their code of values; he ponders "the attribution of different characteristics to the same entity [i.e. his family]: different thoughts, actions, and experiences that might plausibly have belonged to it had it faced different conditions" (Gallagher 12). In other words, family represents the lens through which Roth magnifies and particularizes the possibility of a Holocaust in the US while being, conversely, the object whose features Roth studies and tests against the extreme scenario of the traumatic events. This double dynamic between altered conditions engenders a profitable synergy between family as the organizing principle and history as the backdrop of the novel.

In *The Plot*, the Roths are threatened by a number of governmental policies targeting American Jews and grounded in mounting anti-Semitism; a political situation that, while never getting as far as in Europe, resembles the early years of Nazi Germany (of which Lindbergh is an ally) and reaches its apex in the (fictional) first pogrom in US history. As the narrative unfolds, the Roths' nuclear family proves to be an elastic structure that at times includes more distant individuals and at times distances some of its members. This mechanism functions not only on the basis of consanguinity, but also and more importantly, on individual identification with the ethical, political and religious values considered to be the foundation and the hallmark of the Roths; family principles that, interestingly, are "forged on an American anvil now [in Lindbergh's era] battered" (Cooper 242). The individual identification with the family's code evolves in times of danger and instability and, as a consequence, when the family and its very existence are threatened, the elastic family contours fluctuate, depending from the perspective from which are seen. For some of the characters the family contours will prove to be larger and more inclusive; for others instead, they will be smaller and more exclusive. In this sense, the representation of proto-fascist persecutions of the Jews through the eyes of the nine-year-old "Philip," who is the novel's narrator, constitutes Roth's occasion to reflect upon his family's *counterlife* and upon what could have happened were they seriously endangered; ultimately, he puts pressure on their value system by speculating on who would symbolically sit at their kitchen table in times of high vulnerability for their community.

The centripetal and centrifugal forces within the Roth household seem to me to be driven by a subtle though consistent dogmatic attitude; a mindset that tends to isolate or silence viewpoints that do not conform to the parents' vision – or more problematically, to that of the father.[5] In tune with a patriarchal structure, Herman's stance coincides with that of the entire family. Reading against the background of Roberto Esposito's seminal theorization of community as etymologically and inherently related to the threat of violence (Lemm 2-5), and of immunization as the incorporation of that violence within the very apparatus of the community (Lemm 6), one may argue that "Philip's" father immunizes his family against the fascist threat by building and sustaining his community on "parental love and family loyalty;" an "iron loyalty" that he at once "expects and embodies within his family" (Posnock 23; 27). By enforcing a categorical exclusion of dissent, Herman dramatizes Roth's belief that "family indivisibility [is the] first commandment," and that "Jewish family [is] an inviolate haven against every form of menace" (Roth *The Facts*, 14). Therefore, family unity, understood as unquestioning endorsement of the father's rhetoric on the part of every member, is one of the *foci* of the novel, especially in regard to the necessary renegotiation of the family's ethical values required by political circumstances. The fascist threat, the paternal master narrative implies, must be resisted by always aligning with the Jewish and, most decidedly, familial ethos over societal regulations.[6] Failing to do so entails the removal of the relative from the kitchen table, as a number of episodes in the plot shows. At the beginning of the novel, Aunt Evelyn, Bess' sister, is considered part of the family; although she does not live with the Roths, she is a regular guest at their house and she lively interacts with her kin. This structure of extended family is reconceived when the Roths are confronted with the fascist threat; each of them will be led to fabricate a new frame of reference, as well as new critical tools for reading the traumatic reality, that will disarray family unity, ultimately othering some relatives. The very identity of the Roths as an American family is at stake – as "Philip" notices: "Something essential had been destroyed and lost, we were being coerced to be other than the Americans we were" (108) – and, due to the turmoil of political and ideological reconfiguration, some of the family members distance themselves from the familial

5   The patriarchal structure of the "Roth" family in *The Plot* has been exposed both by Gurumurthy Neelakantan who highlights that "Bess Roth" privileges "the patriarch of the family with authority and control" (133), and by Alex Hobbs who holds that "Herman Roth" "retains control in the family [that] is built along patriarchal lines with Herman making the most consequential decisions" (132). For instance, "Philip" sees his mother crying over their dramatic situation in a couple of occasions, but it is only when he sees his father have the same reaction that he realizes the seriousness of the circumstances. "Philip" thus displays a stereotypical stance according to which crying is a feminine practice, one that undermines masculinity. "It was the first time I saw my father cry. […]. A new life began for me. I'd watched my father fall apart, and I would never return to the same childhood. The mother at home was now away all day working for Hahne's" (344-45).

6   See also the contributions by Brigitte Georgi-Findlay and Lee Herrmann for analyses of TV series and film where the 'circling of the wagons' against outside destructive forces is also central.

set of beliefs, thus becoming unrecognizable (from the Latin *recognoscere*: "to know again") for the rest of their community who distances them in turn.

One of the most debated issues at the Roths' kitchen table is "Just Folks," a program devised by the "Office of American Absorption" and specifically targeting the Jewish population, with the purpose to "encourag[e] America's religious and national minorities to become further incorporated into the larger society" (85). On the one hand, Aunt Evelyn and her husband, rabbi Bengelsdorf – who takes part in Lindbergh's administration because he believes that collaborating with the president, despite his antisemitism, is in the best interest of the Jews – as well as Sandy, who decides to join the program against his parents' will and is sent to Kentucky where he works for free on a farm and lives with a Christian family over a summer, are convinced that "Just Folks" is the occasion for "the Jews of America [to] participate fully in the national life of their country" (106-07). Herman and Bess, instead, take the opposite stance and these political and familial tensions will explode during a family dinner, precisely around the kitchen table.

> Their disagreement only grew more passionate during dinner, my father maintaining that Just Folks was the first step in a Lindbergh plan to separate Jewish children from their parents, *to erode the solidarity of the Jewish family*, and Aunt Evelyn intimating none too gently that the greatest fear of a Jew like her brother-in-law was that his children might escape winding up as narrow-minded and frightened as he was. (86; italics added)

The controversial and treacherous nature of "Just Folks" succeeds in eroding "the solidarity of the Jewish family" even before physically separating its members. Aunt Evelyn's identification with "the dream of President Lindbergh" (107), rather than with the Roths' philosophy of intransigence, will eventually otherize her, with Herman throwing her out of the house physically and metaphorically. Threatened by the FBI, she will be denied shelter by her sister who, at that point, does not recognize her anymore as part of the family whose circle narrowed. When Bess confronts her, the antagonism between two ideas of family comes to the fore: "Why don't you go to the von Ribbentrops' to hide?" my mother said. "Why don't you go to your friend Herr von Ribbentrop for protection? Stupid girl! *What about my family?* Don't you think that we're afraid too? Don't you think that we're in danger too? Selfish little bitch" (339; italics added).

As in the passage above, the rift produced inside the family is linguistically reproduced by the oppositional use of the pronoun "we" versus "you;" a rhetorical device employed also by Sandy who, after his Just Folks experience, comes home with the disquieting habit of addressing his parents as "you people." One night, Sandy has a particularly heated argument with Herman; the son claims that: "the whole country knows Winchell's full of hot air – it's only you people who don't. [...] This guy makes millions selling his shitty hand lotion – and you people believe him!" (230). To these accusations Herman replies by condemning the "you people business," but he simultaneously restates Sandy's estrangement from the family, this time not due to his will but to his father's decision:

> "I told you already about the dirty words, and now I'm telling you about this 'you people' business. Say 'You people' one more time, son, and I am going to ask you to leave the house. If you want to go live in Kentucky instead of here, I'll drive you down to Penn Station and you can catch the next train out. Because I know very well what 'you people' means. And so do you. So does everyone. Don't you use those two words in this house ever again." (230-31)

When perceived as a threat to the family's wellness, even Sandy is otherized; a logic of exclusion that Sandy himself embitters when, after being slapped by Bess, he scornfully resolves: "I'm going to the White House with Aunt Evelyn. I don't care whether you ghetto Jews like it or not" (193).

Political concerns are entangled with domestic matters and at the Roths' kitchen table there seems to be no ideological stance that does not correspond to a reconfiguration of the family circle. Indeed, Roth speculates on what his family's frame of reference would comprehend (i.e. would understand and embrace) under the pressure of vulnerable times not only in terms of exclusion but also of inclusion. The fluidity of the family's contours operates also in including more distant individuals and thus shaping a structure that accommodates a broader but at the same time more selective community, based on unconditional identification with the family's ethos.

This is the case with Seldon Wishnow, a schoolmate of "Philip's" and son of the Roths' neighbors who, orphaned, is welcomed into the Roths' house. Seldon's family is the tragic epitome of the potential destruction of family unity brought about by Just Folks. Indeed, he and his mother are relocated to Kentucky where she is killed in the fictive Louisville anti-Semitic riots; Herman takes it upon himself to go and rescue Seldon because "motherless and fatherless you are vulnerable to manipulation, to influences – you are rootless and you are vulnerable to everything" (358). According to Herman's view, Seldon's rootlessness (motivated by the loss of his parents and, consequently, of his previous frame of reference) makes him like a *tabula rasa* on which Herman can readily project the Roths' code of values. This very condition of adopting Herman's and his family's outlook allows Seldon at the Roths' kitchen table. The doubly vulnerable figure of the orphan is particularly relevant to the novel's construction of analogies between History and familial stories. In accordance with it, "Philip" is convinced that his only option to escape Lindbergh's anti-Jewish plot is becoming an orphan and, therefore, he tries unsuccessfully to flee from home. "I wasn't at all like Sandy, in whom opportunity had quickened the desire to be a boy on the grand scale, riding the crest of history. I wanted nothing to do with history. I wanted to be a boy on the smallest scale possible. I wanted to be an orphan" (232-33).

Ultimately, the autofictional ecology of *The Plot against America* addresses problems of authenticity in American Holocaust texts by reconciling its controversial significance in the US (what is transposed in the alternate history) within the domestic realm of the kitchen table. In particular, by testing his fundamental frame of reference against the "world defined by *action*, by *power*," a world of traumatic upheaval, Roth devises a narrative that puts pressure on the solidity of his family as a threatened community. Confronted with "history's [...] outsized intrusion" (184), the Roths perform mechanisms of exclusion and inclusion that activate their immunization system, whose eventual objective is the very preservation of their community, i.e. their family.

Bibliography

Cooper, Alan. "It Can Happen Here, or All in the Family Values: Surviving *The Plot Against America.*" *Philip Roth: New Perspectives on an American Author*, edited by Derek Parker Royal, Praeger, 2005, pp. 241-53.

Gallagher, Catherine. *Telling it Like It Wasn't: The Counterfactual Imagination in History and Fiction.* U of Chicago P, 2018.

Hobbs, Alex. "Family and the Renegotiation of Masculine Identity in Philip Roth's *The Plot Against America.*" *Journal of American Studies*, vol. 46, no. 1, 2012, pp. 121-37.

Lemm, Vanessa. "Introduction: Biopolitics and Community in Roberto Esposito." *Terms of the Political: Community, Immunity, Biopolitics*, edited by Roberto Esposito, Fordham UP, 2013, pp. 1-13.

Neelakantan, Gurumurthy. "Philip Roth's Nostalgia for the Yiddishkayt and the New Deal Idealisms in *The Plot Against America.*" *Philip Roth Studies*, vol. 4, no. 2, 2008, pp. 125-36.

Novick, Peter. *The Holocaust in American Life.* Houghton Mifflin, 1999.

Posnock, Ross. *Philip Roth's Rude Truth. The Art of Immaturity.* Princeton UP, 2006.

Roth, Philip. "'I Always Wanted You to Admire My Fasting;' or, Looking at Kafka." *American Review 17*, 1973 (Library of America Edition, 2017).

—. *The Ghost Writer.* Farrar, Straus and Giroux, 1979 (Library of America Edition, 2007).

—. *The Counterlife.* Farrar, Straus and Giroux, 1986 (2016).

—. *The Facts: A Novelist's Autobiography.* Penguin, 1988.

—. "The Story behind *The Plot against America.*" *The New York Times*, 19 Sept. 2004. https://www.nytimes.com/2004/09/19/books/review/the-story-behind-the-plot-against-america.html. Accessed 23 Oct. 2019.

—. *The Plot against America.* Houghton Mifflin, 2005.

—. "My Uchronia." *Philip Roth, Why Write? Collected Nonfiction 1960-2013*. Library of America Edition, 2017, pp. 336-45.

Rothberg, Michael. "Roth and the Holocaust." *The Cambridge Companion to Philip Roth*, edited by Timothy Parrish, Cambridge UP, 2007, pp. 52-66.

Worthington, Marjorie. *The Story of 'Me.' Contemporary American Autofiction*. U of Nebraska P, 2018.

Family Crises on the Frontiers
Nation, Gender, and Belonging in US Television Westerns

Brigitte Georgi-Findlay, TU Dresden

US television series aired since the 1950s are, I argue, an ideal subject for the study of family and family crises. Commercial broadcast television has always aimed to reach the widest possible audience, and has, out of commercial necessity, gauged the mainstream. It has thus been serving as a "cultural forum" (Newcomb and Hirsch 564). Studying it can help us to understand how American culture 'ticks' at a particular time. As a domestic medium, early US broadcast television was all about family which was reflected in the formats that defined the TV landscape of the 1950s and 1960s: soaps, animal series, family sitcoms, and western series. This domestic character of TV series certainly makes them an interesting form in which to "observe changing ideas about family" as part of an American value system (Taylor 1). TV series thus 'do' cultural and political work.

In the following, I will focus on constructions of family and family crises with regard to nation and migration in American television westerns aired in the 1950s, 1960s, and 1970s. Let me begin by pointing to 1950s family sitcoms, such as *Father Knows Best*, which idealized a then "qualitatively new phenomenon" (Coontz 25), the suburban nuclear middle-class family. After the Great Depression and World War II, the Cold War defined a new set of social expectations. Family was seen to serve as a bulwark against communism and the Soviet Union, providing security and stability (critics would also say: conformism and consumerism). The interests of family and nation were intricately linked (May 10-11). In family sitcoms, the focus was laid on the performance of family dynamics emplotted in stories of "rupture and crisis" from within and from the outside. Narrative resolutions pointed to sentiments and ideals such as "caring, commitment, loyalty, sacrifice, and permanence" (Chambers 72). As will be shown, Western series sent out similar signals.

The new 1950s ideal of the suburban nuclear middle-class family also involved a more democratic and less authoritarian family structure which was reflected in humorous challenges to patriarchal authority posed by mothers and children, especially teenagers. As scholars have pointed out, the strong role of mothers in these sitcoms reflects not only the concept of the companionate marriage that evolved since the 1920s, but also the movement of women into the workplace during and after World War II (Chambers 61-63). The latter explains why in the family sit-coms the seeming power of wives and mothers is ultimately contained in the way narrative closure is achieved at the end of episodes. Some series thus seemed to address contemporary fears of the dysfunctional family (66). Family was perceived to be under attack, which was also reflected in contemporary debates over juvenile delinquency. In fact, these sitcom families of the 1950s were probably the last in-tact families to be seen on American television screens (71). By the 1960s, the sitcom family had become more diverse, and another serial format imagined non-nuclear types of families: the western television series.

Westerns have served as American founding narratives, dramatizing the con-tradictions within the American historical experience between 'nature' and freedom on the one hand, and 'civilization' and society on the other, between individualism and social responsibility. In this context, the frontier West has been imagined as a formative space for the American nation, for American core values, and for the American 'national character' (mainly represented by male frontier heroes). Within the symbolic logic of many westerns, for instance *Shane* (1953), the core of 'civiliza-tion' is represented by fences, towns, women and children (and thus families). The protection of families functions as the central mobilizing force for the protagonist who enables society but cannot be part of it, who can be a father figure but cannot be a father. Like the American revolutionaries, Shane has eliminated himself from the law of the father: he has no last name (*Shane*). Western 'heroes' like Shane can be seen to embody the contradictions between rugged individualism and "communal domesticity represented by the settlement family" (Ross 7), between "male rest-lessness and familial domesticity" (8), contradictions that also inform the western television series of the 1950s and 1960s.

From 1949 to the early 1970s more than 40 prime time western series were aired on three networks, at first mainly as children's series (Spencer 3). As some scholars have claimed, by the mid-1950s a shift can be observed from juvenile to adult west-ern series, with darker, more troubled and alienated heroes, a shift which was also reflected in movie westerns of the 1950s such as *Shane*, *High Noon*, and *The Searchers*. Women and young adults were now addressed as vital members of the audience (MacDonald 47-48; Boddy 122; Yoggy 77). Within these adult western series scholars have also found distinctions between 'lone wolf' protagonists (in *Lone Ranger*, *Have Gun – Will Travel*, *Maverick*) and characters that define themselves as members of an extended family (*Gunsmoke*), a male group (*Rawhide*), or a family with property (*Bonanza*, *The Big Valley*, *The High Chaparral*).

In my first part, I will focus on how discourses about family and family values are engaged in two series that focus on a propertied frontier family: *Bonanza* and *The Big Valley*. In the second part, I will sketch the discourses on family and family values enacted in *Little House on the Prairie*, a series that was aired between 1974 and 1984.

Part 1

Family Values and Family Crises in *Bonanza*

Bonanza puts a family of men (not a male buddy group as in *Rawhide* that aired on CBS, 1959-1966) at the center. Aired on NBC for 14 years (1959-1973), in 430 episodes, *Bonanza* is a mixture of a western and a family drama. In critical reference to the family sitcom fathers who are challenged by wives and children, the series features a single parent (Ben Cartwright) and his three sons (Adam, Hoss, and Little Joe). Each son has a different mother, since Ben has been widowed three times. Whenever father or sons get ready to tie the knot of matrimony, the female love interest either dies or is eliminated by other means. From time to time, the family takes in children or youngsters in trouble. In Season 12 an adoptive son, Jamie, is added. The series thus features a family constellation that seems unusual for the 1950s, but may be held to reflect the situation on the western frontiers: a patchwork-family of men, aided by a Chinese cook and housekeeper.

Bonanza uses the frontier setting to imagine a family constellation that puts men and masculinity front and center, and thus to comment on the situation of the American family and nation in the 1950s and 1960s, a time "when Americans experienced an exodus of women from hearth and home to the workplace" (Matheson 4). Here, the frontier hero has settled down, ushering in what critics have called the "'suburban' phase" of the western genre, with a close-knit, property-owning, non-nuclear family "as the privileged site of caring, stability, moral authority and emotional security" (Ross 9).

And yet, while this family is 'domesticated', it is so in a 'manly' way, embodying and playing out the ambivalent expectations tied to the sitcom family drama and the western. These ambivalences can be observed in constructions of masculinity and fatherhood. The showrunners apparently put some thought into the conception of the father figure that started out as a strict, patriarchal disciplinarian and gradually became a mentor and mediator figure that showed warmth and emotional sensitivity (Leiby and Leiby 17, 196). This father does not know best, reflecting the move toward a more liberal concept of fatherhood that seems to have hit the spot for viewers of the time: in 1965 the actor embodying Ben Cartwright, Lorne Greene, received the Father of the Year Award from the National Father's Day Committee (292). Viewers sent him letters asking for his parenting advice (Delling 48).

For various reasons, which also had something to do with the star system, father and sons were shown to be on an equal footing. The men were allowed to show love for each other, although they may have had problems expressing this love (see for example season 2, episode 27). Producer David Dortort even maintained that the subject of *Bonanza* was "a love affair between four strong men" which was the reason why no mothers were built into the show (qtd. in Spencer 73; MacDonald

75). In interviews, the actor Lorne Greene reiterated this by explaining the popularity of the show: "One of the reasons is love. The Cartwrights happen to be a family that other families want to be like. ... The Cartwrights love each other" (qtd. in Yoggy 296). One must add, however, that some episodes also feature father-daughter relationships very prominently.

All of the men represent ambivalent masculinities, combining 'old' and 'new' constructions of manhood, and reflecting gender and parenting ideals of the 1950s and 1960s.[1] They are equally strong and sensitive, men of action and interested in education (we often see one of them reading), tough and empathetic, able to exert violence and show emotions. They enjoy freedoms, but are also subjected to constraints. They are able to reign in their rugged individualism in the service of a common good. Due to the frontier setting, they also are seen to assume female-connoted work such as midwifing (see for example season 1, episode 15). They mother each other, and at the end of the day they can always come home, something that is unusual for 'classic' western heroes.

In a similar way as in family sitcoms, family here is about love, caring, loyalty, sacrifice, and permanence in a hostile, dangerous world. Home is where the men can, at least for a while, take off their guns and let their guard down. Family is also shown to be a stage on which social values are enacted and performed in situations of crisis. In fact, most episodes are structured as lessons around growing up, parenting, and learning to be an American. Some episodes focus on how the Cartwrights learn to be a family. Others feature them as a model family in a fictional universe that otherwise seems to be full of dysfunctional, broken, and failing families.

In fact, one of the biggest dangers in this fictional universe is provided by wandering, homeless young men without family, estranged from their families, or in conflict with their fathers. Some are obviously victims of domestic abuse. Family is thus revealed to also be a source of pain, violence, trauma, and dysfunctional behavior due to parents' (but mostly fathers') inability to fulfill their parenting responsibilities. This is where the Cartwrights come in as a positive foil, as advisors or as surrogate parents. However, family may also be a source of violence when families stick together too much, when they pursue feuds in order to uphold a sense of honor, or when individuals are obsessed with seeking revenge for wrongs done to a family member.

Bonanza episodes touch upon all kinds of family issues: child raising, parenting, marital relations, illegitimate births, unwanted pregnancies, interracial love and miscegenation, or domestic abuse. They also engage family-related issues such as

---

1   For an analysis of modern masculinities in some of today's families – in families created with a sperm donor – see Eva-Sabine Zehelein in this volume.

ageing, disability, loss, death, and grief. There are also stories about 'foreign' family concepts: Chinese families selling their children into slavery, Jewish overprotective parents, arranged marriages, 'old world' concepts of family and parenting that entail too strict patriarchal authority, robbing young people of their freedom of choice. Although there are allusions to homoerotic relations, there is no thematization of same-sex marriage yet. In the end, we are told that 'natural' kinship ties do not necessarily have to bind. Sometimes it is better to foster these ties in new family constellations. Thus, we hear Hoss tell a little boy: "It don't matter who your Ma and Pa were, it's more important who you are" (season 1, episode 30). What is suggested in many episodes, is, that the American idea of family is not about heredity, but about the freedom of choice.

Within its discourse on family and family values, *Bonanza* also enacts an American code of values. The Cartwrights stand for the defense and legitimation of private property, the right to liberty, and a fair trial. They represent a strong individualism paired with an equally strong sense of civic responsibility. They call for tolerance and defend the rights of the underdogs and the excluded. They also legitimate the (reluctant and restrained) use of violence in a dangerous world, serving as selfless defenders of these values against violent intruders from outside. Their actions thus provide a filter to look at the real-world Cold War threats.

The Big Valley: A Matriarchal Empire

The family type featured in *Bonanza*, which is that of the combined or patchwork family, also informed *The Big Valley* (ABC, 1965-1969). By imagining a ranching family in 1870s California headed by a widowed matriarch, this series writes women into the history of the frontier family. Barbara Stanwyck plays a mother of three adult sons and a teenage daughter who has accepted and come to love a fourth adult son, the result of her late husband's marital infidelity. Although Stanwyck wanted another story (she wanted him to be her own character's illegitimate son), and although the producers decided against this narrative spin, the series still suggests that birth out of wedlock should not be a problem, thus normalizing it.

Stanwyck's Victoria Barkley is a tough and loving mother willing to argue with her children, but leaving the management of the ranch to her sons and only acting as a mentor. Unlike her daughter, who is often seen trapped in a 'damsel-in-distress'-role, she is capable of taking care of herself beyond her home, displaying mental and physical courage on a volatile frontier that is suggested to demand both conformity to and transgression of gender expectations, as the respective situation demands (see for example season 1, episode 9).[2]

---

2   For an analysis of reversed gender roles in contemporary fiction (short story) see e.g. Margarita Navarro Pérez in this volume.

Although referred to as "*Bonanza* in petticoats" (Marrill 76) or "'Bonanza' in drag" (in Yoggy 328), *The Big Valley* obviously distances itself from its rival. Stanwyck has insisted that the Barkley family "is much tougher" than the Cartwright family. "Our family behaves like any normal family. We fight, argue, discuss things." She emphasizes that the Barkleys are all individuals with "minds of their own" (qtd. in Yoggy 328). A comparison of the two series reveals further differences and similarities. Like *Bonanza*, *The Big Valley* features a powerful and wealthy pioneer family which rose from poverty and established an empire by hard work. The Barkleys share the Cartwrights' strong sense of civic responsibility and stand up for deserving underdogs (white and non-white). Yet, *The Big Valley* lends its Barkley family an aristocratic Southern touch by having them live in a mansion, outfitted with a black servant. However, what Andrew Ross calls, in reference to *Dallas*, an "aristocratic family with a suburban imagination" (Ross 13), could also describe the imagery underlying *The Big Valley* which thus anticipates the television families of the 1980s, yet without their fragmentation and dysfunctionality, without their crises of filial succession and inheritance, without the moral dissolution associated with a leisure class. Moreover, like *Bonanza*, *The Big Valley* clearly distances its Barkley family from 'foreign' or 'old world' conceptions of inheritance (for instance represented by a 'Spanish', i.e. Mexican, father who wants to keep the family blood line 'pure' (season 1, episode 7). In both series, family serves as a bulwark of emotional and economic stability against a hostile, dangerous environment. Both feature concepts of family that seem to be suited more to the Cold War context of the 1950s and 1960s, than to that of the 19th century American frontier.

Most western series were cancelled by the mid-1970s, sharing the fate of the movie western which was pronounced dead by the film critic Pauline Kael in 1974 (Coyne 165). Yet, frontier families survived and were embedded in new formats suited to their times, the 1970s, 1980s, and 1990s, for instance in *The Waltons* (CBS, 1972-1981), *Little House on the Prairie* (NBC, 1974-1984), and *Dr. Quinn, Medicine Woman* (CBS, 1992-1998). In the following, I will sketch the discourses on family and family values enacted in *Little House on the Prairie*.

Part 2

Little House on the Prairie: A Manual for 1970s Families

If *Bonanza* may have functioned as an advisor for 1960s families, its successor series *Little House on the Prairie* could have fulfilled this function for families in the 1970s and 1980s. Based on the semi-autobiographical *Little House on the Prairie* books by Laura Ingalls Wilder, the series follows the young Ingalls family (father, mother, and three little daughters) on their way to a new home in the 1870s West, and then observes the processes of settling into farms and towns where men, women, and children learn to become nuclear families within new communities, leaving behind their extended families back East.

Little House on the Prairie bears the signature of *Bonanza* star Michael Landon. With his character, Little Joe, he had defined the earlier series' countercultural appeal, also including themes such as disability. Like *Bonanza*, the show is structured around a set of lessons, offering itself as a manual for an audience of 1970s families who may have battled cultural and economic crises and may have dreamt of a simpler, countercultural life in a small community. Like those 1970s families, the fictional western 1870s families featured in *Little House on the Prairie* need to find their bearings in an economically and culturally unstable America. Like the two earlier series discussed above, *Little House on the Prairie* offers a "nostalgic and idealized version of the pioneer family" (Matheson 4). Yet, it also seems to address the new demands of the 1970s, provided by countercultural challenges to family structures such as the suburban middle-class nuclear family. *Little House on the Prairie* seems to both answer and contain these challenges. It appeals to nostalgic longings and contains them by repeatedly providing reality checks.

Unlike *Bonanza*, *Little House on the Prairie* focuses less on masculinity than on the particular needs and demands of the different sexes and generations in a close-knit family. The series addresses issues tied to growing up, raising children, marriage, and old age, thus targeting a family audience of all generations, sexes, and ages. Again, family provides the context for enacting learning processes tied to the paradoxes of the American historical experience. Older and young protagonists struggle with the conflicting pressures emanating from peers and community expectations. Stories stress the value of hard work, frugality, discipline, education, compassion, faith, and keeping promises. Protagonists need to balance their individual aspirations against their own capabilities and social responsibilities. Children learn that good grades and winning are not everything, that money cannot buy you friendship and love. All generations need to come to grips with loss, death, and grief. Although the stories suggest that individuals have to deal with these feelings on their own, it is the family that is ultimately shown to enable these processes by providing emotional and economic stability.

All of these seemingly 'old school'-values are updated for a 1970s audience by constructing 'new' types of fathers and mothers, such as fathers who share the parenting and who are capable of expressing affection, and mothers who are trying to hold their own or gradually establishing their independence. The series tells new stories, for example, about marital problems tied to women's professional aspirations, about the problems of single parents (male and female), about adoption, domestic abuse, disability, and drug addiction, about the effect of a parent's addiction on children, about educational challenges tied to minority children. It also tackles issues tied to racial relations. The series thus responds not only to countercultural challenges to family structures but also to the social and political movements of the 1960s and 1970s. It seems to have "painlessly reconciled traditional values of simplicity, decency, and community with visions of progress and modernity" (Taylor 37).

Unlike *Bonanza* and *The Big Valley*, this series shows conflicts to emanate less from dangerous outsiders than from the domestic and community context, such as people striving for higher status. The stories also feature less violence, in a similar way as the Cold War was toned down in real life in the *détente* policies of the 1970s, but also because American audiences may have grown tired of violence, which reminded them of the Vietnam War (see Johnson 210-211). Perhaps one could also argue that *Little House on the Prairie* reflects 1970s sentiments about the limits to American progress and power, about American overextension (for example, in Vietnam), which lead to a move inward, toward the personal and the domestic (see Schulman 79-80). It is the home and the intact family, *Little House on the Prairie* suggests, that provides a bulwark against materialism and all other sorts of false values, in a similar way as suggested by *The Waltons*, where a family is seen to battle poverty and deprivation with dignity and humor.

One episode creates an interesting analogy between the 1870s and the 1970s. Aired on July 4, 1976, it centers on families' anger, in July 1876, at the government's tax policies which threatened to cancel out the upcoming patriotic celebrations. In the end, it is the schoolchildren, together with a Russian immigrant, who remind the adults of the revolutionary founders' sacrifices and the advantages of a free country. Playing on analogies between 1876 and 1976, when a revolt against taxes accompanied a new conservative movement in the US, the series thus uses family stories to engage with a 1970s patriotic fatigue, at a time when television does no longer produce likeable family characters and successful marriages, and when family and marriage as social institutions were seen to be under attack. *Little House on the Prairie* could probably do so without offending anyone because it set its stories in the past.

Conclusion

All of the western series discussed above use the frontier setting not only as an exotic backdrop for adventure and as a premodern setting for the enactment of nostalgia for 'older' values, but also as a backdrop for constructing unusual family constellations. The frontier setting represents a state of exception, providing a crisis situation that serves as a test for families, individuals, and American institutions. It also serves as a setting for not only affirming gender roles but also for imagining transgressions of these roles.

All of these western series suggest that family provides a socializing force, an anchor of economic stability and permanence, and a source of emotional support in a nation where mobility, a strong sense of individualism, and the quest for material success have traditionally served as centripetal forces potentially rending society apart. The focus on family in these popular cultural products can also be explained within the contexts of their respective times. Groups, communities, and families are shown to serve as bulwarks against the threats provided by the Cold War, post-war domesticity, the corporate workplace, the consumer culture, and social and cultural movements for change. All of the series stress the importance of home and belonging beyond a 'natural' birth family. They implicitly explain the emergence of the American combined or patchwork family with a frontier setting that fosters crisis and violence at the same time as it creates a strong sense of individualism. Stressing the performative quality of family life, all of these series suggest that families become such especially or only through crisis.

Bibliography

Boddy, William. "'Sixty Million Viewers Can't Be Wrong': The Rise and Fall of the Television Western." *Back in the Saddle Again: New Essays on the Television Western*, edited by Edward Buscombe and Roberta E. Pearson, BFI, 1998, pp. 119-40.

Bonanza, produced by D. Dortort, NBC, 1959-1973.

Chambers, Deborah. *Representing the Family*. SAGE, 2001.

Coontz, Stephanie. *The Way We Never Were: American Families and the Nostalgia Trap*. Basic, 1992.

Coyne, Michael. *The Crowded Prairie: American National Identity in the Hollywood Western*. Tauris, 1997.

Delling, Manfred. *Bonanza & Co. Fernsehen als Unterhaltung und Politik. Eine kritische Bestandsaufnahme*. Rowohlt, 1976.

Dr. Quinn, Medicine Woman, produced by B. Sullivan, CBS, 1992-1998.

Gunsmoke, produced by N. MacDonnell and J. Meston, CBS, 1955-1975.

Have Gun – Will Travel, produced by S. Rolfe and J. Claman, CBS, 1957-1963.

High Noon, directed by Fred Zinneman, United Artists, 1952.

Johnson, Michael L. *New Westers: The West in Contemporary American Culture*. UP of Kansas, 1996.

Leiby, Bruce R., and Linda F. Leiby. *A Reference Guide to Television's Bonanza*. McFarland & Co., 2001.

Little House on the Prairie, produced by M. Landon and E. Friendly, NBC, 1974-1982.

Lone Ranger, produced by G. W. Trendle and F. Striker, ABC, 1949-1957.

MacDonald, J. Fred. *Who Shot the Sheriff? The Rise and Fall of the Television Western*. Praeger, 1987.

Marrill, Alvin H. *Television Westerns: Six Decades of Sagebrush Sheriffs, Scalawags, and Sidewinders.* The Scarecrow P, 2011.

Matheson, Sue, editor. *Love in Western Film and Television. Lonely Hearts and Happy Trails.* Palgrave Macmillan, 2013.

Maverick, produced by W. T. Orr, ABC, 1957-1962.

May, Elaine Tyler. *Homeward Bound: American Families in the Cold War Era.* Basic, 1988.

Newcomb, Horace M., and Paul M. Hirsch. "Television as a Cultural Forum." *Television: The Critical View*, edited by Horace Newcomb, Oxford UP, 2000, pp. 561-73.

Rawhide, produced by B. Brady, CBS, 1959-1966.

Ross, Andrew. "Families, Film Genres, and Technological Environments." *East-West Film Journal*, vol. 4, no. 1, Dec. 1989, pp. 6-26.

Schulman, Bruce J. *The Seventies. The Great Shift in American Culture, Society, and Politics.* Da Capo P, 2001.

Shane, directed by George Stevens, Paramount, 1953.

Spencer, Kathleen L. *Art and Politics in Have Gun – Will Travel. The 1950s Television Western as Ethical Drama.* McFarland & Co., 2014.

Taylor, Ella. *Prime-Time Families. Television Culture in Postwar America.* U of California P, 1989.

The Big Valley, produced by A. Bezzerides and L. Edelman, ABC, 1965-1969.

The Searchers, directed by John Ford, Warner, 1956.

The Waltons, produced by R. L. Jacks and A. White, CBS, 1972-1981.

Yoggy, Gary A. *Riding the Video Range: The Rise and Fall of the Western on Television.* McFarland & Co., 1995.

Cinematic Violence and Ideological Transgression
The Family in Crisis in the 1977 Horror Film
The Hills Have Eyes

Lee Herrmann, Università di Torino

Since its birth cinema has featured graphic violence, herein defined as the direct visual depiction of injury to the body (Kendrick, *Hollywood* 6). Fiction might be packaged as reality: the staged *Shooting Captured Insurgents*, an 1898 re-enactment of a war crime from the Spanish-American War, uses a documentary presentation making for, in the words of film scholar James Kendrick, "a surprisingly disturbing forty seconds of cinema [...] because the violence is so brutal and uncompromising." The film does not employ cinematic techniques that create distance between the images and the viewer in order to create "conventional action excitement," but offers instead a "cold, hard image of execution" (*Film* 35-38), its artless technique producing visceral affect in viewers.

In American cinema, the major studios created censorship guidelines in the Production Code, enforced from the middle 1930s to the late 1960s, which did not prohibit onscreen violence, but demanded that representations of "[B]rutality and possible gruesomeness" be constrained "within the careful limits of good taste" (qtd. in Kendrick, *Hollywood* 28).[1] People could be strangled or tortured, and bodies could be chopped up or mutilated, as long as certain cinematic techniques and aesthetic strategies, dubbed "substitutional poetics" by Steven Prince, were used to obscure the literal reality of the violence or to produce sufficient emotional distance to avoid disturbing viewers, by keeping the violence just offscreen or displacing it onto an object, for example (205-09, 250).

It was not until the later 1960s that graphic depictions of cinematic violence became acceptable in mainstream cultural production. *The Wild Bunch* (1969) and *Bonnie and Clyde* (1967) are the two examples most often cited as representing this shift (Kendrick, *Hollywood* 45-47), bracketing the year the Code was scrapped for the distributor-governed G/M(laterPG)/R/X rating system. Intellectuals have perceived

---

1   Production Code quoted in Kendrick, *Hollywood Bloodshed* 28.

such violence as transgressive critical engagement. Barbara Klinger describes the development of this critical position:

> There has been strong theoretical and critical attention devoted to the elaboration of the particular relation between cinematic text and ideology . . . Vital to and constant within this primarily textual focus of the cinema/ideology inquiry are the twin interrogatives of what constitutes dominant cinematic practices and then what deconstitutes them. (75)

In this way the deconstitution of a dominant technique, substitutional poetics in the depiction of violence, becomes ideological transgression.

The horror genre particularly has been seen, as Rhona Berenstein characterizes this question, to "function as a site of ideological contradiction and negotiation" (10). Close readings of cinematic texts are indispensable to any ideological mapping of the field of cultural production (see Bourdieu 31-38), and the film scholar Robin Wood has engaged in such close readings of horror films from a consciously Marxist or psychoanalytic perspective. Hence texts are either "progressive" or "reactionary" (192, *passim*), with the former a site of textual challenge to dominant discourses, a challenge that enacts and produces a radical break with manufactured consensus and thereby, in Klinger's words, "produces ideological critique [...] instead of the optimism that characterizes the celebratory or complacent view of the American way of life in the classic text." Cinema is reactionary when the "classic text," a creature of "the dominant mode of production [...] unproblematically broadcasts dominant cultural ideas" (77-79).

The majority of cultural production will be reactionary in this sense, and given the conditions governing production and reception of cinema, films may not have a univocal power to provoke a rupture with celebratory ideological reification. But granting that a text may break with ideological conformity, the notion of progressive depends on a Marxist or modernist teleology, inevitably moving toward a better world through well-meant interventions, which can lead progressive criticism to project qualities onto texts that they do not demonstrate textually. A film that deconstitutes dominant discourse must produce ruptures within the body of the narrative, break with the discourse conventions of its idiom, and be received as antithetical to those traditional discourses. This latter feature leads to the problem that challenges to dominant discourse always seem to be recuperated: the PTA no longer protests the threat to children of 1931's *Dracula* (Kendrick, *Film*, 48).

Wood proposes that the horror genre "became in the 1970s the most important of all American genres, and perhaps the most progressive, even in its overt nihilism – in a period of extreme cultural crisis and disintegration" (84-85). *Variety* reported horror-genre exhibitor rentals over the decade increasing in value from 6.5 to 168 million dollars per year, leading film historian David Cook to concur that "no other genre experienced a greater infusion of creative richness and financial capital during the 1970s" (238). If one may doubt whether the horror genre in general has as "its true milieu, the family," as Wood claims (85), 1970s horror films did take the family as their object. As Vivian Sobchak observes in her discussion of Hollywood horror releases, "the time and place of horror and anxiety [...] has been brought back into the American home." No longer "a place of refuge from the social upheavals of the last two decades [...] the family has become the site of them [and] the site of their representation" (178). Familial crisis and disintegration defined the genre during this period, in studio features like *The Exorcist, The Omen, Burnt Offerings, Carrie, The Fury*, and *The Shining*, and in independent films like *Don't Look Now, The Amityville Horror, Last House on the Left, The Brood*, and *Sisters* – and *The Hills Have Eyes*.

That 1977 cultural commodity has spawned sequels and new-millennium re-makes with their own sequels. Academics have considered it as among the best of its sub-genre: Wood groups it with *Raw Meat* and *Night of the Living Dead* as the "most intense horror films at the exploitation level" (91); Kendrick notes that many critics go so far as to see it as "exemplar[y] of low-budget creativity and social rel-evance" and cites it specifically as a film whose violence emits a "socially inflected resonance that largely defined horror films in the 1970s" (*Hollywood*, 137-39). To the contrary, Judith Hess Wright has argued that the violence of the horror genre is inherently reactionary or conservative (42). Wood allows that "the genre carries within itself the capability of reactionary inflection" and that "perhaps, no horror film is immune from its operations" (191). Kendrick proposes that texts within the genre be seen individually, "with some films expressing more reactionary tenden-cies through their violence, while others deploy violence for explicitly transgressive purposes;" this distinction can be analyzed through the "various ways in which hor-ror violence can be shaped narratively, tonally, and visually to either reactionary or transgressive ends" (*Film* 85). This analysis of what constitutes transgressive tends to rely on metatextual positioning of the artifact in the field of cultural produc-tion and assuming unclassical technique has anti-classical valences of rupture. The schema of ideologically reactionary *vs* transgressive can remain useful to the extent that it demands a close reading of the structure and semantics of the narrative (see Altman), intra- and intertextually, rather than techniques of representation in ef-fects like tone and visual style.

Since many readers may wish to avoid the visceral and psychological bludgeon-ing that viewing the film entails, a brief plot synopsis of *The Hills Have Eyes* follows (for all general references, see Craven). The Carter family detours from their vaca-tion trip to California in search of an inherited silver mine in the Arizona desert, upon the insistence of the patriarch. This extended family unit consists of Big Bob and his wife Ethel, with their children Bobby and Brenda, twin teenagers, and Lynne, along with Lynne's husband Doug and their own infant child, with two pet German shepherds rounding out the retinue of the station wagon and trailer.

A low-flying plane from the adjacent Air Force bombing range and Ethel's panicked reaction cause them to crash, so Big Bob and Doug set off in different directions for help, leaving Bobby with a pistol. The family begins to be tormented by ragged desert-dwellers, who kill one dog. Bob returns to the gas station where the film opened and hears the backstory from the old man there. His wife was killed giving birth to an enormous male child, a "monster kid" who burned down their home, killing his own sister, and despite being beaten and left by the father in the desert to die, he "[stole] a whore nobody'd miss [...and] raised a pack of wild kids:" a "devil kid" becoming a "devil man" (Craven 00.31.00-00.32.00) The devil man bursts through the window, kills his father, and pursues Big Bob until he collapses.

Doug having returned, the family goes to bed (Doug and Lynne have sexual intercourse) only to be awakened by a conflagration: some distance from the crashed wagon-and-trailer Big Bob has been crucified to a tree and is being burned alive, which serves to distract the menfolk while the wild kids, one a sort of mutant, attack the trailer. They shoot Ethel in the stomach, kill Lynne with a gunshot to the head, rape Brenda, and kidnap the infant. Bobby and Brenda lure the devil-man to the trailer using their now-dead mother as bait and blow it up with gas canisters and matches. Doug, aided by the remaining dog and a turncoat girl from the desert family, pursues and kills the rest of them before they can make good on their stated intention to kill and eat the baby.

Respectable mainstream movies like *Ordinary People* or *Kramer vs Kramer* may dramatize fears of inter-familial conflict with greater emotional impact through techniques of realist drama, but the horror film's projection of an exaggerated evil, which must be in some way metaphorically legible, offers its own interpretive meat for critical inspection (Keeler; Sobchak 185-87). Kendrick describes *The Hills Have Eyes* as a film that depicts "deviant family practices" as a "transgressive critique of dominant ideology" accomplished through a "parody of the traditional American family." This element of transgression in violent horror cinema operates by "exposing that which should be hidden, which threatens the proper social order" (*Film* 86-87). Wood describes this exposure as the cinematic construction of a monstrous Other, whose "Otherness represents that which bourgeois ideology cannot recognize or accept" (73).

He quotes *The Hills Have Eyes* director Wes Craven: "The family is the best microcosm to work with [...] A lot of things were not spoken or talked about. If there was argument it was immediately denied. If there was a feeling it was repressed. As I got older, I began to see that as a nation we were doing the same thing" (qtd. in Wood 129). He also mentions a moral failure to confront the realities of the Vietnam War. The representation of the family in *The Hills Have Eyes* is critically engaged in this manner; as one student of a horror seminar observed, in the words of her professor, "the values of the American family in the film (and, by extension, potentially her own family) were inordinately disturbing" (Derry 168). The family is made representative of the nation through the use of the then-president's name, and the proximate cause of the car accident that leads to their deaths is the Air Force flying low over the bombing range, a sort of "bringing the war home," as the Weather Underground had put it in 1969.[2] There are also moments of inter-generational friction between Ethel and Brenda. However, these elements are overwhelmed by the representational totality of the text, such that the reference to war is merely an exterior distraction that puts the family in the position of being attacked by the devil-family.

In another interview, the director claims the film is about intra-familial conflict, through a mirror-image in the text, to the point that each member of one family had an analogue in the other and that the two families act in exactly the same ways. The first point is suggested by some character features, like Big Bob and Papa Jupiter's patriarchal authority, and the second by clear structural equivalencies, like the matched patriarchs dying by fire. Craven conflates the graphic violence enacted onscreen by the two families (Sharrett and Craven 142-43), but structural symmetry can't bridge gaps between rape and consensual sex, or between murder/kidnapping and self-defense. The critical equivalence is not present in the text. Although familial tensions frequently elided are put into the open, neither the family nor their values are the antagonists. Flawed they may be, but they are finally moral, civilized, white Americans pushed to savage violence against a monstrous Other in the name of vengeance and survival.

The Carters' eventual violence affirms dominant cultural ideology by re-establishing the proper social order in the middle-class family, proclaimed by the tagline of the film: "A nice American family. They don't want to kill. But they don't want to die" ("The Hills," Internet Movie Database). Inasmuch as this rhetoric sums up the American fantasy of righteous and deadly victimhood from the Massachusetts Bay Colony to George Zimmerman, Craven's film is a further entry in the crowded field of cultural artifacts that display the narrative structure described in Richard Slotkin's 1973 *Regeneration through Violence*, in which the hero becomes his enemy and, through that becoming, vanquishes the other that threatens to destroy him (Slotkin 55, 91, 119, 132-41). *The Hills Have Eyes* presents this deep structure of American cultural production in a far less sophisticated form, but the final image of the son-in-law/father turning blood-red as he stabs his evil analogue to death with that Other's own homemade knife fits Slotkin's cultural analysis primitively but perfectly.

Frontier mythology is represented in Craven's family-centric 1977 work through an iconography of "the sixties." The tensions of familial intergenerational conflict were famously sensationalized by the mainstream-media-hippie Jerry Rubin with

---

2   In the 2006 remake this gesture of critical engagement is lost, as the mutant cannibals themselves cause the crash.

his 1968 remark that "Until you're prepared to kill your parents, you're not really prepared to change the country" (qtd. in Bates, 175). *The Hills Have Eyes* does present some elements of transgressional ideological negotiation along these lines, in that the parents are killed, in the burning of their bodies, and the use of the mother as bait. Indeed, the "kill your parents" slogan version of Rubin's quote is invoked five times over: first in exposition as backstory, then literally, as Jupiter kills his own father, and three more times metaphorically as the group kills the nationally symbolic patriarch of the nice American family, his wife, and his daughter, herself a mother.

However, savagery is forced on the protagonists, whose imperfect but essentially sound family relationships are established through their dinner scene and prayer circle. The violence is initiated entirely by the antagonists. These Others are represented as hippies through various devices, like their astrological names, Jupiter, Mercury, Mars, and Pluto, which signify not only as a 1970s "swinging liberal" cliché, but also as a reference to the lyrics of the song Age of Aquarius from the musical *Hair*. Jupiter is indeed aligned with Mars: Jupiter and Mars are the leaders of the band, made clear when the former burns Big Bob while the latter leads the assault on the women in the trailer. The matriarch is called only "Mama," which, along with her turquoise amulet, earth-mother wardrobe, and relationship to "Papa" Jupiter, evokes both counterculture slang and The Mamas and the Papas of California Dreaming fame – and the Carter family is dreaming of a California vacation.

While Craven has claimed that the inspiration for the antagonists in his film was a medieval Scottish outlaw band (Cook 230-31), many textual elements on display refer, intentionally or not, to the Manson Family (a successful television miniseries about Manson had aired in April of 1976, a few months before shooting began on Craven's film). The evil killer hippie motif alone would be enough to create that association, given the perception of Manson and his followers as a representation of the death of sixties idealism and a general indictment of the counterculture, but specific details support the analogy. The harsh desert setting recalls the Family's Death Valley redoubt (the shooting location was due south across the Mojave); the use of walkie-talkies, highlighted in the film, was part of the Family's defensive measures; Jupiter's buckskin outfit resembles the cult leader's own; and, perhaps most evocatively, the antagonists repeatedly use the word "pigs" to describe the Carters. The Pig as phrase is not only associated with sixties iconoclasm and rebellion but was a specific obsession of Manson and his "children," appearing scrawled in blood at their three known murder sites. Manson also self-servingly emphasized the interpretation that his followers were society's lost children acting out a metaphorically social parricide (Sanders, *passim*).

Other textual elements, like the name of the family, Bobby's Ohio State t-shirt, and the Airstream trailer, and character details, like Ethel's religiosity and Big Bob's former job as a police officer, identify the protagonists as "nice America," a class and social identity closely resembling broader celebratory elements of 1970s popular culture. Doug, whose longish-hair-with-moustache-and-sideburns mark him as the token liberal, clashes trivially with his father-in-law, who gripes about African-Americans and about his flighty wife, which, along with the extended, more-than-nuclear inclusiveness of the family unit, cannot help but refer, in 1977, to the popular sitcom *All in the Family*. In short, they are *the* American family, representing the white middle-class "silent majority" under attack by forces identified with the counterculture. *The Hills Have Eyes* is a conservative narrative writ over-large, of cannibal mutant hippies-gone-Red-Indian destroying religious, patriarchal, and parental authority, undermining the family, defiling one's daughters, and eating one's babies.

Thus, generically, Craven's text is really a western. Christopher Sharrett at *Literature/Film Comment* calls it an "anti-western," and believes that Craven has employed "renovated conventions from the Western and melodrama" (139, 146), but these conventions are the same as ever. As Tag Gallagher has observed with regard to the Western, the ever-recurring renovations in genres tend to be based on changes in the features of film production overall, so that the structural syntax of the genre remains consistent even if certain semantic features may change (267-68; Altman 34-35, 38); Craven recognizes that in the interview, calling the story not an anti-but a "modern Western." Utilizing Vladimir Propp's functional analysis of folktales as a model, Will Wright has identified recurring structural motifs in the Western genre, and the action of *The Hills Have Eyes* corresponds to the two indispensable functional sequences characteristic of his "vengeance" sub-type: "weakness" then "fight." Of the films discussed by Wright that follow the vengeance pattern, the most similar is 1956's *The Searchers* (155-57, 161; Katz, 97).

The attack on Big Bob, a distraction to facilitate the attack on the trailer of vulnerable women, is a plot development identical to the Comanche diversion-and-attack that kicks off the story of *The Searchers*, and the subsequent rape and murder of one of John Wayne's abducted nieces is his motivation for vengeance (Ford). Wright found that in this functional sequence the weakness stage wherein an attack is suffered tends to be associated with the feminine, as is the attack suffered by the Carter family women in their house-on-wheels. The climactic appropriative and regenerative victory in *The Searchers* comes when John Wayne scalps his indigenous adversary after his brother-in-law killed him, a broadly rendered enactment of Slotkin's frontier mythology: film scholar Douglas Pye insists on this reading, saying that film "is about America – a symbolic representation of the American psyche – as one might discuss the Leatherstocking tales or Moby Dick" (216). Doug's frenzied stabbing makes the appropriative/regenerative point with transgressive violence comparable to Wayne's.

Big Bob has a pointed monologue in which he complains of life as a cop in Cleveland where "niggers shoot arrows at me," (Craven 00.11.48) compressing intertextual allusions into a foreshadowing synecdoche that evokes a modernized Western theme and highlights the most important feature of the symbolic nice American family, its whiteness. This phrase recalls the film's forefathers in settler-colonial narratives and declares the film's politics as conservative/reactionary by asking the audience to identify with the protagonists on the basis of their whiteness, racializing the antagonists. Craven's text is ultimately about the white family under threat from exterior forces, a threat represented by and defeated by extremes of graphically depicted violence.

Not only the syntax but also the semantics of the Western dominate the film. The wagon with a broken axle, the hostile wilderness, the wild men using animal calls, the animal-hide costumes, the kidnapped child, the female captive yearning for civilization, the initial westward movement, the search for a silver mine, and the rape by savages, all hearken back to Western tropes. Cannibalism has been projected onto indigenous Americans as part of settler-colonial narratives of moral and racial superiority, and its use in the film further qualifies the Carter family as representative of the national and historical project of white-supremacist manifest destiny that classic texts like *The Searchers* frequently celebrate, and that the social upheavals of the 1960s and malaise of the 1970s seemed to call into question.

Craven's film deploys the genre tropes of horror in two ways: its treatment of graphic violence, and its identification of the antagonists as devilish and monstrous. Wood classifies the characterization of horror monsters as simply evil, especially when that evil is ascribed to the devil, as the first of the four features that define his reactionary genre text. Even without the literal reference to the devil, the lack of any character qualities except bloodlust in the cannibal family satisfies his rubric (83). James Baldwin, discussing *The Exorcist*, makes the same point: "The mindless and hysterical banality of the evil presented [...] is the most terrifying thing about the film. The Americans [...] know more about evil than that; if they pretend otherwise, they are lying" (122).

He also specifies how this lie encompasses a denial of the "ruined earth of Vietnam" (116), precisely the flashpoint for the most substantial generational conflict of the era, also specifically mentioned by Craven as influencing his representation of the American family in crisis. Craven and Sharrett link these points and those discussed above in the previously quoted interview:

Question: But the importance of [...] *The Hills Have Eyes* – and other horror films of the 70s – resides at least in part in the way they reflect a specific outrage and pessimism about the traditional view of the family, the frontier, the whole civilizing experience as previously portrayed in film.

Craven: Oh yes, certainly the traditional vision has changed [...] I do believe in the family [...] American myth as previously conceived – John Wayne [...] the flag, good guys vs. bad guys – all this has to die, because as it is applied to the real world it clearly doesn't make it; it's failing every time. It didn't make it in Vietnam [...] The basic working model for a lot of us making horror films comes almost out of Mao Tse-Tung. I mean, no one is that rigid in their thinking, but it does become a question of a few people who aren't in the mainstream [...] do[ing] things on a very, very small budget, hitting and moving on (145-46).

It is highly ironic that the director produced a text that formally replicates the American myth as previously conceived – John Wayne included – while representing its monstrous family in ways that intertextually mark the Other with the signs of the counterculture with which he identifies. One might well say of Craven's 1977 film that it had to destroy the family in order to save it.

The remaining horror-genre feature of *The Hills Have Eyes*, its graphic violence, is finally the only locus of the "outrage and pessimism about the traditional view" that "has to die," represented by the attack on the Carter family. Such genre violence played its own role in the cultural conflicts of the period: *Variety* reviewed *Night of the Living Dead* (1968) with moralizing alarm: "The film casts serious aspersions on the integrity of its makers, distrib[utor] Walter Reade, the film industry as a whole and exhib[itor]s who book the pic, as well as raising doubts about [...] the moral health of filmgoers who cheerfully opt for unrelieved sadism" (qtd. in Kendrick *Film* 117n12). Low-budget graphic violence, shown without technique, like the aforementioned 19[th] century *Shooting Captured Insurgents*, was seen as inherently transgressive in an ideological sense.

However, graphic violence, whether or not transgressively opening space for ideological negotiation, was expressed through new kinds of distancing techniques as it became mainstream. *Bonnie and Clyde* showed its apocalyptic finale in slow motion, and *The Wild Bunch* used an incredibly dense montage to present its climactic bloody shoot-out (Kendrick, *Film* 59-60; *Hollywood* 45-47). 1976's *The Godfather* presented realistic murders in the context of lush cinematography and operatic, high-concept storytelling to become the most financially profitable studio film up to its time (Kendrick, *Hollywood* 48). The high production values that were unavailable to the independent horror film provided viewers a new kind of substitutional poetics. As Thomas Atkins says in a 1976 study of cinema violence, "despite the demise of the Code, popular hits like *The Godfather* use the same tactic of appeasing conventional morality while appealing to fundamental but often unacknowledged emotions and fantasies of the audience" (Atkins 8). These stylized violations of classic-text aesthetics came to be seen as a mark of auteurish innovation, and a spur to the kind of progressive break discussed by scholars. This interpretation was not limited to academia, as shown by Pauline Kael's review of *Bonnie and Clyde*: "But people also feel uncomfortable about the violence, and here I think they're wrong. That is to say, they *should* feel uncomfortable [...] The dirty reality of death – not suggestions but blood and holes – is necessary. It is a kind of violence that says something to us [...] in the last few years, our view of the world has gone beyond 'good taste'."

There are no distancing techniques – no "good taste" – in the bargain-base-ment productions of independent horror films, particularly Craven's first films. He was a completely unschooled filmmaker with no auteurish traits and there are no stylized cinematic flourishes. The representation of violence in *The Hills Have Eyes* is devoid of the new substitutional poetics just as much as the old, and only the graphic quality of the violence sets it apart from that of the classic text. Out to kill off the traditional familial and social pieties, the self-styled cultural revolutionary, hit-and-run filmmaker kills the parents as a representation of cultural tension, but because of the formal conventionality of the text, the attack on the Carter family is the only potentially transgressive scene in the film. The technique-free direct-ness gives the attack-on-the-family scene a transgressive veneer, but functionally the attack empowers John-Wayne revenge and the re-establishment of family sta-bility, so that only the visceral effect of its brutally raw representation of violence could be the source of the ideological critique assumed to be present by Craven, *Literature/Film Quarterly*, and others. In the intertextual field of American cultural production, in the last analysis the film is a bare-bones, "counterculture" version of *The Searchers*, with rape and murder not offscreen but right in the viewer's face as a dirty reality. Graphic violence in the arts may be necessary, but some may be disquieted to consider that American culture produces and consumes images of rape and murder in the name of conventional morality.

Kael's reference to the Production Code and her taste for New Hollywood au-teurs presaged the terms by which the dirty reality of death would become block-buster cinema: the departure from classic-text formal limitations would be man-aged by cultural arbiters and produced by the major studios. Discussing the rise of the slasher subgenre from 1979-1981, Vera Dika points out the congruence be-tween the politics of the slasher and the broader shift in Hollywood films away from the facade of liberal consensus and critically engaged social commentary that had characterized the previous decade (Cook xvi): "After the humiliation, pain, loss, and guilt of Vietnam, with the Reagan presidency came the finalization of an al-ready ongoing process that tended to reverse the ideals, aspirations, and attitudes of the 1960s," and the slasher films, like *The Hills Have Eyes*, thus "demonstrate the inefficacy of sexual freedom, of casual, non-goal-oriented activity, and of a non-violent attitude" (97-99). As Cook remarks, Craven's career arc itself mimics the mainstream studio recuperation of unclassical techniques as Hollywood "turned increasingly toward exploitation tactics at the level of both production and distri-bution," in that the director moved from no-budget exploitation with *Last House on the Left* in 1972, to the glossy mainstream-horror production *Nightmare on Elm Street* in 1984 (232). The latter series' evolution, in the course of which the monstrous-other antagonist became a wisecracking anti-hero protagonist, reproduces in microcosm the shift toward graphically violent Hollywood heroes in the action genre in the 1980s (Kendrick, *Hollywood* 79-105, 134), an industry-wide recuperation of representations of violence that had disturbed audiences in the late 1960s and 1970s.

The familial representation of socio-cultural unease in the horror genre of the 1970s has seen its qualities of rupture with dominant ideologies diluted and obscured by such recuperations, especially to the extent that discursive transgression depends on graphic violence. The issues forcing such ruptures have not gone away, even if the reception of cinematic production, most specifically horror films, has given rise to a solipsism (Kendrick, *Hollywood* 153-55) wherein those issues are no longer presented in ideologically challenging forms: The 1984 sequel to *The Hills Have Eyes* is derivative of the first film, the 2006 remake is narrative-functionally identical to the original, and the 2007 sequel to that remake replays the action as a military, not familial, crisis. Such recuperation of a representational strategy might offer a warning to any would-be cultural neo-Maoists fetishizing violence as a gesture of protest.

Bibliography

Altman, Rick. "A Semantic/Structural Approach to Film Genre." *Film Genre Reader III*, edited by Barry Keith Grant, U of Texas P, 2003, pp. 27-41.

Atkins, Thomas R. "Introduction." *Graphic Violence on the Screen*, edited by Thomas R. Atkins, Monarch P, 1976, pp. 5-18.

Baldwin, James. *The Devil Finds Work*. Dial P, 1976.

Bates, Milton J. *The Wars We Took to Vietnam: Cultural Conflicts and Storytelling*. U of California P, 1996.

Berenstein, Rhona J. *Attack of the Leading Ladies: Gender, Sexuality, and Spectatorship in Classic Horror Cinema*. Columbia UP, 1996.

Bernard, Mark. "Cannibalism, Class, and Power: a Foodways Analysis of the Texas Chainsaw Massacre Series." *Food, Culture, and Society*, vol. 14, no. 3, 2011, pp. 413-32.

Bourdieu, Pierre. *The Field of Cultural Production: Essays on Art and Literature*. U of Columbia P, 1984.

Cook, David A. *Lost Illusions: American Cinema in the Shadow of Watergate and Vietnam*. Scribners, 2000.

Derry, Charles. "More Dark Dreams: Some Notes on the Modern Horror Film." *American Horrors*, edited by Gregory A. Waller, U of Illinois P, 1987, pp. 162-74.

Dika, Vera. "The Stalker Film, 1979-1981." *American Horrors: Essays on the Modern American Horror Film*, edited by Gregory A. Waller, U of Illinois P, 1987, pp. 86-101.

Gallagher, Tag. "Shoot-Out at the Genre Corral: Problems in the Evolution of the Western." *Film Genre Reader III*, edited by Barry Keith Grant, U of Texas P, 2003, pp. 262-86.

The Hills Have Eyes. Internet Movie Database, www.imdb.com/title/tt0077681/. Accessed 7 Oct. 2019.

Kael, Pauline. "Bonnie and Clyde." *The New Yorker*, 29 Oct. 1967, www.newyorker.com/magazine/1967/10/21/bonnie-and-clyde. Accessed 7 Oct. 2019.

Katz, Thomas. "The Structural Influence: New Directions in Film Study." *Film Genre Reader III*, edited by Barry Keith Grant, U of Texas P, 2003, pp. 92-102.

Keeler, Greg. "*The Shining*: Ted Kramer Has a Nightmare." *Journal of Popular Film and Television Studies*, no. 8, 1981, pp. 2-8.

Kendrick, James. *Film Violence: History, Ideology, Genre*. Wallflower, 2009.

—. *Hollywood Bloodshed: Violence in 1980s American Cinema*. Southern Illinois UP, 2009.

Klinger, Barbara. "Cinema/Ideology/Criticism Revisited: The Progressive Genre." *Film Genre Reader III*, edited by Barry Keith Grant, U of Texas P, 2003, pp. 75-91.

Prince, Steven. *Classical Film Violence: Designing and Regulating Brutality in Hollywood Cinema, 1930-1968*. Rutgers UP, 2003.

Pye, Douglas. "The Western Genre and Movies." *Film Genre Reader III*, edited by Barry Keith Grant, U of Texas P, 2003, pp. 203-18.

Sanders, Ed. *The Family*. 3rd ed. Hachette Books, 2002.

Sharrett, Christopher, and Wes Craven. "'Fairytales for the Apocalypse': Wes Craven on the Horror Film." *Literature/Film Quarterly*, vol. 13, no. 3, 1985, pp. 139-47.

Slotkin, Richard. *Regeneration Through Violence: The Mythology of the American Frontier, 1800-1860*. Wesleyan UP, 1973.

Sobchak, Vivian. "Bringing It All Back Home: Family Economy and Generic Exchange." *American Horrors: Essays on the Modern American Horror Film*, edited by Gregory A. Waller, U of Illinois P, 1987, pp. 175-94.

Wood, Robin. *Hollywood from Vietnam to Reagan*. U of Columbia P, 1986.

Wright, Judith Hess. "Genre Films and the Status Quo." *Film Genre Reader III*, edited by Barry Keith Grant, U of Texas P, 2003, pp. 41-79.

Wright, Will. *Sixguns and Society: A Structural Study of the Western*. U of California P, 1975.

Filmography

The Hills Have Eyes Collection, directed by Wes Craven et al., 1977; 1985; 2006; 2007. Twentieth Century Fox, 2009.

The Searchers, directed by John Ford, 1956. Warner Home Video, 1997.

Kinship at the Margins
Punk-Rock Modes of (Dis-)Association

Stefano Morello, The Graduate Center (CUNY)

Following two decades of social turmoil, Ronald Reagan's presidencies (1981-89) revived fantasies of innocent bliss enjoyed by white America in the 1950s. Reaganomics, conservative morality, and a return to traditional family values were to restore the integrity of a national project that had been disrupted by the political and social uprisings that shaped the previous two decades. Needless to say, just as the 1950s myth never really squared with reality, neither did the depiction of itself that America painted during the conservative ascendancy of the 1980s. Despite economic and technological flourishing, polarization and social fragmentation skyrocketed throughout the decade and well into the 1990s (Hartman; Hunter).

While we are accustomed to media representations of the 1980s that celebrate the abundance of the era, boost narratives of American heroism, and praise the quest for independence of suburban white teenagers (Hoberman),[1] turning to the lived experiences of marginalized subjects and their cultural production allows for the emergence of a set of dissonant narratives. Subcultural formations such as hip hop and punk-rock stemmed as allergic reactions to both the logics of consumer culture and previous subcultures to propose otherwise and oppositional modes of cultural production. In this essay, I am interested in exploring punk's rejection of the myth of the nuclear family – as produced by, as well as producing and repro-ducing, a national project – in favor of alternative modes of kinship,[2] togetherness, and solidarity. To explore what I call punk kinship, I turn to an ephemeral and eclectic archive that depicts communal living in punk houses, dwellings occupied

---

1   See, among others, *Wall Street* (1987), *Top Gun* (1986), the *Die Hard* and *Indiana Jones* estates, *Risky Business* (1983), and just about every John Hughes comedy from the era.

2   In line with thinkers such as Kath Weston, Margaret K. Nelson, and Dawn O. Braithwaite, whose scholarship is also deeply engaged with the subject of kinship, I am reluctant to use the expression "fictive kinship." Despite being a term of choice in the field of anthropology, the adjective "fictive" prefigures consanguineal and legal kinship as natural, as opposed to chosen kinship as fictional, already foreclosing the authenticity of extra-familial and tran-sient modes of belonging, care, and solidarity.

by punks where domesticity is subverted and subcultural participants collectively create alternative worlds, modes of sociality, and forms of desire.

I

A paperboy on his bicycle. White collar workers *en route* to the office. A family walking into their new suburban home. A young couple at the altar, fulfilling every-parent-in-America's fantasy. Campers raising the flag in front of daydreaming children. It's 1984 and, in one of the most popular political campaign ads in US history, imagery reminiscent of 1950s American sitcoms such as *Father Knows Best* and *Leave it to Beaver* is rendered to the music of sentimental strings. The montage evokes a sense of nostalgia for the middle-class tranquility, prosperity, and sense of the possible that preceded the social and political unrests of the countercultural revolution. The voice-over narrator, ad man Hal Riney, boosts Ronald Reagan's alleged accomplishments in his first presidential term: unprecedented purchasing power, record employment levels, and low inflation are associated with high marriage rates and framed as the gateway to a prosperous future for young Americans ("Prouder, Stronger, Better"). Despite the fantasies projected by Reagan's campaign, the reality behind this façade is much less sunny.

Throughout the decade, rising averages obscured increasing economic and social polarization. While some families made gains in living standards, these gains were not distributed evenly. High-income households enjoyed above average financial growth, while incomes of low-income families stagnated or declined. In other words, the rich grew richer, but the poor grew poorer (Bradbury 25). One of the most immediate consequences was that it became more difficult for younger generations to achieve the house in the suburbs that had been an integral part of the postwar American dream. Affordable rentals were no easier to come by. By 1987, as a consequence of neoliberal policies, more than a third of American households were "shelter poor," unable to buy enough food, clothes, and other necessities after paying for their housing (Coontz, *The Way We Never Were* 262). Furthermore, in accordance with Reagan's less-government intervention views, domestic welfare spending – including Social Security, Medicaid, Food Stamps, and federal education programs – was cut or experienced periods of reduced funding throughout his presidencies. A shrinking state added more weight on the shoulders of existing networks of care and especially family units that had become increasingly fragile due to both increasing divorce rates and a post-war shift from bigger and interconnected extended households to smaller and detached nuclear families. A combination of falling incomes, deteriorating social capital, and cutbacks in public support programs fostered a growing sense of alienation and discontent among both, new and older generations. On the one hand, family and community relations became harder to maintain, as more household members worked longer hours to keep up with the Joneses at a time when inflation hit record highs. On the other hand, family and community were further burdened with the weight of being sole sources of support in the shift away from public welfare and toward private networks of economic relief.[3]

As Stephanie Coontz has observed, across the 1980s and through the '90s, "the 'crisis of the family' became the key to explaining the paradox of poverty amid plenty, alienation in the midst of abundance" ("On the Edge"). The perennial epidemic of family breakdown was, and still is, often identified as the major cause of poverty and inequality in the United States, with discourses around divorce and single motherhood relying on racialized and gendered narratives, of which the Reaganite myth of the "Welfare Queen" is a prime example. For the state, the family is a critical resource due to its central role in the social reproduction of the economic structure that sustains the cheery, white, heteronormative middle-class version of palatable patriarchy in which Reaganite fantasies are steeped. As Cindi Katz and others have proposed, drawing from Marx's *Das Kapital*, the family – together with the state, the workplace, and the institutions of civil society – is one of the central sites where most of the social relations and material bases of capitalism are produced and reproduced (712). If that is the case, for individuals and communities who are not left "Prouder, Stronger, Better," as the title of Reagan's ad proposes, by the tyranny of success of liberalism, a loud rejection of the nuclear family model and a disruption of its underlying logics of individualism represented a mode of resistance that mimicked the sonic interruption that punk, as a music genre, produced.

II

It is hardly surprising that, ever since punk's early days, the family, like all institutions, became a target of its histrionic critique of normativity. In 1982, *We Destroy the Family*, a five-part documentary on punk-rock's alleged deleterious effects on youth and society aired on Los Angeles' KABC News. The show alternates live footage from punk shows to interviews with subcultural participants, concerned parents, and Serena Dank, founder of Parents of Punkers, a group whose work focuses on bridging the gap between generations. Punk antics, fashion, lyrics are deployed and juxtaposed to images of suburban homes, aiming to produce a semantic cacophony, capitalize on the subculture's spectacle, and feed moral and social panic to the audience. The show opens with Lee Ving, singer for Fear, reciting to the

---

3   See Maurizio Vaudagna's contribution in this volume on America and welfare politics, especially between Reagan and Trump.

camera the lyrics to the band's track that gives the show its title: "Steal the money from your mother/Buy a gun/We destroy the family/Kill your mother/and father/we destroy the family." With a quasi-childlike smile, Vinn asks to an amused camera-woman, "Isn't that nice?" The show then cuts to a live performance of the song and scenes of bodies flying across the stage – young punks slam dancing, moshing, crowdsurfing – while the host, Paul Moyer, suggests that "this is not just another foolish teenage fad" but a daily crisis and a "frightening subculture." As the show unfolds, it becomes clear that the parents, as well as Moyer himself, are blaming the teenagers for the structural dysfunctions of their households. The possibility that the tendencies manifested by the adults – lack of empathy, burdensome parental projections, loveless marriages, and evident inability to cope with the major shifts that occurred in American culture and society in the previous two decades – could be the causes of the kids' rebellion is hardly entertained. Both the rhetoric of the show and its literal repurposing of punk texts and imagery fall in line with the wave of hysteria that, according to Dick Hebdige, characterizes early media coverage of youth subcultures – a process that eventually leads the symbolic challenges posed by subversive communities to be trivialized, naturalized, or domesticated as part of a transaction into commercial and ideological incorporation (92-99).

Penelope Spheeris' 1981 documentary *The Decline of Western Civilization* – also featuring Fear, among other bands such as Black Flag, the Germs, X, Alice Bag Band, the Circle Jerks, and Catholic Discipline – provides a more nuanced testimony of punk subcultural belonging. Spheeris' film covers the daily happenings at the Canterbury Apartments in Los Angeles, one of the focal points of the scene in the late 1970s and early 1980s. The Hollywood depicted by *The Decline* is far removed from the larger than life American dream incubator personified by the movie-star-turned-president figure. At the Canterbury, punks from across gender, generational, race, and class lines live alongside other marginalized communities. Residing in undesirable urban areas, occupying spaces in the margin, with complete disregard of living, social, and sanitary standards, serves as a symbolic rejection of domesticity, a disavowal of neoliberal bourgeoise ideology, and a disruption of its narratives of success. The gaze of the camera does not steer away from the oddities of the punks' lived performances: Darby Crash's interactions with his pet tarantula, a peanut butter and Jello sandwich in the making, the fury and *gobbing* at punk shows. However, beyond the performative nihilism and behind the self-caricatures punks draw *of* and *for* themselves, what emerges from the interplay among the interviewees (and between them and Spheeris) is the desire for a sense of belonging that many found in their shared rejection. On several occasions, José Muñoz has commented on the feeling of commonness fostered by that very subcultural space.

In the scene, people encountered one another in ways that felt new and unpredictable. They arrived at venues and stages where they could realize their plurality. And through punk as genre (or, more nearly, antigenre) they found a way to, in a sense, "pause" a temporal moment, allowing people hailed by a mode of negation associated with the outsider's trajectory, the space to find an otherwise elusive mode of being-with. ("Gimme Gimme This" 97)

The mode of negation invoked by Muñoz is one that functions as "a modality of the possible" (*Cruising Utopia* 12), one that, by rejecting the limited affordances of one's positionality, opens up to a range of previously unimagined possibilities. If punk is, as Greil Marcus would have it, a voice "that denied all social facts and that denial affirmed that everything was possible" (2), then its obliteration of the values and norms that *make* society produces "a regression to the infinite" (*Cruising Utopia* 12), a clean slate upon which a new world can be built.

In one of the most referenced studies on the subject, David Schneider argues against an understanding of kinship that rests solely upon consanguineal relationships, in favor of one based on performance. Social scientists, laments Schneider, have historically imposed an understanding of the world through a Euro-centric notion of kinship, one closely related to genealogy and upon which traditional understandings of "family" rest. However, the anthropologist suggests, some forms of kin-belonging are to be understood as a kind of *doing* restated over time, as a kind of iterative and performative act, rather than a product of qualities or legal ties alone (*A Critique* 72). While not all forms of subcultural belonging lead to kinship, punk modes of association are often born out of a common desire for disassociation from the dominant logics of the present social and political milieus. As subcultures often do, punk treats the everyday as a scene and exerts its political value of interruption from without, by embracing aesthetic and political practices, such as the antics and oddities documented in *The Decline*, deemed detrimental from within. Drawing from Schneider and Muñoz, I propose that punk kinship is always and inevitably grounded in a kind of iterative symbolic performance of negation, a kind of undoing – acts of communal conscious disruption, both on and off the stage.

III

Fast-forward to the late years of the Reagan presidency, zoom out of Southern California, and onto the eastern shores of the San Francisco Bay. In continuity with the countercultural movements of the previous decades, the local scene here has developed into the historical realization of a punk ideal: a sustainable and self-reliant community of dissensus rooted in territoriality and its own alternative institutions. The Gilman Street Projects is the epitome of the local punk-rock commons and its autonomous cultural apparatus. A non-profit, all-ages, collectively organized music venue, Gilman opened its doors in Berkeley in 1986 and has, ever since, hosted punk shows, art exhibits, speakers, poetry readings, plays, and other events. The club emerged as the epicenter of a punk scene informed by codified promises of inclusivity – No Homophobia, No Sexism, No Racism, No Alcohol, No Drugs, No Fighting – aimed to translate into practice the ideology that grew out of a generation that bristled at the macho hardcore scene that punk had become by the mid-1980s.

The story of Robert "Eggplant's" involvement with Gilman is the story of many-a-one kids in many-a-one punk scenes in America. In Eggplant's zine *Absolutely Zippo*, Lawrence Livermore sketches a profile of his two-decades younger fellow punk:

> Gilman Street was a whole new world. "I smiled a lot more, talked to a lot more people. Everyone was like me; they did not fit in either. But they were hungering for oneness, too. They wanted a feeling of community."
> Until then Eggplant's social life had centered around his parents and their friends. His dad was usually stoned on pot or speed or whatever was available. Life was a constant party, though not always a festive one. Eggplant remembers the time one of his dad's friends died in the living room from a morphine overdose.
> His mother lived nearby. On weekends she liked to take Eggplant to motorcycle races. Technically he was living with her, but that ended one weekend when she insisted that he come with her instead of going to the punk-rock show. "I called her from Gilman and said I wasn't coming home." ("A School Paper")

Through punk, Eggplant made his way out of Pinole, a suburban town 13 miles north of Berkeley, and into a life-shattering world of possibilities. At Gilman, he came into contact with other strange and estranged punks who enabled his ascent into underground publishing and music. By 1989, *Absolutely Zippo*, the punk-zine that he had started in the 9th grade as a 12 digest-sized page DIY publication, had evolved into 32 full-sized pages. Two years later, the zine reached a circulation of 2,000 copies and international distribution through Lookout Records, the label that Livermore and David Hayes had started in 1988 to document and distribute the local punk scene. Lookout also recorded and distributed Eggplant's band, Blatz. *Zippo*, like most zines, was a communal effort in both its material and literary production, including contributions by Aaron Cometbus, Michelle Cruz Gonzales, Billie Joe Armstrong, Jesse Michaels, and Livermore, among others. Stephen Duncombe has proposed that "in an era marked by the rapid centralization of corporate media, zines are independent and localized [...] They celebrate the every-person [...] in a society that rewards the best and the brightest" (7). Through music, publishing, and artmaking, punk enabled alternative forms of communication that allowed individuals to escape social fragmentation, while defying what is generally understood to be "work." Punks set out their labor as an antidote against the exploitation of the working class in favor of another's profit, while also challenging ever-increasing alienation by forging communities of singularities through their labor.

Figure 1. Robert Eggplant playing with Blatz at the Old Fang House in Oakland. October 21, 1990. Murray Bowles.

In his 1968 study of the symbolic meanings of kinship in American Culture, David Schneider identified in love, understood as "diffuse, enduring solidarity," its distinctive feature (*American Kinship* 51). Unable to perceive love in either (and sometimes neither) broken or authoritarian households, punks sought it and found it in alternative kin formations. Despite its negationism, solidarity and the desire for a different kind of community are the driving forces behind punk's very DIY ethos. Whether it's playing in a band, putting up shows, running a venue, editing a zine, or performing nihilism on stage (at which few acts can outplay Blatz), in punk, DIY is never a "do it yourself alone," but rather a "do it yourselves," a "do it collectively." Even though punk's promises of inclusivity have not always lived up to their expectations, individuals disillusioned with or unable to access, and sometimes even dream, the American dreams they were fed, turned to themselves, then to each other, and collectively crafted alternative worlds, modes of sociality, and forms of desire.

IV

At once experiments in communal living, music venues, social centers, and training grounds for radical community organizing, punk houses emerged from the legacy of hippie communes across the United States, and especially in the Bay Area. In the late 1960s, as baby boomers enacted a reverse White Flight, foregoing regular jobs and careers and leaving their parents' suburban dreams, Utopian communes arose in both rural and urban areas as attempts to exist outside of the hegemonic system. For both punks and hippies, communal living fostered artistic expressions that were key to their world-making praxis. Punk houses were one of the sites in which punks collectively imagined a world free from heteronormativity, imperialism, capitalism, racism, and governmental authority. In overcrowded and dilapidated houses, subcultural participants offered a new kind of prefigurative politics and articulated an already revolutionized society through their everyday social practices. Not unlike hippie communes, some punk houses were consciously structured, but far more common was the situation where young people wound up together in the same apartment or house and discovered they had become a family through a set of mutual practices and beliefs or, as Schneider would have it, through a kind of communal *doing*. Each punk house was different and developed its own culture, personality, and rules (or lack thereof) over time. While some had overriding ideologies that allowed them to flourish longer, many degenerated fast, when the balance between the desires to burn the world to the ground and to build one anew was tipped towards the former.

Regardless of their inner functioning, punk houses created the conditions of possibility for a punk life. In an era when wages for many did not suffice to own or rent a home, subcultural participants recurred to communal living. As seen with the Canterbury, punks crammed houses with occupancy that far exceeded their capacity. Doing so, they rejected the logics and imperatives of the time: living together – sometimes eight people in a two-bedroom apartment – and sharing resources allowed artists, anarchists, and intellectuals to live on a lower income, and hence work less and make time for community relations, self-education, DIY art making, and social protesting. Punk kin shared meals, money, and other assets, cared for each other in illness, spent holidays and created rituals together. Punk houses also made up for the lack of safe spaces where communal activities (such as making, rehearsing, and playing music, crafting zines, skateboarding, or just being with each other) could be carried out. By the 1990s, they had come to be nodal points of an autonomous cultural apparatus based on solidarity weaved by punks. In the East Bay, punk's subcultural infrastructure also comprised record labels, music venues, printing and merchandise companies, independent publications, radio programs, and even an alternative high school.

V

The Maxi-Pad was a 2-story punk house in North Oakland rented by three women in 1990. Kate Knox first conceived of establishing a house that functioned on the same premises as the European squats she had visited while on tour with the local band Fang. Its main operating principle was that the house would always be open to traveling and touring punks. Knox recounts: "There was one bathroom [...] and there were usually seven or eight people living there. We had bands staying in the living room. We had people tattooing out of the closet. At one point, I had 13 Germans staying in the attic" (Boulware and Tudor 357). While living at the Maxi-Pad, Knox ran Holden High School, an institution rooted in the alternative education movement of the 1960s, from which many punks graduated across the decades.[4] In her leisure time, she put on benefits for the school, attended punk shows, and organized protests against racism, the Gulf War, and anti-abortion laws, among other causes.

Adrienne Droogas and Michelle Cruz Gonzales, respectively vocalist and drummer of the all-women feminist hardcore punk band Spitboy, complemented Knox's vision.[5] Gonzales recalls: "we wanted a woman's house. [...] it's risky dating and living with someone because as soon as you break up, there's no place to live. We rented the Maxi-Pad to avoid all that" (Interview). Droogas also edited *Too Far*, a feminist zine that far pre-dates riot grrrl, the underground movement that, in the following years, became the symbol of punk's feminist awakening.

Punk houses' names contributed in inscribing these, often ephemeral, sites in the scene's own mythology. The name Maxi-Pad, not unlike the signifier "punk," aligned with the movement's provocative, aggressive, and parodistic aesthetics.[6] An obvious double-entendre pointing to both a large bachelor pad and a highly absorbent menstrual pad, the name was originally coined by artist Pete Inc and embraced by the trio, as Butler suggests, to "rework [...] abjection into political agency and thus as a kind of demanding resignification" (21).

At the Maxi-Pad, the three women set up a support system for daily life and created kinship through intimate intellectual, emotional, and embodied relationships. Like the politics of Spitboy, who in 1992 disassociated from riot grrrl's separatist practices (Gonzales, *The Spitboy Rule* 7-10), the prefigurative politics of the Maxi-Pad did not consist of creating a women-only safe space, but rather in providing a model of lived relationality that defied normative understandings of female

---

4   The school's name is an obvious homage to J.D. Salinger's icon of teenage rebellion and angst.

5   The band was named after a "female-body-centric creation story, a story that didn't involve god, a rib, or a man" from Anne Cameron's *Daughters of Copper Woman*, a retelling of northwest coast Native myths (Gonzales Interview).

6   On the etymology of "punk" see Tavia Nyong'o.

Figure 2. Gonzales, Droogas, and Knox at the Maxi-Pad, circa 1990. Michelle Cruz Gonzales.

friendship – favoring collaboration to the perceived competitiveness that informed female friendship outside of the scene (Knox) – patriarchal society, and the sexism of an inclusive, yet still mostly-male-dominated punk scene. Not only did the three women explicitly demand higher standards of language and behavior from men visiting or participating in the many social gatherings at the house, but also by mere mutual exposure, enabled the exploration of different kinds of social interactions and dialectics among genders.[7] Although the Maxi-Pad only lasted three

---

7   For example, every Sunday, the Maxi-Pad hosted Simpson's night – an informal gathering irregularly attended by dozens of punks, at a time when Matt Groening's irreverent animated sitcom had become a target of conservative politicians' critique for its celebration of everyday American failures and depiction of the nuclear family as flawed and dysfunctional. At the 1992 Republican National Convention in Houston, Texas, then-President George H. W. Bush, whose campaign platform had strongly relied on family values, insisted: "We are going to keep on trying to strengthen the American family, to make American families a lot more like the Waltons and a lot less like the Simpsons" (Office 1455).

years in its original configuration – the kin formations that ensued were starting blocks for future punk families.[8]

VI

As Knox recalls: "once part of the punk scene, once given the space to figure out who I was, and be accepted for it, the other side of the world stopped making sense from within" (Interview). In the topography of the East Bay, punk houses operated as counter sites, spaces to explore alternative forms of social relations, and, as such, cracks though the system. At a time when, as Michael Stewart Foley has argued, "free markets and individualisms overcame ideals of community mobilization and activist government" (4), punks created non-places where people came together and practiced being with each other; where people made time and space to understand themselves and their relationship with society; non-places in which one found oneself in spite of oneself, and where a multiplicity of singularities produced discord and noise, a collective plan, calls to disorder.[9]

At a time when the mainstream soundscape was monopolized by vapid MTV pop and television bombarded with nostalgic and cheery accounts of suburban family life, punk kinship fostered the development of alternative social worlds that offered new nurturing relationships, meaning-making practices, and a sense of belonging in an especially alienated and disillusioned youth. Punk's disavowal of traditional family structures is not to be read as a rejection of family values, but rather as a rejection of national values inevitably embodied by the figure of the parents, as both quintessential authority figures and makers of the present inherited. Similarly, punk kinship shows us that punk anti-sociality is but a negation of the dominant neoliberalist ideology that sees competition as the defining characteristic of human relations, but not of sociality altogether.[10] Through punk kinship, we learn to look at punk not only as a music genre, or as a youth subculture revolting through style, as Hebdige would have it, but also as a meeting ground for those rejected by society and those who reject it *as is*. As a mode of belonging in unbelonging, punk seeks alternative modes of lived care and relationality free from the self-perpetuating motives of capital and the nation.

---

8   For instance, in 1996, Knox founded B.O.B, a transnational collective that organizes punk festivals in Bath, Oakland, and Bremen, extending punk-kinship across transnational lines, and producing a kind of punk counter topography. As of 2019, members of the B.O.B. family, one made of hundreds of individuals, are debating how they will take care of each other in old age.

9   On "non-places" see Lefebvre (164-68).

10   On punk anti-sociality, see Muñoz ("Gimme Gimme This"), Nyong'o, and Halberstam (128-31).

Bibliography

Bradbury, Katharine. "The Changing Fortunes of American Families in the 1980s." *New England Economic Review*, July/August 1990, pp. 25-40.

Braithwaite, Dawn, et al. "Constructing Family: A Typology of Voluntary Kin." *Journal of Social and Personal Relationships*, vol. 27, no. 3, 2010, pp. 388-407.

Boulware, Jack, and Silke Tudor. *Gimme Something Better: The Profound, Progressive, and Occasionally Pointless History of Bay Area Punk from Dead Kennedys to Green Day*. Penguin, 2009.

Butler, Judith. *Bodies That Matter*. Routledge, 1993.

Coontz, Stephanie. *The Way We Never Were: American Families and the Nostalgia Trap*. Basic Books, 1992.

—. "On the Edge." *Chicago Tribune*, 11 Oct. 1992, https://www.chicagotribune.com/news/ct-xpm-1992-10-11-9204020356-story.html. Accessed 1 Nov. 2019.

Duncombe, Stephen. *Notes from Underground: Zines and the Politics of Alternative Culture*. Verso, 1997.

Foley, Michael S. *Front Porch Politics: The Forgotten Heyday of American Activism in the 1970s and 1980s*. Hill and Wang, 2013.

Gonzales, Michelle Cruz. *The Spitboy Rule: Tales of a Xicana in a Female Punk Band*. PM P, 2016.

—. Personal interview. 25 Oct. 2019.

Halberstam, Jack J. *The Queer Art of Failure*. Duke UP, 2011.

Hartman, Andrew. *A War for the Soul of America: A History of the Culture Wars*. The U of Chicago P, 2015.

Hunter, James Davison. *Culture Wars: The Struggle to Define America*. Basic Books, 1991.

Hebdige, Dick. *Subculture: The Meaning of Style*. Taylor & Francis, 1997.

Hoberman, J. *Make My Day: Movie Culture in the Age of Reagan*. The New P, 2019.

Katz, Cindi. "Vagabond Capitalism and the Necessity of Social Reproduction." *ANTIPODE*, vol. 33, 2001, pp. 709-28.

Lefebvre, Henri. *The Production of Space*. Blackwell, 1984.

Nelson, Margaret K. "Fictive Kin, Families We Choose, and Voluntary Kin: What Does the Discourse Tell Us?" *Journal of Family Theory & Review*, vol. 5, no. 4, 2013, pp. 259-81.

Knox, Kate. Personal interview. 26 Oct. 2019.

Livermore, Lawrence. "A School Paper." *Absolutely Zippo* [Zine], Robert Eggplant, Ed., 21, Berkeley, CA, 1995.

Marcus, Greil. *Lipstick Traces: A Secret History of the Twentieth Century*. Harvard UP, 1988.

Muñoz, José Esteban. *Cruising Utopia: The Then and There of Queer Futurity*. New York UP, 2009.

—. "'Gimme Gimme This... Gimme Gimme That'." *Social Text*, vol. 31, no. 3, 2013, pp. 95-110.

Nyong'o, Tavia. "Punk'd Theory." *Social Text*, vol. 23, no. 3-4, 2005, pp. 19-34.

—. "Do You Want Queer Theory (or Do You Want the Truth)? Intersections of Punk and Queer in the 1970s." *Radical History Review*, no. 100, 2008, pp. 103-19.

Office of the Federal Register, National Archives and Records Service, General Services Administration. "Remarks at the Bush-Quayle Welcoming Rally at the Republican National Convention in Houston, Texas." *Weekly Compilation of Presidential Documents*, 1992, pp. 1452-57.

"Prouder, Stronger, Better." Ronald Reagan and George Bush Presidential Campaign. 1984, www.livingroomcandidate.org/commercials/1984/prouderstronger-better. Accessed 1 Nov. 2019.

Schneider, David Murray. *American Kinship: A Cultural Account*. U of Chicago P, 1968.

—. *A Critique of the Study of Kinship*. U of Michigan P, 1984.

Spheeris, Penelope, dir. *The Decline of Western Civilization*. Shout! Factory, 1981.

Weston, Kath. *Families We Choose: Lesbians, Gays, Kinship*. Columbia UP, 1991.

Donald the Family Planner
How Disney Embraced Population Control

Andrea Carosso, Università di Torino

The Population Bomb

In the 1960s a new kind of fear spread across America: the idea that human population was outstripping the Earth's ability to support mankind and that dire consequences would ensue if swift action was not taken. Media reports warned that the US could be bursting out at the seams by the end of the century and that if America would not, by humane means, limit its population, then the population would be limited by famines and shortages and consequent social conflicts. The prophet of doom was Stanford entomologist Paul Ehrlich, who had an epiphany in the summer of 1966, when he visited with his wife the crowded streets of Delhi during a research trip to study butterflies. During that visit, Ehrlich came to formulate a very persuasive argument: "the underdeveloped countries of the world face an inevitable population-food crisis [as] each year food production in these countries falls a bit further behind burgeoning population growth" (Ehrlich 3). To put it in other words: on a finite planet with finite resources, you can't have infinite population growth.

Ehrlich laid out his hypothesis in a paperback entitled *The Population Bomb*, published in 1968. The book opens with a narrative of the Ehrlichs riding on a "stinking hot night" through a crowded slum area in Delhi teeming with "[p]eople eating, people washing, people sleeping. People visiting, arguing, and screaming. People thrusting their hands through the taxi window, begging. People defecating and urinating [...] People, people, people, people" (Ehrlich 1). To Ehrlich, this "disease of overpopulation" would eventually spur poor people to attempt "to overwhelm us in order to get what they consider to be their fair share" (Ehrlich 177, 128-29). Ehrlich's concern was shared by many. In 1968, he co-founded an organization called Zero Population Growth (ZPG, now Population Connection, which dubs itself "the largest grassroots population organization in the United States"), dedicated to the idea that population control begins at home, and called for population control for the United States, also by coercion if necessary (Connelly 248). Other groups and organizations were active in similar ways.

This paper discusses Disney's 1967 propaganda animation film *Family Planning* and contextualizes it within the fears of world overpopulation that Ehrlich's book graphically evoked. It looks at the ways in which women's rights advocates, neo-Malthusian activists and proponents of eugenics joined forces in post-World War II America to promote reproductive control campaigns, mostly aimed at third world subjects in key Cold War locales around the world and how Disney seamlessly integrated its pro-family agenda in campaigns aimed at establishing a global vision of what "family" should ultimately look like.

The Population Control Movement

As it turned out, Ehrlich was only the poster child of a much larger movement brewing underneath. He had written *The Population Bomb* at the suggestion of David Brower, the executive director of the Sierra Club, an environmental organization of considerable influence based in California, which at that time attempted, as its in-house publication has recently acknowledged, "to enact an anti-immigration agenda by trotting out the overpopulation bogeyman" (Bollay). When it was published, *The Population Bomb* spearheaded a crowded population control movement whose history went back at least 150 years to the theories of a British minister named Robert Malthus, whose *Essay on the Principle of Population*, published in 1797, had argued that societies should not interfere (e.g. though welfare programs) with the barriers that biology puts in place (in the form of famines and diseases) to prevent population from outstripping food production (see Franks 130).

The roots of the idea of overpopulation are complex. The concept had, in the words of Laura Briggs, "a tangled history born of politics, statistics, and struggles over professional legitimacy" (Briggs 81). Beginning with the early days of the British Malthusian League in the mid-19th century, birth control advocates had been spreading the notion that excess reproduction caused poverty. As historians have pointed out, these ideas were popularized in the United States beginning in the 1920s as two discrete groups, which had been separately promoting reproduction control under quite different agendas, began to join forces. Reformers associated with the birth control movement, or "neo-Malthusians" as they were called, closed ranks with the overlapping sciences of eugenics and population demography and gained new prominence. In the United States, population demography stressed class, racial, and geographical differences with respect to reproduction. Eugenicists such as Madison Grant who, concerned about low "Nordic" birth rates, spoke of "race suicide," and Lothrop Stoddard, whose *The Rising Tide of Color* (1921) described the collapse of white supremacy and colonialism due to population growth, and popularized a kind of reproductive racism according to which high birthrates among non-"Nordics" constituted a threat to America. Demographers, for their part, were concerned more about class than racial difference. The American birth control movement, which began in the early 1900s out of concerns by Margaret Sanger and her associates for women's welfare and rights of reproductive choice, shifted in focus over the decades from women's rights to controlling supposedly excessive birthrates. As Briggs has pointed out, "by 1937, the paradigm of reproduction as a significant form of racial, class-based, and geographic difference was firmly established," one that would bear significant consequences for US population policies both domestically and internationally (Briggs 82-83). The issue of overpopulation began to be seen as an international cause: the "unchecked reproduction" of more and more people around the world came to be perceived as a threat to international peace, as migrants began to flow out of poor and largely populated nations. At the 1927 World Population Conference in Geneva, ILO Director Albert Thomas suggested that the right of overpopulated nations to occupy underpopulated territories should be granted on the condition that they first try to solve their own population problems (Connelly 65-76).

From Population Control to Family Planning

As world population continued to grow through the years of the war and its aftermath, significant extensions of average lifespans were seen throughout the world thanks to the wide-scale adoption of life-saving medicines (antibiotics, vaccines) and the emergence of a baby boom in the West. These and the beginning of widespread migration patterns led demographers to associate population growth with increased dangers of new wars and famines (Connelly 115-16). In the years that immediately followed World War II, early intimations of a "population bomb" extended the atom bomb imaginary and intensified fears that the earth would soon be unlivable. The authority of the new international institutions emerging after the war was called upon in citing projections of future growth and focusing international attention on so-called "differential fertility," i.e. the fact that underprivileged social groups around the world were having too many children whereas the more affluent were having too few. This, combined with increasing migrations, was feared to cause a decline in the "quality of population" (Connelly 116).

The post-World War II period saw the emergence of a host of international initiatives – some under the jurisdiction of international organization, others stemming from national governments, others yet, especially in the US, emanating from private groups – tasked with specifically addressing world population and "family planning," an emerging concept promoting "family oriented" policies to improve and regulate reproductive choices. Every organization had its own history and its own approach to the problem and contradictory responses and solutions on the part of national and international bodies were the norm (Connelly 115-55). On the one hand, activists and governments in as diverse parts of the world as Sweden, India and Mexico were advocating international measures for limiting overpopulation. On the other, advocates and governments in just as diverse parts of the worlds (Lebanon, Ireland, Italy, just to name a few), coalescing around the Catholic Church, fiercely resisted the implementation of international measures. Standing in the middle, international organizations found themselves powerless to mediate any sort of compromise.

This is when a loosely-knit coalition of organizations, including philanthropic foundations and activist groups, emerged at the helm of the population movement. In the US, the Population Council and the Ford Foundation stood out among the former; the Population Crisis Committee and Planned Parenthood Federation of America were among the most prominent among the latter. Although divided over strategy, these organizations cooperated in an intense lobbying effort to involve the federal government in family planning. Ranging from groups promulgating a neo-Malthusian vision, such as the Population Crisis Committee, to organizations focusing on women's reproductive rights, such as Planned Parenthood, the population movement in America converged around the figure of John D. Rockefeller III, the grandson of the oil tycoon John D. Rockefeller and a major supporter of birth control.

In 1952, the same year that the International Planned Parenthood Federation was established thanks to the efforts of Margaret Sanger and her associates,[1] Rockefeller organized the Population Council, which he envisioned as a way of providing leadership to the population movement. The Council's stated aim was to support medical research into reproduction and to train demographers and population professionals who could be employed in the developing nations of the world. Joined by the Ford Foundation, the Population Council played a major role in establishing an international network of experts who shared a set of assumptions about overpopulation and technical intervention, loosely based on the idea that state-imposed family fertility control programs were the key to the rapid reduction of fertility in crisis areas such as Japan (which was undergoing at the time a major overpopulation problem) and elsewhere in Asia (Takeuchi-Demirci 147; Critchlow 4-5).

As the Baby Boom raged in America in the early 1950s, Hugh Moore, the founder of the Population Crisis Committee and a social scientist who believed that more coercive measures were needed to control the rate of population growth, undertook a campaign to educate the American public about the impending "population explosion." Influenced deeply by William Vogt, research director at Planned Parenthood of America, Moore saw world peace and population control as strictly connected. An entrepreneur who had amassed a huge fortune after co-founding

---

1   See Claudia Roesch in this volume on Planned Parenthood / Pro Familia in Germany during the 1980s.

the Dixie Cup Corporation, a company that early in the 20th century had pioneered the production of paper cups as a solution to the spreading of germs by people sharing glasses, Moore published the widely read pamphlet "The Population Explosion" in 1954. Moore warned of an immediate social and economic crisis caused by global overpopulation. Adopting Cold War terminology, he called for population control as a necessary tool to prevent the spread of communism in the newly-defined Third World – a category that had recently been broached in a famous article that French demographer Alfred Sauvy had written for a French weekly in August 1952. One decade later, it was to Moore's pamphlet that Ehrlich turned for inspiration to write *The Population Bomb*.

More in general, the population movement shared the belief that the post-war bonanza – a mixture of economic growth, international stability, and domestic tranquility – required keeping population growth in check. If, in the 1950s, the Eisenhower administration had avoided any involvement in population problems to avoid a backlash from US Catholic bishops, under the Johnson administration the population lobby's efforts to shift American policy toward family planning assistance domestically and internationally began to produce results. As part of the Great Society policy, domestic population stability came to be understood as essential to addressing an array of social problems, including poverty, welfare, crime, urban decay, and pollution (Critchlow 5). Family planning became closely linked with the War on Poverty, and the newly instituted Deputy Assistant Secretary for Population relied on Planned Parenthood, the Population Council, and the Ford Foundation to set up family planning clinics and demonstration programs (Critchlow 6). The Population Council, in particular, was tasked to address world overpopulation, at a time when the atmosphere of alarm, even hysteria, surrounding the population issue made coercive policies seem inevitable, as Ehrlich's book and ZPG would soon persuasively advocate.

Calling on Disney

In the 1960s, initiatives to persuade "third world" countries to control their ever-growing families multiplied. In India, the Ford Foundation aimed at making "people ashamed of having more than three children." All over the world, posters, films, flip charts, and folk performances depicted the "unplanned family" as unclean, unhealthy, violent, and ugly. Ever focused on reducing global population, particularly in developing countries, the Population Council's president Bernard Berelson published a paper in 1969 entitled "Beyond Family Planning" in which, citing Ehrlich, he suggested "mass use of [a] 'fertility control agent' by government" in the water supplies of urban areas (Roberts 147).

In 1967, the Population Council decided to commission a documentary to be used in developing nations to raise awareness among farmers of the dangers of overpopulation, and explain the existence of contraceptive solutions for family planning. To produce the documentary, the Council called on Disney, a now global entertainment company whose expertise in animated and documentary filmmaking, including propaganda and public health campaigns, would prove a useful asset. During the war, Disney had received a government contract to make 32 patriotic propaganda films aimed at getting Americans behind the war effort. Some of these films attracted immediate criticism: *Victory Through Air Power*, the most controversial of all, was designed to support the theory of the "effectiveness" of bombing population centers (Dorfman and Mattelart 19). Between 1941 and 1943, Disney also produced two dozen films in Spanish, Portuguese, and English versions, mostly educational shorts for Latin American audiences on the subject of health and sanitation (Cartwright and Goldfarb 169-80). After the war, Disney continued its commitment to public health campaigns, at home and abroad, most notably with a 1946 animation entitled *The Story of Menstruation*, made under contract with the Kimberly-Clark Corporation and (in)famous for pioneering onscreen use of the word "vagina."

The educational shorts produced by Disney in 1941-43 for Latin American audiences set the template for Disney's later public health interventions. Made in response to the US government's interest in educating developing nations about personal and household diet, grooming, and sanitation, these wartime films fixed intently, as Jon Lewis has argued, "on the private bodies and domestic lives of the subjects," focusing on a set of "colonialist imaginings and desires" (Lewis 170). Characterized as innately lazy and/or ignorant, the Latin American subjects and families created in these animated health shorts were held "individually responsible for their own states of disease and poverty" and their attitudes became "the subject of a repetitive and paternalistic discourse" (Lewis 170).

This time around, Disney's film aimed at leveraging the soft power of American popular culture to persuade peoples in the developing world to learn about and adopt newly available "voluntary methods" of population control, mostly the contraceptive pill. To achieve this purpose, Disney chose to base the documentary upon its well-honed tropes of 1950s family rhetoric, in ways that continued, but were also at odds with, a powerful imaginary of family wholesomeness that the company had been shaping since the end of the war. By the 1950s, Disney had transitioned into a family education and entertainment company (Watts 58), having become the standard bearer of a veritable "mystique" in which family became, according to Eleanor Byrne and Martin McQuillan, "synonymous with a certain conservative, patriarchal, heterosexual ideology which is loosely associated with American cultural imperialism" (Byrne and McQuillan 1). Despite its rather narrow notion of what family was, Disney's powerful hegemonic hold over children's literature, family entertainment, mainstream taste, and Western popular culture was expanding its potential to propagate that vision worldwide. The inauguration of Disney's first theme park, Disneyland, in 1955, "the happiest place on earth," catalyzed an image of the company as one that focused on visions of childhood innocence and family togetherness. Disney's family model, rooted in post-World War II family ideology, encapsulated the vision, in the words of historian Elaine Tyler May, of "the nuclear family in the nuclear age: isolated in their newly-discovered suburban seclusion [...] cushioned by abundance, and protected against impending doom by the wonders of modern technology" (May 3). As cultural scholar Susan Willis has pointed out, Disney viewed family as the nexus for social relations, "subsumed by the primary definition [...] as the basic unit of consumption" (Willis 128), the ethical referent, in the words of Henry Giroux, "for linking consumerism, gender roles, motherhood, and class chivalry" (Giroux 142).

Family Planning: the Documentary

Disney's 10-minute animation for the Population Council was released in December 1967 under the title *Family Planning* and translated into 24 languages. That families were, especially in "third-world" nations, becoming too large to enjoy the prosperity of the modern world was the central assumption of the film. As in the earlier health and sanitation propaganda films for Latin America the pedagogical strategy had been to didactically associate illness and poverty with particular bodily "customs," and health and prosperity with Western scientific standards of hygiene (Cartwright and Goldfarb 170), in *Family Planning* the same approach was applied in persuading developing nations to keep family size small.

Written by Bill Bosché, a Disney writer famous for films such as *Lady and the Tramp* (1955), and directed by veteran Disney animator Les Clark, the film was designed, according to a short companion article appearing in the Population Council journal *Studies in Family Planning* in January 1968, "primarily for men and women of reproductive age in the developing countries of Asia, Africa, and Latin America," but to be used "in the United States as well." According to the paper, the film made "about 15 elementary but important points about family planning." Among the vast stable of Disney characters, it chose Donald Duck as the "guide to the content of the film" and tasked him with interrupting the narrative with humorous interludes. Choosing the duck was not by chance. According to David Kunzle, "Donald Duck represented a new kind of comedy, suited to [the post-war] age: a symbol not of courage and wit, as Mickey had been to the '30s, but an example of heroic failure, the guy whose constant efforts towards gold and glory are doomed to eternal defeat." In other words, Donald Duck provided the perfect allegory of the colonial condition and was therefore deemed ideal to evoke empathy among the documentary's implied audience, "the perfect embodiment of the age of capitalism at its apogee, an age presented (by the media) as one of opportunity and plenty, with fabulous wealth awarded to the fortunate and the ruthless competitor, like Uncle Scrooge, and dangled as a bait before the eyes of the unfortunate and the losers in the game" (Kunzle 19).

The animation opens rephrasing the central refrain of Disneyland's most ideological ride, "It's a Small World" (King 128; Kuenz 63-88), with a narrator claiming that, irrelevant of external physical features, "basically, all men are the same." It therefore postulates a universal "common man" prototype, "just like you and me," who rises above all other animals "by his ability to reason," and may eventually "master [...] all he surveys" (all quotations: *Family Planning*). At man's side "of course, is woman," and together they face the challenge of post-war societies when, in the space of a single generation, great progress in medical science, more food and better distribution, and vastly improved methods of health and sanitation have radically upset the balance between the number of babies born each year and the number of people who died. It is within this Malthusian framework that *Family Planning* sets its discussion of the "population bomb."

Focusing on Disney's favorite trope, the "happy family" in its traditional postwar gender roles (the husband is the breadwinner; the woman never speaks, and happily welcomes the choice to adopt birth control), the film goes on to illustrate two possible scenarios for its ideal "common man" (and woman): the small family, enjoying the ease and comforts of modernity because the resources available suffice to provide for everyone, set *vis à vis* the large family, doomed to starve with "no money for modern conveniences," where the mother "will have too much to do, [will] be tired and cross and her health will suffer" and "the children will be sickly and unhappy with little hope for the future" since "no one will have enough." Warning that "this picture can be true for countless families if the number of children born is left to chance", the film suggests that "fortunately, this need not happen anymore." Now donning a surgeon's gown, Donald wields a large golden key, symbolizing that "today things have changed," because "modern science has given us a key that makes possible a new kind of personal freedom – family planning!" The documentary now reaches its climax: explaining that "you can decide in advance the number of children you will have and when you will have them" thanks to newly available contraceptive methods that "will improve the health of mother and children." The film ends on the promise that family planning will restore the balance between births and deaths, and eventually build "a better life, not just for [oneself], but for people everywhere" (all quotations: *Family Planning*).

Visually, the documentary is very explicit in locating its "common man" (and woman) prototype: these are "third world" subjects, certainly not white, a composite of ethnic features from the major regions of the world, with distinct Latino and Asian ethnic traits. Donald Duck's personas, first as painter, then as medical doctor, his canvas eliciting animations within the animation, makes no secret of the documentary's indoctrinating aim: the colonial subjects are instructed upon the best reproductive options available to them. And the recurrent application of classic visual tropes from the 1950s, the so-called "television circle" in particular, in which the presentation of domestic bliss is codified via the family members sitting around the television set (a radio receiver, in fact, in this case), serves the purpose of creating an aspirational model onto which to project the colonial subjects' desires and eventually contributing to halt the proliferation of the population.

Conclusion

As Laura Briggs has convincingly argued in *Reproducing Empire*, the US drive to control the population bomb in developing nations was predicated on two visions of nationalism. On the one hand, it was the product of a US-centric vision that "sought protection for the (white, US) nation from too many of 'them' – working-class and/or dark-skinned people – the result of an exclusive nationalism derived from 'hard' eugenics which feared the reproduction of the lower classes and, indeed, all non-'Nordics'." On the other, it was a "modernizing nationalism [...] associated with missionaries, social workers, reformers, and public health professionals [suggesting that] the family was the key to the world's well-being, and that reducing large families, the number of irregular marriages, and the high maternal and infant mortality rates of the rural farmers and urban and agricultural working classes" was crucial to improving economic conditions in the developing world (Briggs 75).

Some have remarked that Disney's collaboration with the Population Council ran contrary to the family image around which Disney developed its corporate identity after the war, an image rooted in the post-World War II definition of a nuclear family imagery. Attracting attention from several conservative concerns in the US and internationally, *Family Planning* has been seen as contradictory and dangerous. A blogger for Campaign Life Coalition, a pro-life media organization based in Canada, has written that Disney "did not seem to comprehend the irony of allowing itself (and Donald Duck) to be used for this nasty anti-family agenda that has caused great social damage over the past several decades, resulting in today's moral and demographic collapse." Rather, I would argue that Disney's association with the Population Council was ultimately coherent with the company's worldview – one that, in typical Disney fashion, speaks for an America that "dreams and redeems itself, and then imposes that dream upon others for its own salvation" (Dorfman and Mattelart 95). *Family Planning* promotes a vision compatible with the company's goal of appealing not to "family" in the abstract, but rather to a specific "family-consumer," this time to be shaped in the Third World to promote global corporate interests. The film's vision of family aspiring to middle class propriety where family size and gender roles were functional to the production of, to borrow Liz Cohen's term, new "citizen-consumers" (Cohen 8) in the developing world, is consistent with Disney's ultimate understanding of family – affluent, consumption capable, ever aspiring to middle class status. It is to this wholesome nuclear family that Disney, consorting with the overpopulation-obsessed, appealed to defuse the population bomb.

Bibliography

Bollay, Brittney Bush. "The Overpopulation Myth and its Dangerous Connotations." *Sierra Club Washington State*, 21 Jan. 2020, https://www.sierraclub. org/washington/blog/2020/01/overpopulation-myth-and-its-dangerous-connotations. Accessed 18 March 2020.

Briggs, Laura. *Reproducing Empire: Race, Sex, Science, and U.S. Imperialism in Puerto Rico*. U of California P, 2002.

Byrne, Eleanor, and Martin McQuillan. *Deconstructing Disney*. Pluto P, 1999.

Cartwright, Lisa, and Brian Goldfarb. "Cultural Contagion: On Disney's Health Education Films for Latin America." *Disney Discourse: Producing the Magic Kingdom*, edited by Eric Smoodin, Routledge, 1994, pp. 87-105.

Cohen, Lizabeth. *A Consumers' Republic: The Politics of Mass Consumption in Postwar America*. 1st ed. Knopf, 2003.

Connelly, Matthew. *Fatal Misconception: The Struggle to Control World Population*. Harvard UP, 2009.

Critchlow, Donald T. *Intended Consequences: Birth Control, Abortion, and the Federal Government in Modern America*. Oxford UP, 1999.

Dorfman, Ariel, and Armand Mattelart. *How to Read Donald Duck: Imperialist Ideology in the Disney Comic*. International General, 1984.

Ehrlich, Paul R. *The Population Bomb*. Ballantine Books, 1989.

Family Planning. Directed by Les Clark. Produced by Walt Disney Productions for The Population Council, 1967.

Finch, Christopher. *The Art of Walt Disney: From Mickey Mouse to the Magic Kingdoms*. Abrams, 1995.

Franks, Angela. *Margaret Sanger's Eugenic Legacy: The Control of Female Fertility*. McFarland, 2005.

Giroux, Henry A. *The Mouse That Roared: Disney and the End of Innocence*. Rowman & Littlefield, 1999.

Jalsevac, Steve. "1968 Disney family planning cartoon reveals cooperation with population control zealots." *Life Site News*, 2 Aug. 2013, https://www.lifesitenews.

com/blogs/1968-disney-family-planning-cartoon-reveals-cooperation-with-population-con. Accessed 18 March 2020.

King, Margaret. "Disneyland and Walt Disney World: Traditional Values in Futuristic Form." *Journal of Popular Culture*, 1981, pp. 116-40.

Kuenz, Jane. "It's a Small World After All: Disney and the Pleasures of Identification." *South Atlantic Quarterly*, vol. 92, 1993, pp. 63-88.

Kunzle, David. "Introduction to the First English Edition." *How to Read Donald Duck: Imperialist Ideology in the Disney Comic*, Ariel Dorfman and Armand Mattelart, International General, 1984, pp. 11-21.

Lewis, John. "Disney after Disney: Family Business and the Business of Family." *Disney Discourse: Producing the Magic Kingdom*, edited by Eric Smoodin, Routledge, 1994, pp. 87-105.

May, Elaine T. *Homeward Bound: American Families in the Cold War Era*. Basic Books, 1988.

Roberts, Dorothy E. *Killing the Black Body: Race, Reproduction, and the Meaning of Liberty*. Vintage Books, 2014.

Stoddard, Lothrop. *The Rising Tide of Color Against White World-Supremacy*. Scribner, 1921.

Takeuchi-Demirci, Aiko. *Contraceptive Diplomacy: Reproductive Politics and Imperial Ambitions in the United States and Japan*. Stanford UP, 2018.

The Population Council. "The Disney Film on Family Planning." *Studies in Family Planning*, vol. 1, no. 26, 1968.

Watts, Steven. *The Magic Kingdom: Walt Disney and the American Way of Life*. Houghton Mifflin, 1997.

Willis, Susan. "Disney World: Public Use/Private Space." *South Atlantic Quarterly*, vol. 92, 1993, pp. 119-37.

Of Turkish Women and Other Foreigners
Family Planning and Guest Workers in 1980s West Germany

Claudia Roesch, GHI Washington

"Of Turkish Women and other Foreigners" was the title of a 1982 special issue of the *Pro Familia Magazin*, the bi-monthly journal of the West German family planning association. The issue was dedicated to immigration and family planning. Its cover shows a Turkish-origin woman seated in a room decorated with old-fashioned knickknacks ("Türkinnen" 1). A girl about four years old, probably her daughter, sits in her lap and holds a doll. The mother is wearing a plain T-shirt and a long floral skirt. She has a simple hairstyle, little jewelry, no make-up, no headscarf. The daughter has a fashionable 1980s haircut and wears a nice, short dress and stockings. The doll is blond and fair-skinned and wears a similar dress with a checkered pattern that looks like a Bavarian dirndl. As the doll alludes to the daughter's future role in motherhood, the image shows three generations of Turkish-origin women. While the mother and her old-fashioned clothes depict the first generation that was born in Turkey and was slow to assimilate, the daughter represents the second in-between generation, where differences were slight, but still visible. The doll stands for the future third generation, which would be no different from German mainstream culture. The cover photo displayed a positive and optimistic narrative to Turkish family migration into West-German society that assumed complete assimilation to German gender and family norms within two or three generations.

The cover photo, and the special issue generally, were a response to two debates regarding Turkish migration and family structure in German society. On the one hand, a documentary film by Iranian exile film makers Mehangis Montazami and Reza Dabui called "Männerrecht – Frauenleid" (men's rights/women's suffering) drew attention to the difficulties of Turkish-origin women in Germany (Littkowski 2). It depicted Turkish-origin housewives as isolated in their homes and their teenage daughters as juxtaposed in between Turkish cultural norms, which emphasized honor and purity, and German social practices, which accepted sexual freedom.

On the other hand, a group of right-wing professors and former minister of expellees Theodor Oberländer (CDU), who had had to step down in 1960 due to his involvement with the Nazis' ethnic cleansing policies in Eastern Europe, pub-

Figure 1: Cover Pro Familia Magazin vol. 10, no. 2, 1982, Copyright "Archiv pro familia Bundesverband"

lished a manifesto against immigration (Kühnert 13).[1] They argued that the identity and Christian-western heritage of Germany were under threat, if German families continued to have fewer children than Turkish immigrants ("Heidelberger" 31). The manifesto claimed that each "Volk" presented a biological and cybernetic system of

---

1   The German weekly newspaper *Die Zeit* actually published the manifesto in the context of an investigative article about racism among German academics, *Pro Familia Magazin* reprinted the *Die Zeit* clipping (*Pro Familia Magazin* 3, 1982, p. 31).

order and had the right to self-preservation, which is why different people should not mingle. Therefore, it demanded the expulsion of all foreigners to ensure the future of Germany and Europe. Instead, "lebensvolle und intakte deutsche Familien" (vivid and faultless German families) should have more children. While the authors distanced themselves from Nazi population policies, their manifesto was still a highly racist document that drew on white replacement theories and positive eugenics. When Helmut Kohl (CDU) became chancellor in 1982, his Christian-liberal coalition started a remigration program that offered incentives to Turkish-origin families to return to Turkey. Historian Michelle Kahn has interpreted this as a political response to xenophobia and anti-Turkish sentiments in German society (Kahn 16).

Pro Familia's attempt to present Turkish immigration to Germany as a promise of successful integration stood between the racist anti-immigration discourse that identified Turkish-origin women's reproduction as a danger, and a feminist discourse that described Turkish families as patriarchal and problematic. They drew on assimilation theory and modernization theory that were both outdated in academic circles by the 1980s (Harzig and Hoerder 57; Latham 24), but remained a guiding principle of social work in Germany.

This paper assumes that the reproduction of Turkish-origin women stood at the center of controversies on immigration in the 1980s Federal Republic of Germany. It will examine how Pro Familia positioned itself within these controversies, and how it drew on concepts of modernization and feminist self-help to support Turkish immigrant women. First, it will give a background on the founding of Pro Familia and its ties to the American Planned Parenthood association. Then, it will discuss how Turkish immigrant women moved into their center of attention. A third part will trace the learning curve that Pro Familia counsellors experienced in the early 1980s when reaching out to Turkish-origin women. In the conclusion, my paper will argue that Pro Familia counsellors learned that most problems that Turkish families faced were tied to their position as part of the urban working class with an insecure migration status rather than their rural or religious backgrounds.

The West German family planning association Pro Familia was founded in 1952, when female doctors and social workers from Berlin and Kassel decided to form a national network to promote contraceptives. They obtained financial support from the American Planned Parenthood founder Margaret Sanger and foundations that supported population control globally.[2] However, since the beginning, Pro Familia and Planned Parenthood differed in their goals. Sanger considered the global fight against overpopulation paramount, while Pro Familia activists consid-

---

2   See Andrea Carosso in this volume for the analysis of Disney's involvement in family planning propaganda abroad.

ered promoting contraception to fight illegal abortions their most important goal (Roesch, "Love" 107).

Under the overpopulation paradigm, American family planning activists began targeting immigrants in 1953, when affiliates from Texas called attention to the "illegal immigration of illiterate people from Mexico who were in bad health and in need of contraceptive services" ("Minutes"). They depicted immigrant families as uneducated and completely ignorant of birth control. Brochures, comics and films in Spanish that targeted Mexican immigrants and Puerto Ricans described their families as patriarchal, too large, and with a rural mindset ("Ustedes"). Their message was that while large families were an advantage in a pre-modern, rural setting, in the urbanized industrial United States, smaller families promised affluence and better educational opportunities for each child (Roesch, "Planning" 222).

Immigrants were not a great concern for West German family planners until the late 1970s, since birth rates were declining, and Pro Familia assumed that only immigrants held reproduction rates above the zero-population growth level (Harmsen 4). Guest worker programs in West Germany had started in 1955 with agreements with Italy. Spain and Greece followed in 1960, Turkey in 1961. Later, the Federal Republic also signed agreements with Morocco, Korea, Portugal, Tunisia and Yugoslavia (Severin-Barboutie 226). The programs originally intended for male workers to return home to their families after a few years; therefore, Pro Familia did not address guest workers at all. But labor contractors hired both male and female workers individually. Some of them then married in Germany, others had spouses in their home country (Miller 26). The *Anwerbestopp* (recruitment halt) of 1973 meant that guest workers were not granted new work visas anymore. This made circular migration of family fathers impossible, so that transnational couples were faced with the choice to either return to their home country permanently, stay in Germany permanently, or live in a permanent long-distance marriage. About 62% of all foreign workers chose to stay and bring along their families (Thomsen Vierra 38; Oltmer 192).

While individual Pro Familia activists had suggested campaigns for immigrants since 1971, the organization only began to reach out to them in 1978, triggered by the abortion reform in 1976. Pro Familia collaborated with the Federal Agency for Health Education to provide mandatory pregnancy crisis counselling. This meant that Pro Familia opened 102 new clinics within nine years, for which they had to hire new staff, most of whom were women that had studied social sciences or pedagogy and had been involved in the student and feminist movement on campus (Roesch, "Love" 108). Some of them had also gone to the United States as exchange students, where they had been introduced to the principles of feminist women's health centers. Through training sessions and constant evaluations, they changed the set-up of the counselling practice within Pro Familia from providing women with top-down information and contraceptives, to enabling them to "make informed decisions" as "mature citizens" ("Selbstdarstellung" 3).

Immigrant women entered the feminist counsellors' radars since they attended abortion counselling in higher proportions than the average population. The Hamburg family planning center wrote in its annual report that 13% of its clients were immigrant women, while only 8.4% of the general population of Hamburg were immigrants ("Familienplanungszentrum" 8). Centers in other large cities like Berlin or Munich reported similar findings. The centers interpreted the findings as evidence that Turkish-origin women had more unwanted pregnancies and therefore needed sex education. A study from Berlin that will be discussed in detail further on in this paper showed that Turkish couples often practiced contraception with the withdrawal method and abortion as a back-up, which explained their higher abortion rates (Tietze 35).

The first initiative to reach out to immigrant women was a glossy brochure in several languages called "Familienplanung: Warum – womit?" (Family Planning, why and how?; see Familienplanung Arbeitsvorlage 1). Versions existed in Italian, Spanish, Turkish, Portuguese, Croatian and Greek, later also in a Kurdish translation. Pro Familia obtained funding from the Federal Agency for Health Education and the World Health Organization for the project ("Familienplanung Warum" 18).

The underlying assumption of the brochure was that immigrant women had more abortions than German women because they were ignorant about family planning. Therefore, it featured all available contraceptives and information on how to obtain a legal abortion in Germany in factual language. Pro Familia worked together with local family planning associations, and in the Spanish version they used either correct terms in Iberian Spanish or direct translations from German, rather than the direct translations from English and simple language that the American brochures for Hispanics used (Planificación 9-13, Roesch, "Love" 97).

Deliberately, the brochures did not suggest that there was any ideal number of children, as they wanted to convey the message that immigrants had the right to have as many children as they "wanted and needed" ("Familienplanung Warum" 18). But all the photographs – which were supposed to show typical families of the respective country, even though the Spanish and Portuguese families were portrayed by the same models – depicted modern families with two or three children. All of the children looked happy and had lots of toys. Especially in the Italian and Croatian brochure, the mothers had modern haircuts. Here, family planning promised happy children, modern mothers, access to consumer goods and middle-class lifestyles. The brochures were a great success, and social institutions in Germany, as well as family planning associations in Belgium and Switzerland, used them to reach out to immigrants. Activists in Spain, Portugal, and Greece, where there were no nationwide family planning associations, and in Italy, where the local association was underfunded, circulated the brochure. Even in Yugoslavia, where a well-funded family planning association with its own resources existed, activists used the brochure ("Familienplanung Warum" 19).

In contrast to the other brochures, the Turkish version showed a family with three children and a mother who was dressed more modestly (Aile 2). It used photographs from the same photoshoot as the 1982 magazine cover described above. Also, the brochure contained a diagram to use for natural family planning with the Billings temperature method, which was not included in the other brochures. A report by Pro Familia counsellors on their experience with Turkish women revealed that they were concerned about Turkish cultural attitudes towards modesty and bodily functions (Klöss and Krasberg 16; Wunderlich and Schlüter 27). Since Turkish culture considered menstruation to be unclean, this was a hindrance to Turkish women getting to know their bodies. The Turkish concept of modesty stood in contrast to the feminist ideals of emancipation and empowerment through knowledge and self-examination (Kline 2-5). Therefore, counsellors promoted the Billings Method among Turkish-origin women, which meant checking their vaginal temperature each morning, as an entrance into getting to self-empowerment through touching their genitals. This shows that Turkish-origin women were perceived as especially ignorant and disempowered by their own culture.

Even though Turks made up less than one third of all immigrants in West Germany, nearly all Pro Familia activities focused solely on them.[3] In 1979, Lili-Lore Schmidt-Schiek, an experienced medical counsellor from Cologne who had helped set up abortion counselling in 1974, assumed that the German pattern of individual counselling would not work for Turkish-origin women ("Thema Beratung" 18). She argued that most of these women came from rural Anatolia, where they were used to meeting in groups in their homes. The term "rural Anatolia," which encompasses the Asian part of Turkey, often appeared in descriptions of these immigrant women, and symbolically stood for backwardness and rural poverty, even though Turkish migrant workers were more skilled than other immigrant groups and 50% came from urban areas (see "Fragen" 12, Miller 14). Social workers, who worked with second generation Turkish-origin women in secondary schools and job training, learned that Turkish women tended to open up more easily in larger groups than in one-on-one conversations with a counsellor (Wunderlich and Schlüter 30). Therefore, Pro Familia Berlin Kreuzberg set up a new outreach program to meet Turkish-origin women in their own living rooms, since living rooms were important meeting spaces for these women (Thompson Vierra 79).

In the program, two female counsellors, who were either trained social workers or physicians, a sociologist, and a Turkish interpreter would arrange a visit

---

3   According to the German Federal Labor Office, in 1974, 26.4% of foreign workers were from Turkey, 10% from Greece, 14.6% from Italy, 3.5% from Portugal, 6.8% from Spain and 20% from Yugoslavia (Akgündüz 104).

to the home of a Turkish-origin client (Tietze 12). That woman would invite her mother-in-law and other female friends, neighbors and relatives to the meeting, and they would have an informal chat about reproduction. Counsellors brought along brochures, suitcases with contraceptives and a pelvic model to illustrate their information ("Beratung" 18). The interpreter guided the conversation, while the German-origin counsellors took a passive role. If a woman reported a specific problem (such as infertility or a fear of being pregnant) they would arrange an appointment at the Pro Familia clinic later on.

At the events, counselors emphasized on taking part in Turkish practices of hospitality, such as using rose water and accepting tea and snacks. In the conversations, they were surprised that most of the women were actually quite fluent in German and that they talked openly about abortions and infertility ("Beratung" 19). They also learned that reproduction was often not their most pressing problem. Housing and work-related problems, the need for childcare, and general medical issues, such as high blood pressure, back pain, or headaches, often took a higher priority to family planning. Many requested help with issues that were not directly related to reproduction, such as assistance with their immigration status or conflicts with a landlord (Tietze 27).

Through the program, Pro Familia met with 78 Turkish-origin women in Berlin Kreuzberg and learned that most of them had or wanted two children (Tietze 35). 60 out of 78 women used some kind of birth control, the rest were either pregnant, wanted to be pregnant, were not in a relationship, or in menopause; only three women did not practice family planning at all. Among the women, the pill was by far the most popular method. They and their partners were concerned about side-effects but did not seem to be aware of the feminist debates on this topic. When women experienced side-effects of the pill, couples often returned to the insecure withdrawal method. Abortion served as a back-up when the method failed. Therefore, a large number of the participants in the program had had abortions, most of them illegally in Turkey before it became legal in Germany in 1976. One woman reported that she regularly went to Turkey to get Depo Proveda, a long-term hormonal contraceptive that was not approved in Germany due to long-term health risks (Tietze 35). This shows that these women, rather than being linguistically and religiously isolated, had their own agency. They had knowledge about family planning and desired to keep their families small. They knew about some modern contraceptives, as well as outdated practices, and were able to access methods in their home country that were unavailable in Germany.

The approach of the Berlin counsellors relied on the feminist concept of consciousness-raising, where women gathered to relate their own experiences with sexism, in order to raise awareness about their oppression as women (Echols 10). But the counsellors perceived their clients as even more oppressed than the average German woman. Therefore, the informal gatherings served not to raise political awareness, but to circulate information about contraception and counselling. At the same time, as they encouraged women to invite members of their extended families, they relied on traditional knowledge transmission through extended family networks.

Learning from this experiment, Pro Familia affiliates hired Turkish interpreters, social workers, and nurses. Affiliates in Munich and Heidelberg published Turkish language versions of their abortion brochures and materials for teenagers ("Faltblatt" 17; Ludwig 25). In special groups for teenage girls, counsellors prepared them for their first visit to a gynecologist. They taught self-examination practices for girls to prove that they were still virgins, or passed out referrals to hymen-restoration surgeries if families expected girls to marry as virgins (Wunderlich and Schlüter 28).

In Frankfurt, Pro Familia hired two social workers – one Turkish and one German – who set up Turkish women's groups in social housing projects and cultural clubs with the focus on general preventive healthcare (Erhan and Hirschberger 27). In most sessions, they did not even reach the topic of family planning, as women were most interested in learning massages and means of stress reduction. In classes on family planning, the social workers reported that participants were most interested in getting a pill prescription. They learned that mothers-in-law proved to be the biggest impediment to promote birth preparation classes, as they considered child-birth a natural phenomenon. In order to promote family planning among more women, the Frankfurt team suggested to set up German, alphabetization, and sewing classes. These were similar to classes proposed to get Mexican immigrant women in the US out of their isolation in the early 20th century, and the plan contains notions that these women were uneducated and cared only for housework (Ziegler-McPherson 82).

Social worker Doris Dunkel from Hanau, who had promoted family planning among German-origin women in homeless shelters, reported in 1985 that Turkish-origin families had moved into the shelter because they could not find a home on the regular housing market (Dunkel 6). According to Dunkel, the Turkish-origin women suffered from the same health issues as German women, which is why she and her coworkers set up a Turkish women's health group. There, she learned again that women needed general medical care rather than contraceptive counselling, as many suffered from high blood pressure, headaches and back pain due to their workplace conditions, insecure housing situations, or an insecure immigration status. The social worker was also shocked to learn "that some of the Turkish women had been sterilized without their knowledge during a hospital stay" (Dunkel 7). While coercive postpartum sterilizations of Mexican-origin women in Los Angeles had caused a huge outcry among civil rights activists and feminists in the 1970s US (Gutiérrez 33), coercive sterilizations in Germany did not become public knowledge beyond Dunkel's report in the Pro Familia journal. Pro Familia Bremen president

Gerhard Amendt had complained in the early 1980s that women underwent unwanted sterilizations in hospitals when requesting an abortion without disclosing their ethnic origin (78) and a court case against a doctor in Nuremberg for performing abortions without prior counselling revealed that he had coerced working class and immigrant women to use IUDs or consent to a sterilization after an abortion (Gast 5; Soltau). But those are the only traces of coercive sterilizations in the Pro Familia archives. Therefore, it is unknown how widespread the practice of sterilizing poor Turkish-origin women without their consent actually was – whether this was the action of single doctors or a more wide-spread practice, and whether this happened in the context of a legal abortion or Caesarean birth. Nevertheless, it shows that there were doctors in West Germany who acted on the margins of legality and pushed sterilizations and permanent contraceptives on poor and minority women. It also shows that Turkish women could not trust the medical establishment to give them all necessary information to determine their own fertility.

Conclusion

When Pro Familia counsellors approached Turkish immigrant women to teach them about family planning, they acted on stereotypical depictions of Turkish women as uneducated, isolated, and coming from rural backgrounds. They soon had to learn that these women were less isolated and more informed than they had expected. Through their programs, Pro Familia counsellors learned that formal knowledge networks of doctors and hospitals in Germany failed them. Social workers needed to make an extra effort to reach them through group work or home visits. Instead, immigrant women relied on informal networks of families and neighbors to receive information on birth control or used formal networks in their home countries when they obtained abortions or Depo Poveda in Turkey.

While in the US, Planned Parenthood had reached out to Mexican and Puerto Rican migrants with a population control focus, the concept of overpopulation did not hit fertile grounds in Germany due to a population decline and concerns about illegal abortion. Pro Familia counsellors since the late 1970s targeted immigrant women with feminist motivations to promote empowerment through knowledge, to counter a racist anti-immigration discourse, and to offer practical help to women who experienced a disproportionately high number of unwanted pregnancies. But the counsellors mixed their feminist ideals of self-help and consciousness-raising with images based on outdated assimilation and modernization theory that depicted Turkish families as rural and pre-modern. The goal was to assimilate them to German mainstream culture so that differences became invisible. This meant that women's groups or natural family planning did not serve as democratic forms of empowerment, but a one-sided circulation of modern knowledge about family planning.

Yet, the experiments of counselling Turkish-origin women presented a learning curve for Pro Familia counsellors. They learned that these women faced more severe health and housing problems, and that they were connected to bad working conditions and insecure immigration statuses. They also learned that most women wanted two children and actively requested the pill or abortions, they proved their own agency and subscribed to the Western concept of the nuclear family. But these women were cut off from feminist discourses of the side-effects of the pill and faced dangers including coercive sterilization when visiting hospitals. This shows that Turkish-origin women in 1980s West Germany were not isolated in a rural mind-set, but were actually working-class members of an urban society, who experienced discrimination, but made use of personal networks of families, neighbors, and sympathetic counsellors to negotiate their own reproductive wishes.

Bibliography

Akgündüz, Ahmet. *Labor Migration from Turkey to Western Europe, 1960-1974. A Multidisciplinary Analysis*. Routledge, 2008.

Amendt, Gerhard. "Vom Beichtstuhl zum Gynäkologenstuhl." *konkret* 1981, pp. 77-81.

Dunkel, Doris. "Familienelend und die Gesundheit der Frauen." *Pro Familia Magazin* vol. 13, no. 4, 1985, pp. 4-7.

Echols, Alice. *Daring to be Bad: Radical Feminism in America, 1967-1975*. U of Minnesota P, 1989.

Erhan, Şebnem, and Marie-Louise Hirschberger. "Gesundheitsberatung für türkische Frauen bei der Pro Familia Frankfurt." *Pro Familia Magazin* vol. 14, no. 3, 1986, pp. 27-29.

Gast, Wolfgang. "Abtreibungen dienen der Bedarfsdeckung." *TAZ*, 4 Apr. 1987, p. 5.

Gutiérrez, Elena. *Fertile Matters: The Politics of Mexican-Women's Reproduction*. U of Texas P, 2008.

Harmsen, Hans. "Zum Geburtenrückgang in der Bundesrepublik Deutschland." *Pro Familia Informationen* vol. 1, no 2, 1971, p. 4.

Harzig, Christiane, and Dirk Hoerder. *What is Migration History?* Polity P, 2009.

Kline, Wendy. *Bodies of Knowledge: Sexuality, Reproduction, and Women's Health in the Second Wave*. U of Chicago P, 2010.

Kahn, Michelle. "Between Ausländer and Almancı: The Transnational History of Turkish-German Migration" (working title) *GHI Bulletin*, vol. 66, Spring 2020, pp. 1-39 (forthcoming).

Klöss, Cornelia, and Ulrike Krasberg. "Gesundheitsberatung türkischer Frauen in einem Mutter-Kind-Zentrum." *Pro Familia Magazin* vol. 10, no. 3, 1982, pp. 15-16.

Kühnert, Hanno. "Rassistische Tendenzen." *Die Zeit*, 2 Feb. 1982, p. 13, https://www.zeit.de/1982/06/rassistische-klaenge. Accessed 20 Feb. 2020.

Latham, Michael E. *Modernization as Ideology: American Social Science and 'Nation Building' in the Kennedy Era.* U of North Carolina P, 2000.

Littkowski, Ingrid. "Zwei persische Filmer: Ein Portrait." *Pro Familia Magazin* vol. 10, no. 3, 1982, pp. 2-3.

Ludwig, Bruni. "Broschüre für türkische Mädchen." *Pro Familia Magazin* vol. 10, no. 6, 1982, p. 25.

Miller, Jennifer A. *Turkish Guest Workers in Germany: Hidden Lives and Contested Borders.* U of Toronto P, 2018.

Oltmer, Jochen. *Migration: Geschichte und Zukunft der Gegenwart.* Konrad Theiss Verlag, 2017.

Roesch, Claudia. "Love Without Fear: Knowledge Networks and Family Planning Initiatives for Immigrant Families in West Germany and the United States." *Bulletin of the German Historical Institute*, vol. 64, no. 1, 2019, pp. 93-113.

—. "Planning a Puerto Rican family in New York: Symbolic violence and reproductive decision-making in the Planned Parenthood film *La Sortija de Compromiso* (1965)." *International Journal of Culture & Media Politics*, vol 15, no. 2, 2019, pp. 213-29.

Severin-Barboutie, Bettina. "Multiple Deutungen und Funktionen: Die organisierte Reise ausländischer Arbeitskräfte in die Bundesrepublik Deutschland, 1950er-1970er Jahre." *Geschichte und Gesellschaft*, vol. 44, no. 2, 2018, pp. 223-49.

Soltau, Heide. "Es war immer sehr voll." *Die Zeit*, vol. 20, 8 May 1987, https://www.zeit.de/1987/20/es-war-immer-sehr-voll. Accessed 20 Feb. 2020.

Tietze, Getrud. "Jahresbericht zum Modellprojekt Familienplanung für Ausländer: Familienplanung bei türkischen Frauen in ihrer Wohnung." Dec. 1981. Bundesarchiv Hans Harmsen Nachlass N 1336 (hereafter cited as "BArch N 1336") 870.

Thomsen Vierra, Sarah. *Turkish Germans in the Federal Republic of Germany: Immigration, Space and Belonging, 1961-1990.* Cambridge UP, 2018.

Wunderlich, Marion, and Gerline Schlüter. "Ich glaube manchmal, ich bin verrückt. Türkische Mädchen auf der Suche nach einer anderen weiblichen Identität." *Pro Familia Magazin* vol. 10, no. 3, 1982, pp. 25-30.

Ziegler-McPherson, Christine A. *Americanization in the States: Immigrant Social Welfare Policy and National Identity in the United States 1908-1929.* U of Florida P, 2009.

"Aile Planlamasi nasil ve ne gibi usullerle?" 1978. BArch N1336/605.

"Faltblatt auf Türkisch." *Pro Familia Magazin*, vol. 12, no. 5, 1984, p. 17.

"Familienplanung – Warum – Womit? Deutschsprachige Arbeitsvorlage." 1978. BArch N1336/605.

"Familienplanungszentrum Hamburg Erfahrungsbericht 82." BArch N 1336/757.

"Familienplanung: Warum? Womit? Broschüren für Ausländer in sechs Sprachen."
Pro Familia Magazin, vol. 10, no. 3, 1982, pp. 17-18.

"Fragen an: Lieselotte Funcke. Staatsminister a. D. Beauftragte der Bundesregierung für Ausländerfragen." *Pro Familia Magazin*, vol. 10, no. 3, 1982, p. 12.

"Heidelberger Manifest." *Pro Familia Magazin*, vol. 10, no. 3, 1982, p. 31.

"Minutes of the Board of Directors Meeting." 1954. Margaret Sanger Papers, Library of Congress, Washington DC, Reel 120.

"Planificación familiar ¿Por qué y Cómo?" 1978. BArch N1336/605.

"Pro Familia Selbstdarstellung." ca. 1972. Pro Familia Verbandsarchiv: Ordner "Geschichte Pro Familie: Dokumente," p. 3.

"Thema Beratung (II): Familienplanungsberatung bei türkischen Frauen in ihrer Wohnung." *Pro Familia Magazin*, vol. 9, no. 4, 1981, pp. 18-20.

"Ustedes Pueden Planear Su Familia." 1968. *Planned Parenthood Federation of America Records II*, Sophia Smith Library, Smith College Northampton, Box 100, Folder 50.

"Von Türkinnen und anderen Ausländern." *Pro Familia Magazin*, vol. 10, no. 3, 1982, p. 1.

Closing Remarks - By a Family Lawyer

Anatol Dutta, Ludwig Maximilians Universität München

Many concepts discussed in this book – filiation, marriage, partnership, adoption, divorce – are predominantly legal categories. They are, in most modern societies, defined and created by family law. Therefore, reading the present book – the results of an "interdisciplinary, multiperspectival, European-American transatlantic comparative project" (Zehelein, "Introduction" p. 21) – must be particularly interesting for a family lawyer. As the law should always serve societies and their families, family law is in constant change, unlike many other areas of law. Ideas and theories on family and family relations developed within other disciplines are (or at least should be) directly relevant for legal studies and legal policy.

What is the relationship between families (as a societal phenomenon) and the law? Of course, family and family relations are not determined by legal norms. Law in general, and family law as part of private law in particular, can only indirectly influence the family life of the citizens. Even if the law creates private rights between family members – for example, common property or maintenance rights between spouses during their marriage – the law does not play a major role in the daily life of the family members. This is true at least as long as the relationship is intact and the behavior of the family members towards each other is driven by mutual altruism. Spouses or partners of a couple relationship, to stay with this example, use and administrate their property commonly, and support each other not because the law requires them to do so, but rather, because they live in a common household with or without children, and share the same interests – based on love or other motives. The law only enters the scene if the altruism between the family members ceases in case of crisis or the end of the family relationship, if the spouses or partners separate, or one of the spouses or partners dies. Then – because altruism does not guide the behavior within the relationship anymore – the law has to regulate the rights and duties between the family members. It mainly does so by dividing the advantages (for example, wealth acquired during the marriage by the spouses) or disadvantages (for example, the economic dependency of one of the spouses because of family work) justly and fairly (which often means equally) between the departing family members by creating rights and duties (for example, joint shares in the accrued wealth or maintenance duties of the economically stronger family member towards the weaker part). The law, of course, also interferes with family relations if the law maker comes to the conclusion that interests of third persons or public interests are affected. This mainly concerns care relationships, such as the parent-child relationship, but also guardian- and custodianship where the state (and the law) supervises the parties – for example, the parents, when exercising their parental responsibility for the child and the state safeguards that the best interest of the child is protected. Against this background, the papers collected in this impressive volume focusing on potential crises of the family are a treasure trove for family lawyers, as a brief look at three topics covered by the book shows:

Poverty and families (see the contributions by two Italians, the sociologist Chiara Saraceno, and the Americanist Maurizio Vaudagna) raise legal policy questions, if the state shall use public welfare to incentivize a certain family model. A liberal social welfare system should, of course, treat families impartially, and should not try to influence the family models lived by persons in need. In a system based on freedom, it can hardly be justified that the state encroaches on the private sphere of its citizens, even more so, if the state does so only with the poor. Interesting questions of family law also arise when the law has to delineate the financial responsibilities for weaker members of society between state and family: who has to care financially for family members first, for example, for parents in need – the state, or the children? The German legislator has recently solved this conflict by releasing a child of maintenance duties towards parents if the child earns an annual income below 100,000 Euros.

Much insight for lawyers (and lawmakers) provides also the chapter by the Spanish anthropologist and social worker Gloria Álvarez Bernardo. Assisted Reproductive Technologies should be available irrespective of the family model. The only limit placed on the intended parents – also from a human rights perspective – should be the best interest of the child. Gloria's conclusions regarding same sex parents very much reflect the prevailing opinion that the child's well-being is not endangered if his or her parents have the same gender. Therefore, many legal systems who opened marriage for same-sex couples also allowed adoption for such couples. Regarding the right to know the identity of the gamete donors, one can also only agree with her analysis, and the observations made by Eva-Sabine Zehelein in the context of her analysis of an American TV series featuring sperm donor families. Research in the area of adoption as well as on donor conceived children shows that the truth regarding the biological and genetic links is always in the best interest of the child. This includes, that the child does not only know that the legal parent(s) is/are 'only' (an) intended parent(s) (and that there is/are also (a) genetic parent(s), but the child should also (have the right to) know the identity of the donor(s).

Family planning – as shown from two different angles by Andrea Carosso (American and cultural studies), and Claudia Roesch (history) – was for decades focused on keeping families small and nuclear. In times of demographic changes, families with more than two children are in some Western societies the new ideal and symbol of wealth. Nevertheless, the law does rarely treat families differently depending on their size. Especially the rules on parentage and its legal consequences work well not only in multi-children families, but also in one-child or two-children families. Actually, in Germany the law distinguishes only in the area of succession between families with many and less children. Here, the law provides that in case the deceased is survived by his or her spouse, as well as by one child or two children, the intestacy share of the children shall not be larger than the share of the surviving spouse – a rule which does not apply to families with more than two children. However, we also learn in this volume that the law increasingly focusses on families where there are more than two parents: multiparentality – a rather new concept which is explored by Josep Ferrer-Riba. It appears that – to cite the book title chosen by a German colleague – "in the past parents had many children – today children have many parents" (*Früher hatten Eltern viele Kinder – heute haben Kinder viele Eltern*; Martin Löhnig, Baden-Baden, 2015).

To conclude: This volume is a good example that interdisciplinary exchange works, and that the different disciplines dealing with, and thinking about, and caring for families should cross national, as well as disciplinary borders, and listen to each other.

About the contributors

Gloria Álvarez Bernardo is a lecturer in Social Work at the Universidad de Granada where she also earned a PhD in Gender Studies (*Etnografía de las relaciones de parentesco en familias encabezadas por parejas del mismo sex*; PhD Extraordinary Award). She holds a Bachelor's degree in Social and Cultural Anthropology (Universitat Rovira i Virgili; with distinction) and Master's degrees in Social Work, Welfare State and Social Intervention Methodologies (Universidad Nacional de Educación a Distancia) as well as in Gender Studies (Universidad de Oviedo). She has published widely on family diversity, same-sex families and LGBT bullying in schools. Currently, she is taking part in a project on teachers' LGBT knowledge, attitudes and beliefs.

Alice Balestrino holds a PhD in American literature from Sapienza Università di Roma. Her dissertation *Extra-Vacant Narratives. Reading Holocaust Fiction in the Post-9/11 Age* examines the philosophical concept of vacancy as a narrative strategy for Holocaust uchronias and autofictions published in the aftermath of 9/11. She has published on Holocaust literature and postmemory, on alternate histories, on post-9/11 fiction, and on the representation of memory in graphic novels. She currently holds an appointment as Research Assistant at the International Forum for US Studies, University of Illinois at Urbana Champaign, where she is also pursuing a second PhD in Italian Studies.

Andrea Carosso is professor of American Literature and Culture at the Department of International Languages and Literatures of the Università di Torino, where he coordinates the post-graduate program in English and American Studies. He is former director of the "Piero Bairati" Center for American Studies. He is the author of *Cold War Narratives. American Culture in the 1950s* (2012), *Urban Cultures in the United States* (2010), *Invito alla lettura di Vladimir Nabokov* (1999), *T.S. Eliot e i miti del moderno. Prassi, teoria e ideologia negli scritti critici e filosofici* (1995) and has edited, among other volumes, *Decostruzione e/è America. Un reader critico* (1994). His current research focuses on representations of the backlash on ethnic (especially Arab and Muslim) communities in the US after 9/11, family and reproductive policies in early

Cold War America, and the transatlantic circulation of the blues. Forthcoming is a monograph on the US South-West.

Sonia Di Loreto is Associate Professor of American Literature at the Università di Torino. She has published widely in journals on topics from archives and the Digital Humanities, to epistolarity and transatlantic relations. Her most recent publications are "Margaret Fuller's Archive: Absence, Erasure and Critical Work" in *19. Interdisciplinary Studies in the Long Nineteenth Century*; and "Kinship, Affiliation and Adoption. Catharine Maria Sedgwick's *Hope Leslie* and Nineteenth Century American Literature" in *CoSMo – Comparative Studies in Modernism*. Her current research focuses on Margaret Fuller's transnational network, and aims at reconstructing the network of communication and the circulation of revolutionary ideas generated during Margaret Fuller's European years. She is project manager of a Northeastern University based DH project, the "Margaret Fuller Transnational Archive" (MFTA). She serves on the editorial board of *Acoma, Rivista Internazionale di Studi Nordamericani*.

Anatol Dutta is Professor of private law, private international law and comparative law at the Ludwig-Maximilians-Universität München. Previously, he was Fellow at the Max Planck Institute for Comparative and Private International Law in Hamburg (2003–14) and Professor at the Universität Regensburg (2014–17). In 2009, he was a visiting fellow at the University of Cambridge. Dutta is a corresponding member of the Cambridge Family Law Centre, a member of the German Council of Private International Law, and co-editor of both, the *Zeitschrift für das gesamte Familienrecht (FamRZ)*, a leading family law journal for practitioners and academics in Germany, and the *Zeitschrift für Europäisches Privatrecht (ZEuP)*. He has a special interest in family and succession law, from a private international law as well as a comparative and interdisciplinary perspective.

Josep Ferrer-Riba is Professor of Private Law at Universitat Pompeu Fabra (Barcelona, Catalonia) and a member of the Catalan Law Commission for the Codification of Catalan Civil Law. He has been a Visiting Scholar at the Universities of Göttingen, Yale, Bologna, Leuven and Cambridge. His teaching and writing have mainly focused on child and family law, succession law, non-profit organizations, and comparative private law.

Brigitte Georgi-Findlay is Professor of North American Studies at the Technische Universität Dresden. She is co-editor of the periodical *Zeitschrift für Anglistik und Amerikanistik – A Quarterly of Language, Literature and Culture*. Her major publications include two monographs on Native American literature and one on *The Frontiers of Women's Writing: Women's Narratives and the Rhetoric of Westward Expansion* (U of

Arizona P, 1996). In recent years she has published on Western films and Western television series (new and old).

Lee Herrmann was born in West Germany and grew up in Indiana. He received Bachelor's degrees in history and English from Western Washington University, a Master's degree in American Studies from the Università di Torino, and a PhD in Comparative Modern Social and Political History from the Universitat Autònoma de Barcelona. His article "'Bothersome Forms, of Course, Were Mechanically Exterminated': Colonialism, Science, Racial Dysgenia, and Extermination in the Work of H.P. Lovecraft, Intertextually and Beyond," was published in the 2019 issue of *Comparative Studies in Modernism*.

Antonio Legerén-Molina (PhD in Law) is Assistant Professor at the Civil Law Department, Universidade da Coruña (Spain). As a researcher, his fields of expertise are the rights of persons, family law, smart contracts and blockchain, and succession law. He has taught in several universities in Europe and the US, and has also enjoyed several research stays at Columbia Law School (New York) and Oxford (UK). Among his publications are four books with deep impact – one of them awarded the XI Prize Aequitas, granted by the Spanish National Council of Notaries–, as well as more than 15 papers and 25 book chapters.

Stefano Morello is a doctoral candidate in English at The Graduate Center, CUNY, and a Teaching Fellow at Queens College, CUNY. His academic interests include American Studies, pop culture, poetics, and digital humanities. His dissertation, *Let's Make a Scene! East Bay Punk and Subcultural Worlding*, explores the heterotopic space of the East Bay punk scene, its modes of resistance and (dis-)association, and the clashes between its politics and aesthetics. He serves as co-chair of the Graduate Forum of the Italian Association for American Studies (AISNA) and is a founding editor of its journal, *JAm It! (Journal of American Studies in Italy)*. As a digital humanist, Stefano focuses on archival practices, with a knack for archival pedagogy and public-facing initiatives. He created the East Bay Punk Digital Archive, an open access archive of East Bay punk-zines. He is currently working on a book with architectural historian Kerri Culhane on urban and public health policy responses to poverty and disease at the turn of the 20th century. The book is based on "The Lung Block: A New York City Slum and Its Forgotten Italian Immigrant Community," an exhibit they curated at the Municipal Archives of the City of New York in 2019.

Margarita Navarro Pérez holds a PhD in English and Cultural Studies from Universidad de Murcia (2015) and works as an associate professor and researcher at the English Department of the Universidad de Murcia. Her main research interests are the representation and interpretation of the moving image, questions of national identity, ethnicity, civil wars, belonging and the impact of media in the constructions of cultural identities. She has been a visiting researcher at the Centre for Research in Media and Cultural Studies (University of Sunderland, UK) and at Universidad Alberto Hurtado (Santiago de Chile). Her publications and papers, delivered at national and international conferences, mainly focus on the teaching of culture, the study of national identity, gender, and media studies.

Virginia Pignagnoli is Postdoctoral Research Fellow at the Department of English and German Philology of the Universidad de Zaragoza (Spain). Her publications include articles in *Narrative, Poetics Today,* the *European Journal of English Studies (EJES), Contemporary Studies in Modernism (CoSMo),* the *Amsterdam International Journal of Cultural Narratology (AJCN),* and *RSA Journal (Rivista di Studi Americani).* She edited "Rethinking 1968 and the Global Sixties" (2019, *Jam It!* special issue), "Teaching American Studies in Europe: Challenges and New Directions for the Twenty-First Century" (2018, *RSA Journal* Forum section), and *Open Literature. La cultura digitale negli studi letterari* (2016, Università di Torino). Her current monograph project is titled *Narrative Fiction in The Digital Age: A Rhetorical Approach.*

Claudia Roesch is a research fellow at the German Historical Institute in Washington, DC. Her research focusses on the history of family and migration, the history of knowledge and transatlantic relations. She obtained her PhD from the Westfälische Wilhelms-Universität Münster as a member of the junior research group "Family Values and Social Change" with a dissertation on Mexican immigrant families in the United States. She recently finished her second book project on a transnational history of family planning in West Germany and is embarking on a new project about social reform and knowledge circulation in the early 19th century.

Chiara Saraceno, former professor of Sociology at Università di Torino, Italy, and research professor at the Wissenschaftszentrum Berlin für Sozialforschung, is at present honorary fellow at the Collegio Carlo Alberto, Torino. From 1999 to 2001, she was the chair of the Italian Poverty Commission. She has published extensively, in Italian and English, on families, gender and generations relations, welfare, poverty and social exclusion. Her latest, coauthored, book, *Poverty in Italy: Features and Drivers in a European Perspective,* is forthcoming with Policy Press.

Maurizio Vaudagna is Emeritus Professor of Contemporary History at the Università del Piemont in Italy, and former director of CISPEA, the Americanists' consortium of the universities of Bologna, Florence, Triest, and Eastern Piedmont. He has been a member of the coordinating committee of the Italian Fulbright Program and of the Italian Academy for Advanced Studies at Columbia University and has given summer courses at Cornell and Columbia University, as well as at different European universities. As a specialist in 20th century American political and social history, he has coordinated national and international research groups dealing with European-American relations. His most recent book is *The New Deal and the American Welfare State: Essays from a Transatlantic Perspective (1933-1945)* (2014), and his edited book, *Modern European-American Relations in the Transatlantic Space. Recent Trends in History Writing* (2015) has won the Transatlantic Studies Association Book Prize.

Eva-Sabine Zehelein is currently adjunct professor of American Studies at Goethe Universität Frankfurt and Visiting Scholar at the Women's Studies Research Center at Brandeis University (supported by the Fritz Thyssen Stiftung). She specializes in 20th and 21st century North American literatures and (popular) cultures, leads an international and interdisciplinary research group on "Family Matters," and in her own current research project investigates the (bio)politics of reprogenetics and ARTs in transnational (auto/biographical) texts through a reproductive justice lens. She has published monographs on John Updike (2003) and Science Plays (2009). Her most recent publications include "Reproductive Justice and (the Politics of) Transnational Gestational Surrogacy – review essay" (*American Quarterly*, vol. 70, no. 4, 2018, pp. 889-901), "Mothers, ART and Narratives of (Be)longing" (*CoSMo*, vol. 12, Spring 2018, pp. 74-91), "Love, Marriage and Family in the 21st Century: *All We Had* (Annie Weatherwax), *The Nest* (Cynthia D'Aprix Sweeney)" (*The American Novel in the 21st Century: Cultural Contexts – Literary Developments – Critical Analyses*, edited by Michael Basseler and Ansgar Nünning, EVT, 2019, pp. 215-30), as well as "Mummy, me, and her podcast – feminist and gender discourses in contemporary podcast culture" (*International Journal of Media & Cultural Politics*, vol. 15, no. 2, 2019, pp. 143-61).

Cultural Studies

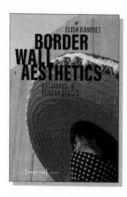

Elisa Ganivet
Border Wall Aesthetics
Artworks in Border Spaces

2019, 250 p., hardcover, ill.
79,99 € (DE), 978-3-8376-4777-8
E-Book: 79,99 € (DE), ISBN 978-3-8394-4777-2

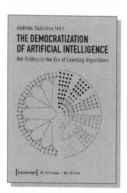

Andreas Sudmann (ed.)
The Democratization of Artificial Intelligence
Net Politics in the Era of Learning Algorithms

2019, 334 p., pb., col. ill.
49,99 € (DE), 978-3-8376-4719-8
E-Book: free available, ISBN 978-3-8394-4719-2

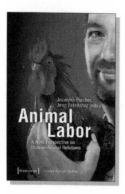

Jocelyne Porcher, Jean Estebanez (eds.)
Animal Labor
A New Perspective on Human-Animal Relations

2019, 182 p., hardcover
99,99 € (DE), 978-3-8376-4364-0
E-Book: 99,99 € (DE), ISBN 978-3-8394-4364-4

Cultural Studies

Burcu Dogramaci, Kerstin Pinther (eds.)
Design Dispersed
Forms of Migration and Flight

2019, 274 p., pb., col. ill.
34,99 € (DE), 978-3-8376-4705-1
E-Book: 34,99 € (DE), ISBN 978-3-8394-4705-5

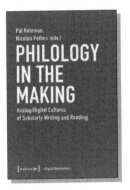

Pál Kelemen, Nicolas Pethes (eds.)
Philology in the Making
Analog/Digital Cultures of Scholarly Writing and Reading

2019, 316 p., pb., ill.
34,99 € (DE), 978-3-8376-4770-9
E-Book: 34,99 € (DE), ISBN 978-3-8394-4770-3

Pablo Abend, Annika Richterich,
Mathias Fuchs, Ramón Reichert, Karin Wenz (eds.)
Digital Culture & Society (DCS)
Vol. 5, Issue 1/2019 –
Inequalities and Divides in Digital Cultures

2019, 212 p., pb., ill.
29,99 € (DE), 978-3-8376-4478-4
E-Book: 29,99 € (DE), ISBN 978-3-8394-4478-8

**All print, e-book and open access versions of the titles in our list
are available in our online shop www.transcript-verlag.de/en!**